Education reform in democratic Spain

Oliver Boyd-Barrett and Pamela O'Malley have brought together a collection of the best recently published and specially commissioned articles that chart the rapid and extensive process of education reform in Spain since 1970.

The articles cover in detail all the key measures of reform and the relevant changes in legislation and government policy since the 1970 *Ley General de Educación*. They also set these changes within their historical context. The book shows that the process of reform in Spain has been characterized by both idealism and conflict, and has been notable for its sheer pace. Topics covered include democratization and decentralization, curriculum reform, vocational and technical education, and the leading partners in education such as the Ministry of Education and Science, teacher unions and governors.

This book is a significant contribution to the study of worldwide processes of education reform and will be of interest to comparative educationists, those who have a professional interest in education in Spain, and also anyone with a more general interest in modern Spain.

Oliver Boyd-Barrett was Sub-Dean at the School of Education of the Open University until 1994, and is currently Director of Distance Learning at the Centre for Mass Communications Research, University of Leicester. **Pamela O'Malley** has taught for many years at the British Council School in Madrid. She was active in the anti-Franco resistance. She has worked in an advisory capacity with the *Partido Comunista de España* (PCE) and subsequently with the Parliamentary Education Commissions of *Izquierda Unida* (IU). She is President of the *Fundación por la Escuela Pública Angel Díaz Zamorano* of one of the leading teacher unions (CCOO).

International developments in school reform
Series editor: Bob Moon

Other titles in this series include:

Education in Germany: Tradition and Reform in Historical Context
Edited by David Phillips

Education and Reform in France: The Mitterrand Years 1981–1995
Edited by Anne Corbett and Bob Moon

Education reform in democratic Spain

Edited by Oliver Boyd-Barrett and Pamela O'Malley

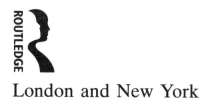

London and New York

First published 1995
by Routledge
11 New Fetter Lane, London EC4P 4EE

Simultaneously published in the USA and Canada
by Routledge
29 West 35th Street, New York NY 10001

Selection and editorial material © 1995 Oliver Boyd-Barrett and Pamela
O'Malley; articles © the individual contributors

Phototypeset in Times by Intype, London

Printed and bound in Great Britain by
TJ Press (Padstow) Ltd, Padstow, Cornwall

British Library Cataloguing in Publication Data
A catalogue record for this book is available from the British Library

Library of Congress Cataloguing in Publication Data
A catalogue record for this book has been requested

ISBN 0–415–09148–9

Contents

vi *Contents*

Contributors

Vicente Alvarez Areces was former Director of Education for Asturias, former Director of the Central State Inspectorate and is at present Mayor (PSOE) of Girón, Asturias.

Mark Blaug is Professor of Economics at the University of Exeter.

Oliver Boyd-Barrett was Sub-Dean at the School of Education of the Open University (UK) until 1994, and is currently Director of Distance Learning at the Centre for Mass Communications Research, University of Leicester. He has published widely in both the fields of education and the communications media.

Angel Chico Blas, secondary teacher of mathematics, formerly worked for the Ministry of Education as Section Head of Pedagogic Reform. He is Consultant to the Federation of Teachers' Unions (CCOO) and a Member of the Federal Area of Education of *Izquierda Unida*.

Francisco Bosch is Professor of Economics, University of Alcalá de Henares.

Arturo Pérez Collera is a teacher of vocational education, and Chief Provincial Inspector of Oviedo, Asturias.

Javier Díaz is an economist and government inspector.

Javier Doz Orrit, a secondary mathematics teacher, was General Secretary of the Federation of Teachers' Unions (CCOO) until 1988, and is currently a Deputy (*Izquierda Unida*) in the Regional Parliament of Madrid.

Mariano Fernández Enguita is Professor of Sociology of Education in the University Complutense of Madrid. He is author of various publications, including: *Integrar o Segregar*; *Trabajo, Escuela e ideología: Marx y la* *crítica de la educación*; *Trabajo, escuela y ideología*; *Juntos pero no revueltos*. He is also editor of the review *Educación y Sociedad*.

Joan Carlos Gallego Herrerz is General Secretary of the Federation of Teachers' Unions (CCOO) of Cataluña. He is an economist and an FP (Formación Profesional) teacher.

Antonio Guerrero is Lecturer in Sociology of Education at the University Complutense of Madrid. His publications include *El Magisterio en la Comunidad de Madrid*.

Juan José Sanchéz de Horcajo is Professor of Sociology of Education at the University of Salamanca.

Diego M. Justicia is a primary teacher, physics graduate and teacher in adult education.

Pamela O'Malley taught for many years at the British Council School in Madrid, and was active in opposition to General Franco. In 1990 she was awarded a doctorate by the Open University for her thesis concerning the role of teachers in the opposition movement in the Franco years, and the development of an educational reform movement.

José María Maravall is Professor of Sociology of the University Complutense of Madrid. He was Minister of Education from 1982 to 1988 and is a member of the Executive of the PSOE. He is author of many publications including: *Trabajo y Conflicto Social*; *Sociología de lo Posible*: *Dictadura y Disentimiento Politico*; *La Politica da la Transición*.

Sara Morgenstern de Finkel is Lecturer in Sociology of Education in UNED (Universidad Nacional de Educación e Distancía – Spanish Open University), Madrid.

Antonio José Gil Padilla is a civil engineer and formerly worked in the vocational education section of the Ministry of Education. Publications include: *Electrónica General I and II*; *Electrónica Analógica*; *Materiales curriculares del area de Electrónica del Bachillerato Tecnológico*; *Tecnología y empleo*.

José Jimeno Sacristán is Professor of Didactics and School Organization in the University of Valencia. He is the author of various publications, which include: *El Curriculum: una reflexión sobre la práctica*; *Comprender y transformar la enseñanza*.

Foreword

In nearly all parts of the world there is an interest and fascination with the way other national systems of education are organized and worked. Demographic change, economic transformation, technological innovation and the explosion of knowledge have created a veritable maelstrom of ideas within which schooling and education generally are centrally situated. The important shifts in political and ideological structures over the last decade have contributed a further dimension to this complex interplay of ideas. How others educate their children, young people and, increasingly, the population as a whole, is now the subject of intense intellectual curiosity amongst the media, politicians and the increasingly aware generation of parents.

On these issues there is also a vast array of expertise working in the fields of comparative, development and international education. Strong academic bases exist for these interrelated fields through institutions of higher education and within national and trans-global agencies. Journals and other publications, as well as the new technological means of accessing data and information, provide a forum for theoretical and methodological debate.

This present series of books seeks to provide a range of sources to inform both the policy making and political community as well, it is hoped, as contributing to debates amongst specialists in the field. The word source is important. The series, and the individual selections made by editors, do not seek to provide a comprehensive account of the structure of any particular education system. A number of educational encyclopaedia and guides, as well as international publications, now serve that purpose. Rather, the series seeks to give readers an inside view of the issues and arguments that characterize contemporary debate. For that reason a strong emphasis has been placed on the translation of key texts, where the normal language of debate is other than English, or alternatively the selection of contributors who, while writing in English, either work within the system or have a detailed working understanding of the context. Translation, of course, poses problems in its own right, as indeed does a series framework based on nations or regions, but giving access to the ways of understanding, habits of thought and assumptions from within a specific cultural context is an important aim of the series. And in that respect it is hoped to remedy the imbalance in the exchange of ideas that global access to the English-speaking medium can bring.

Editors who are specialists in the area have made their own choices about the organization of the different volumes and the selection of contributors. Many of the others go beyond specifically educational concerns to touch on the social, political and economic influences that are intertwined with the process of change and reform. In this sense the series provides a source to stimulate curiosity, examine wider social and cultural issues, and provide a starting point for further study and exploration.

Bob Moon
The Open University

Introduction

This volume is a contribution to the study of worldwide processes of educational reform. Although few chapters have adopted a specifically comparative framework, we believe that taken together the volume yields data and insight of considerable interest to comparative educationists. We also believe that Spanish education is of interest in and for itself, both for those who have a professional interest in Spanish education and for that much wider audience which has an interest in the study of modern Spain. Two characteristics of Spanish education stand out as particularly worthy of mention in this general introduction: one is the sheer pace of reform activity since the 1970 *Ley General de Educación* (LGE) and the second is the distance from autarky to modernism that has been travelled since the government and the philosophy of General Franco was at the peak of its influence and authority. In the study of Spain since 1970 can be traced, albeit within a much shorter span of history, some of the journeys that other industrial nations made from the nineteenth to the mid-twentieth centuries.

Education has probably attracted a greater measure of idealism and determination than have other spheres of modernization in the period since 1982, presided over by the governing party of Spain, the *Partido Socialista de Obrero Español* (PSOE) – its power considerably weakened, at the time of writing, by the 1993 general election and by a succession of major corruption scandals in 1994. Education figured prominently in the national constitution signed in 1978 and although there are complaints of inadequate resourcing and of irresolute speed, there can be no doubt that firm directions for change have been projected, which are being implemented, and will be realized within the next few years. Measuring the gap between the rhetoric of intention and the reality, certainly no less urgent a task in Spain than in any other European country, is a part of what this volume is about. Nor are there too many such books, for academic analysis of the political economy of education in Spain is relatively recent. In the 1980s there would have been even fewer sources of analysis or of data, a dearth which now promises to be eradicated with the gathering commitment to formal evaluation and analysis of education practice.

The editors have provided separate chapter introductions, where they also note any recent developments of significant relevance for matters discussed within the chapters they introduce, as most of the contributions for this volume were first written between 1990 and 1993.

The recent history of education in Spain and the transformations that have been experienced since the ending of the Franco regime are introduced by Boyd-Barrett in Chapter 1, which describes the key measures of the reform process, particularly those introduced by the 1990 legislation *Ley Orgánica de Ordenación General del Sistema Educativo* (LOGSE), as it affects each level of the educational system up to but not including the universities. A more extensive and more passionate historical background is provided in Chapter 2, by PSOE's celebrated former minister of education, José María Maravall, author of two particularly important pieces of educational legislation, the *Ley de Reforma Universitaria* (LRU) and the *Ley Orgánica del Derecho a la Educación* (LODE). O'Malley in Chapter 3 investigates the critical turning point which was represented by the 1970 legislation, *La Ley General de Educación*, often dubbed 'technocratic' yet of vital importance in establishing an infrastructure of educational provision that could begin to respond to the growing demand of both industry and the public for improved quantity and quality of provision. Throughout the 1960s and 1970s, often in clandestine activity, radical elements of the teaching profession in alliance with opposition parties had begun to debate and to promote new models for teaching and learning. This period, which is described by O'Malley in Chapter 4, represents an epoch of fertile intellectual challenge to the then ruling ideas, which was later to feed directly into mainstream politics as well as into the development of progressive groups within the teaching profession. The latter were to spearhead reform experiments in the early years of the Socialist Government and to provide a lead in the implementation of reform legislation.

The period of most recent reform is represented by the publication of LOGSE in 1990, and the preamble to this, which is translated and reproduced in Chapter 5, outlines the Ministry's own rationale for the reforms, and offers a summary of its objectives. Its key-note features are flexibility, participation and consensus. In Chapter 6, Boyd-Barrett identifies some of the major dimensions of reform in Spain (democratization; decentralization; comprehensivization; curriculum standardization; vocationalization; multi-culturalism; and professionalization) for the purpose of comparative analysis with England and Wales. Javier Doz Orrit predicts the most likely sources of trouble for the implementation of the Spanish reforms in Chapter 7. Evaluation of the progress of reform is in part constrained by severe limitations of historical data, the implications of which are the preoccupation of Chapter 8 by Blaug, Bosch and Díaz.

The process of decentralization of responsibility for educational provision from Central Government to the autonomous communities, a process that is due to be completed by 1997, is the focus for Joan Carlos Gallego Herrerz in Chapter 9. Turning to issues of educational content, Jimeno Sacristán in Chapter 10 looks at the reform in terms of what it means for the curriculum and for teaching and learning. A flavour of the reform debate, as it affected the design of option systems in the reformed secondary education of Catalonia and the implications of optionality for authentic comprehensivization, is offered by Fernández Enguita in Chapter 11. Angel Chico Blas in Chapter 12 reviews the expanding range of devices for the evaluation of education in Spain, including a national institute for quality control. One aspect of this changing landscape of evaluation is the evolving role of the Inspectorate away from functions of control towards greater emphasis on reporting and advisory functions; this trajectory is traced by Alvarez Areces and Pérez Collera in Chapter 13. The role in reform of the teacher unions and associations is discussed in Chapter 14 by Antonio Guerrero. Morgenstern de Finkel in Chapter 15 assesses the teachers' centres, viewed by government as one of the principal channels for improvements in teaching, and she judges them less than promising for the preparation and inspiration of practising teachers in the implementation of curriculum and pedagogic reform. In Chapter 16, Juan José Sanchéz de Horcaja reviews the history of troubled relations between Church and State. The Church is the single largest provider among the substantial private and grant-aided sector of Spanish education which accounts for roughly a third of all provision. The following Chapter 17, by Boyd-Barrett, outlines the issues that have been raised by the introduction of teaching *in* and *through* official languages of the Spanish communities other than *castellano*. Two subsequent chapters, 18 and 19, by Diego Justicia and Gil Padilla, respectively, examine the rhetoric and reality of reform in vocational education and training, while in conclusion Chapter 20 by Boyd-Barrett focuses on university reform.

STATISTICAL SUMMARY

In the year 1992–3 there were 19,887 pre-school and primary schools (catering for the 6 to 14 age range in pre-reform education) in Spain, with 275,557 teachers and 5,501,081 pupils. Approximately 8,000 of these schools were within the territory controlled by the Ministry (but soon to be decentralized to the remaining ten autonomous communities of Spain which do not as yet have responsibility for educational provision). The remainder were controlled by the autonomous communities. Areas with the highest numbers of schools were Cataluña (3,053), Andalucia (3,020) and Castilla-Leon (2,070). Of the total number of schools, 14,655 were state schools, with 193,378 teachers and 3,572,009 students. There were 5,232 private schools with 82,199 teachers and 1,929,072 students.

There were 5,185 secondary schools (BUP, COU, FP – see glossary for definitions of acronyms – and schools already offering the reformed educational programme) with 171,383 teachers and 2,560,522 students. Of these schools, 2,878 were state schools, with 130,838 teachers and 1,861,237 pupils; 2,307 schools were private with 40,545 teachers and 699,285 students. Of all secondary school students, 1,489,384 were BUP or COU students (studying for the *Bachillerato* or for the one-year pre-university course) and 860,015 were FP students. A further 693,585 were following courses in pilot forms of the new *Bachillerato*, and 104,936 were in the newly established regime of reformed secondary schools.

There were 519 special schools with 6,226 teachers and 33,498 pupils; 220 were state schools with 3,752 teachers and 17,024 students; 299 were private with 2,474 teachers and 16,474 students.

By 1993–4, more than a million students between the ages of 8 and 10 were embarking on the second cycle of the new primary education (6 to 12 years), and 125,000 were starting – in its still experimental form – the new system of comprehensive secondary education and the different modalities of *Bachillerato*. Teaching of modern languages from the age of 8 years was generalized from this year. At ages 4 and 5 years (*educación infantil*) 100 per cent of children now received schooling (within those communities still the direct responsibility of the Ministry). Ten thousand, three hundred new places were also being made available for children of 3 years, and the anticipated rate of schooling for 3-year-olds was 47 per cent.

Pupil–teacher ratios for 1993–4 were expected to be around 20.5 in the first cycle of primary education and 22 in the second cycle. Within the Ministry's area of direct responsibility, about one-third of all secondary schools, 364, were expected to be offering the new secondary education, with pupil–teacher ratios of 14.2:1 in the state sector and 17:1 in the private sector. According to OECD data for 1991, ratios of students to teaching staff were 22.5:1 in pre-school education, 19.7:1 in state primary, 17.6:1 in lower secondary and 14.7:1 in upper secondary (15.8:1 for all secondary). But they are higher when public and private sectors are combined: 24.8:1 for pre-school education, 22:1 for primary, 18.1:1 for lower secondary, 16:1 for upper secondary and 16.9:1 for all secondary.

In terms of educational attainment, 10 per cent of the 25 to 64 age group in the population had completed tertiary education and 12 per cent had completed upper secondary, well behind other OECD countries with the exceptions of Portugal and Turkey, although there has been significant expansion in provision for and participation in tertiary education over the past 10 years. Net enrolment in public and private university education was 21.3 per cent for 18–21-year-olds, higher than for all OECD countries other than Canada and the USA, 14.2 per cent for 22–25-year-olds and 5.3 per cent for 26–29-year-olds.

Younger age groups show more impressive rates of education completion but are more likely to be unemployed. In 1991, 30.8 per cent of the total population was aged between 5 and 24. The overall unemployment rate was 15.9 per cent (higher than any other OECD country with the exception of Ireland), but 30.5 per cent among the 15 to 24 age group (higher than all other OECD countries).

Spain spends approximately 5.6 per cent of gross national product on all provision for education, both public and private (4.5 per cent excluding private). The OECD average was 6.1 per cent (or 5.4 per cent with private education excluded). Spain had one of the lower levels of national income per capita in 1991, higher only than Ireland, Portugal, Greece and Turkey. Eight per cent of Spanish educational expenditure went to pre-school education, 21.8 per cent to primary (experiencing falling school rolls), 51.6 per cent to secondary (experiencing rising school rolls) and 18.5 per cent to tertiary. State sources provided 80.1 per cent of expenditure (the figure is 86.7 per cent for primary and secondary education alone) and 19.9 per cent (13.3 per cent) came from private sources; approximately half of all state expenditure was central, the other half coming from regional (mainly) and local sources. Current expenditure was 88.6 per cent (of which 66 per cent was for staffing), 11.4 per cent capital expenditure.

SOURCES

Centre for Educational Research and Innovation (1993) *Education at a Glance. OECD Indicators*, Paris: CERI.
Eurydice (1990) *Structures of the Education and Initial Training Systems in the Member States of the European Community*. Brussels: Commission of the European Communities.

1 Structural change and curriculum reform in democratic Spain

Oliver Boyd-Barrett

Originally written to coincide with the passage of important new reform legislation (Boyd-Barrett, 1990) this chapter outlines the principal features of education in the Franco period, and the major directions of change that have been introduced since the 1970 Ley General de Educación *(LGE) onwards to the 1990* Ley Orgánica de Ordenación General del Sistema Educativo *(LOGSE). Successful passage of LOGSE through the Spanish parliament was followed by a process of phased implementation. This has been subject to delay as a direct consequence of the economic recession of the early 1990s. It is still envisaged that the reform will be complete by the year 2000, by which date all children will receive compulsory comprehensive education to the age of 16. The government of Cataluña has endeavoured to anticipate the reform, amid union fears that the necessary preparations have not been undertaken. Economic difficulties notwithstanding (after increasing every year from 1983 to 1991, education spending then declined for three consecutive years), the rhetoric of reform has been sustained. To hostile union comment early in 1994 the Minister for Education, Gustavo Suarez Pertierra, introduced a consultative document outlining seventy-seven measures to improve the quality of education. The year 1994 also saw the establishment of the* Instituto Nacional de Calidad y Evaluación, *which will have responsibility for educational evaluation in general and evaluation of the implementation of reform in particular. A substantial number of schools, some of them involved in experimental pilots during the 1980s, have been allowed to anticipate the reforms.*

INTRODUCTION

The period 1972–90 was one of intense legislative activity in the area of education, a period of heady rhetoric as well as real change, bitter controversy as well as cynical apathy. The intensity of change was experienced at every level of the educational system, from infant to university and vocational education. It affected, most noticeably, the scale and framework of provision; the structure of educational government and management; the representation and involvement in educational management of the community, parents, teachers and pupils; and last, but of course not least, the specific contents and processes of education as such, namely the curriculum.

THE FRANCOIST LEGACY

The 1970 *Ley General de Educación*, coming as it did only a few years before Franco's death, is widely regarded as marking the beginning of a transition from one model of education to a qualitatively different one, informed by distinctive ideological and pedagogical precepts. The transition itself did not occur all at once, and with each subsequent legislative initiative there is a tendency to measure progress in terms of how far Spain has moved away from the Francoist era at its reactionary peak. This era may be described in terms of a number of prevailing features; from each of which there has been considerable movement over the past two decades.

From 'Subsidiariedad' to state control

The Francoist state increasingly and deliberately assumed a subsidiary role in educational provision. The principal role was ceded to the Catholic Church, most notably at secondary (voluntary) level, where the growing power of the Church as provider exacerbated a tendency for provision to concentrate in the wealthy city centres or prosperous suburbs, while very many pupils in remote communities were not even provided for at the supposedly obligatory level of primary education up to the age of 12 (cf. Maravall, 1984; Puelles, 1980; O'Malley, 1990).

Church influence waned in the 1960s. A technocratic administration wanted to expand state provision. This was to meet both the demands of new industrial employers and the rise of demand from upwardly mobile migrants to the industrial fringes in city areas. These fringe areas had not been well served by the Church. In an increasingly urban and secular society, the Church was unable to attract sufficient numbers of new (and cheap) religious staff (Maravall, 1984). While numbers attending church schools remained static, pupils in state schools rose dramatically: there were more children, more parents were seeking education for their children, and girls were forming an increasing proportion of the school population.

In the period 1960–80, the population of the primary sector rose by 60 per cent, while at secondary (*Bachillerato*) level, the rate of increase was 753 per cent. Numbers of *Bachillerato* students rose by 30,000 in the private sector as against 450,000 in the state sector in 1975–83. The proportion of children attending private schools at primary level (aged 6 to 14) in the period 1970–87 fell from 72 per cent to only 35 per cent. In technical secondary education (FP), the proportion of students educated at private institutions fell from 57 per cent to 37 per cent. Overall, private education now caters for approximately one-third of all students up to university level (which is predominantly public).

Not all private provision is religious. There are many secular providers, especially at pre-obligatory levels. A wide range of secular provision developed in the 1960s and 1970s to meet, in however rudimentary a fashion, both the growing demand for secondary education and the demand at primary level for education in regional languages (e.g. the *ikastola* schools in País Vasco). Secular provision now accounts for roughly half of all private education, although the Church remains the single largest private provider. The principal representative body for the Catholic schools, Educación y Gestión, claimed to represent more than 60 per cent of private schools in 1992, and among these were more than 70 per cent of all direct-grant schools (Boyd-Barrett, 1991).

Grant-aided private education

While the power of the Church has waned, however, it still carries weight. Church interests successfully campaigned for a system of government subvention for private provision of basic compulsory education. Grant totals increased from 1,385 million pesetas to 70,000 million in 1973–82, a rate of increase of 4,954 per cent. Despite the historical enmity of the *Partido Socialista Orbrero Español* (PSOE) to private education, grants continued to rise under PSOE government in the 1980s, by 112 per cent between 1982 and 1988 (CE, 6 July 1988).[1] By 1988, 91 per cent of all private schools at this level were grant-aided, covering 100 per cent of relevant costs (i.e. of provision of compulsory education), so that the State now bore the expense of educating 96 per cent of all school children. Grants were further increased in line with the extension of obligatory education from 1993.

Why did the Socialist Government maintain grant-aid policy? PSOE was a major signatory to the historic compromise on education consolidated in the Constitution of 1978. The Constitution committed all parties to a system of mixed provision, and guaranteed some form of subvention to private schools, subject to fulfilment of certain conditions. Without the active involvement of the private system the State may not have been able to capitalize the required expansion in educational infrastructure. The grant system also provided a mixture of sticks and carrots which the Government could manipulate to bring about reforms in grant-aided schools, for example, comparability of conditions between private and state schools; democracy in management through participation of teachers, parents and students on governing bodies; adherence to state-defined norms; and freedom of conscience for both teachers and students (on condition they respect the basic character of the school and the need to live together in harmony). All confessional practice must be voluntary.

As the price of subvention, therefore, the autonomy of the Church and other private schools is diminished. Recipients must be non-profit-making institutions. Grants are awarded for four-year periods and may not be renewed where there has been a failure to meet the conditions of grant, or even where there is a local surplus of places (especially threatening in a period of falling primary rolls). Members of the community are represented on governing bodies. Pupils and teachers can excuse themselves from confessional practice.

Catholic nationalism to pluralist capitalism

The doctrine of Catholic nationalism comprised a variety of elements, most important of which was the Francoist commitment to renovation of Catholic tradition, a vision of social justice that involved both the end of liberal capitalism and of Marxist materialism. All teaching was to accord with Catholic dogma. Church schools were eager beneficiaries of a system of tax exemptions, judicial immunity and exemption of religious staff from military service.

Processes of industrialization and accompanying secularization, together with increased state provision of education, created a growing rift between Church and State. The era of Catholic nationalism has left few traces in state education. In its place is a changing ideological context within which the following values appear to be strongly acclaimed if not always practised, namely democracy; Europeanization; modernization; prosperity; equality of opportunity; and individual development.

Elitism to equal opportunity

The decline of church influence is a mark of the decline of élitism in education, although there remains a 'hard core' of completely private provision catering for some 4 per cent of the school population. Education in grant-aided schools in the obligatory stages is generally provided free, although supplementary charges of dubious legality are sometimes demanded. Free provision has reduced but not removed the social class differentials between the population of state schools and those attending grant-aided private schools.

The 1970 education law brought to an end the previous *Bachillerato* system of secondary education whereby children from the wealthier families tended to begin their secondary studies at the age of 10, while others continued in the state system to the age of 12 or 14 before making the transition. But this legislation substituted a new division: between the *Bachillerato* route of secondary education, for most of those who had passed their primary studies, and the FP route, catering for those who had not. The reforms introduced in 1990 have attempted to remove the division between academic and technical secondary education, but have retained the concept of failure at the end of the period of obligatory secondary education.

As in many other countries, the reform movement in Spain has looked at pre-compulsory education to reduce the force of class influence. There has been a significant shift away from the concept of nursery provision as child-minding towards a varied system of provision in which genuinely educational objectives are much more pronounced. This process is confirmed by the 1990 reform legislation which, for the first time, incorporates provision for the 0 to 6 age range as subject to state regulation, and for which the State guarantees to provide as many places as necessary to meet demand, while stopping short of declaring such education to be either free (though much of it is, especially where supported by city governments; but the right-wing municipal government in Valencia withdrew public grants from infant schools in 1994), or obligatory. However, well over fourth-fifths of all 4–5-year-olds now have nursery provision and increasingly this is in the context of primary schools (exploiting space released by falling rolls).

There is a growing range of compensatory programme measures, resources and grants; for example, free textbooks for low-income families; free school libraries for rural schools; and special courses for young people who have dropped out of education before the end of or immediately after basic education. The monetary value of such categories of support has increased geometrically in recent years. Significant increases (as high as 50 per cent in 1987–8 alone) in educational expenditure were experienced in the 1980s. A much proclaimed medium-term ambition was expenditure on education at 6 per cent of gross national product to bring Spain in line with the European average, and it was hoped that this would be achieved over the phasing-in of the reform programme during the 1990s. The economic recession of the 1990s slowed the process of reform. Spending on education remained at 4–5 per cent of GNP, while as a percentage of public spending education slipped back to 3.5 per cent in 1993–4.

Centralization to devolution

Seven of the seventeen autonomous communities into which Spain is divided enjoy 'full powers' with respect to education and the others are set to follow by 1996–7. In practice these powers appear to have more significance in administrative terms than in the generation of policy, and the scope for discretion is probably less than the rhetoric of community autonomy might seem to promise. But it is a feature of much educational legislation today that the door is open for the autonomous communities to adapt nationally agreed measures to community conditions. One important example is the incorporation of community languages where these are other than *castellano*, both in the sense of requiring the teaching *of* community languages as subjects on the curriculum, and in the sense of teaching *through* community languages.

Teaching of and teaching through the community language is now a significant factor of educational provision in Cataluña, Valencia, Islas Baleares, País Vasco, Navarra and Galicia. This development has generated many interesting policy issues (Boyd-Barrett, 1990).

At school level, governing bodies now comprise roughly equal numbers (according to size of school) of teachers, on the one hand, and parents and pupils on the other. Each of these categories is elected from their various constituencies, together with representatives of the school's management and local government. Parents and students have their own associations with local, regional and national offices, and their freedom of association has been guaranteed by law since 1984. Since 1988 teachers have been able to vote in their own union elections. In state schools the school's director is elected from among the teachers by the members of the governing body. There are also community and national educational consultative committees on which parents, teachers and students are represented.

All these elements of the democratic process, therefore, contribute to a growing participation in decision-making and decentralization of control in education. In elections for categories of representative on school governing bodies, however, the voting turn-out among parents has been considerably less than for any other category of representative, and the quality of their participation is in many cases restricted by unfamiliarity and lack of confidence. Governing bodies generally focus on management issues, leaving curriculum development to the province of the teachers' council (*claustro*). Teachers' and employers' associations, and the *Consejo Escolar del Estado* (in its report on the year 1989–90, which called for a profound debate about the functioning of the governing bodies), have expressed a range of (not altogether consonant) reservations about the operation of the governing bodies to do with politicization; disenchantment with democratic process; insufficient dialogue between the sector representatives, or between representatives and those represented; misunderstanding by members of their role; absenteeism; insufficient respect for their decisions by the administrations; perception that they are merely rubber-stamping bodies; insufficient powers with respect to key areas of school life, including curriculum; and the frequency and timing of meetings (CE, 11 November 1992). More recently it has been argued (Bolivar, 1994) that the introduction of democratic management by LODE has not in itself substantially altered the organizational culture of schools or given them greater control over working and curricular conditions. A 1993 survey suggests that school heads and teachers are by far the most influential voices on governing bodies (Fernández-Enguita, 1993).

The elected position of school director has not carried a substantial allowance and in many schools where no candidates have come forward the local administration has had to nominate directors without election. It has been estimated that three out of four school directors are nominated by the administrations for lack of candidates (Jímenez, 1992). The same source reports studies which show that 50 per cent of school directors find the work unfulfilling or frustrating. Ministry proposals in 1994 suggest that the elected character of the role will be retained, but that the range of candidates may be broadened to include candidates from other schools, that the role will be strengthened, with greater authority over selection of other members of the management team, and that training and rewards for directors will be enhanced.

The implementation of LOGSE (Ministerio de Educación y Ciencia (MEC), 1990) will continue a process initiated by LODE (MEC, 1985) towards more participative but also more professional school management. In the new secondary schools (Educación Secundaria Obligatoria: ESO), for example, management will comprise the governing body, director, chief of studies, administrator, teachers' *claustro*, teaching and pastoral departments, department of complementary and extra-scholastic activities, teaching co-ordinating committee (which brings together senior management and the co-ordinators for each cycle) and the tutors. The governing body of a state secondary school, with variations according to size, comprises the elected director (chair), chief of studies, a municipal councillor or representative, seven teachers elected by the *claustro*, three parents, four students, a representative of the administrative and service personnel and the school administrator acting as non-voting secretary. The director, along with the administrator, one teacher and one parent nominated from the governing body, form the school's economic committee (*consejo económica*). The duties of the governing body are to establish guidelines for the annual development of a global educational programme (*projecto educativo*), to approve and assess this annually, elect the director and approve the management team which he proposes, to decide on admissions, approve school rules and the budget, resolve conflicts, impose sanctions, adopt criteria for school planning, promote the maintenance and renewal of installations, and analyse student progress. It is the responsibility of the teachers' *claustro* to propose criteria for curriculum development (*proyectos curiculares*) at each level, and these are co-ordinated by a teaching co-ordinating committee in relation to objectives, context, methodology and evaluation (CE, 23 June 1993).

THE CURRICULUM

While it is not easy to say with confidence what exactly are the *accomplishments* of curriculum reform over the past twenty years, it is possible to identify consistencies and departures in the problems which the reformers are posing, both from within positions of power and without, and to identify the directions of change. I would single out the following features:

- Less reliance solely on educational theory as a basis for policy-making and greater emphasis on consultation, research and development;
- Moves towards a unified comprehensive curriculum up to the age of 16;
- Educational ideology giving increasingly greater weight to the concept of individual development within the context of political democracy and industrial, secular society, at the expense of conceptions of social morality and Catholic nationalism;
- Education is seen increasingly in terms of constructivist notions of learning and skills-related processes rather than in terms of the transmission of important knowledge;
- The curriculum is conceptualized in terms of concepts (facts and principles), procedures (knowing *how*, in theory and in practice), and attitudes, norms and values;
- A process of decentralization within the context of a national curriculum which increases the scope for communities, provinces and individual schools and teachers to modify the curriculum in the light of local and individual needs; and
- A broad approach to evaluation, conceived not only in relation to student outcomes, but also to the teaching–learning process and to the implementation of reform.

Basic education: *Educación Básica General* (EGB)

The main achievement of Education Minister Villar Palasi's 1970 *Ley de Educación* was the introduction of a single, unified period of free, obligatory education from ages 6 to 14. It unified the voluntary *Bachillerato* system at secondary level by removing the previous separation of letters, sciences and technology. But it introduced what proved to be a new, debilitating division between the *Bachillerato*, on the one hand, and what was intended to be a more vocationally oriented system of *formación profesional*, on the other.

The 1970 law attempted to revolutionize curriculum and pedagogy within a centrally determined structure. The new teaching guidelines which followed on the heels of the legislation established what was to be studied and the level to be reached at each stage (MEC, 1970). It suggested appropriate teaching approaches, and specified the forms of assessment to be adopted.

The new guidelines attempted to focus attention on pupil attitudes, social integration, home–school liaison, inter-disciplinarity and pupil-centredness. Subjects were grouped into 'areas of experience'. There was a move away from end-of-year written tests in favour of continuous assessment. Children were to move up from one class to another each year, and those who had not performed adequately the previous year would be given remedial work. Teachers were recommended to set up teaching teams for each class and also to establish subject departments.

A watershed it may have been, but the 1970 law was fatally flawed. Political opposition contrived to prevent the *Cortes* (the Spanish parliament) from voting through specific financial provision. Despite the trenchant criticism of the old order in the 1968 *Libro Blanco* (MEC, 1968), and the progressive tone of the law itself, this legislation still represented a very top-down model of educational change. There was no research and development, no piloting. There was very little prior consultation outside charmed circles of ministry officials, inspectors and panels of appointed 'experts'. There was no accompanying provision for teacher retraining. While many teachers welcomed the thinking behind the report, at least as many others were embedded within a structure and culture with which it could not possibly mesh. Many of its recommendations simply failed to take root. Twenty years on, for example, 'continuous assessment' is generally interpreted as the substitution of lots of formal tests *throughout* the year for sole reliance on end-of-term written examinations. Repetition of years is still generally practised for low achievers. Such concepts as child-centredness, inter-disciplinarity and team-teaching too often failed to pass beyond mere rhetoric. Even a reliable machinery for appraising grass-roots practice was lacking. The Inspectorate was small, aloof, centralized and largely acted as a kind of police force to ensure that schools observed narrow legal requirements.

Misgivings accumulating through the 1970s were used as justification for a return to tighter curriculum control in 1981. A 'failure' rate of 30 per cent at the end of compulsory schooling, lack of teacher preparation to handle the consequences of the 1970 law and shortage of materials to support the new curriculum were among some of the concerns.

Regulatory changes in 1981 divided basic education into three stages or cycles, with pupils assessed at the end of each year: each child had to meet specified minimum levels of attainment. There were detailed prescriptions for the type of teaching materials to be used in each subject at each stage. Conventional subject divisions were restored, with a weekly time allocation for each (MEC, 1981; McNair, 1984).

EGB under the PSOE

The transition to a socialist PSOE government from 1982 changed the prevailing climate of concern. The PSOE's foremost interests were in broad issues to do with the management and control of education, particularly favouring greater participation of parents, students and teachers in school management, the election of governing bodies and school directors, and the freedom of conscience of both teachers and pupils (all featuring in its legislation, *La Ley Orgánica del Derecho a la Educación* (LODE), 1984).

Towards curriculum reform

With the struggle over educational management and control resolved in PSOE's favour by LODE (despite unsuccessful appeals to the constitutional tribunal by the opposition) the principal anxieties about education switched to the increasingly divisive character of the split between the *Bachillerato* (BUP) and *Formación Profesional* (FP) at the stage of primary–secondary transition after age 14. FP had clearly become the majority destination of students who had failed to achieve their *graduado escolar* at age 14. Despite the intention that it should provide a more vocational education, FP was still far too academic and the failure rate as high. Although students were required to follow at least the first year of FP to the age of 15 (the minimum legal working age), a substantial minority of children were effectively leaving education illegally at 14, and some were even giving up earlier. These concerns were recognized as interlinking with the structure and content of primary education. Already, the socialists had undertaken a wide range of experiments, covering reform of the final cycle of EGB and the first cycle of BUP/FP.

Under the guidance of PSOE Education Minister, José Mariá Maravall, the government returned to the curriculum with its 1987 *Proyecto para la Reforma de la Enseñanza: Propuesta para Debate* (MEC, 1987), the beginning of possibly the most thoroughly considered and democratic period of educational consultation in Spain. A sister document appeared early the following year (MEC, 1988), dedicated to the sector of *Formación Profesional: Proyecto para la Reforma de la Educación Técnico Profesional*. In 1989 the Ministry published a glossy, colourful and substantial volume, *Libro Blanco Para la Reforma del Sistema Educativo* (1989a), which took account of the debates and consultation that had occurred the previous year, and which served as a further stage of the consultative process, leading in 1990 to publication of the *Proyecto de Ley Orgánica de Ordenación General del Sistema Educativo* (LOGSE) (MEC, 1990). Allowing for some further modifications that occurred in last-minute negotiations, this was the proposal upon which the *Cortes* was to be required to vote in 1990.

These documents were essentially concerned with the restructuring of education:

- Extending the age of free, compulsory and comprehensive education to 16;
- Incorporating the age range 0 to 6 years within the framework of educational regulation;
- Reducing the period of primary education to the age of 12 years and

starting a new, obligatory, secondary phase of education from ages 12 to 16;

- Introducing a new, modular *Bachillerato* from ages 16 to 18 (and eliminating the old pre-university year, *Curso de Orientatación Universitaria* (COU)); and
- Introducing a new system of professional and technical training that would start during the period of obligatory education and continue both within the *Bachillerato* and as a separate pathway.

These publications established the basic structure of primary and secondary education and the general principles which would inform its organization and delivery. Specific attention to the detail of curriculum content was left to a further round of consultative documents, the *Diseños Curriculares Bases* (DCB) (MEC, 1989b).

Reform: primary education

The 1989 *Libro Blanco* sets out the aims and objectives of primary education from 6 to 12 years of age, mainly in terms of the skills which students should acquire. This stage is to be divided into three two-year cycles. It is intended that for the duration of a cycle students should have the same form teachers and that the ministry-approved textbooks will adjust to this pattern. The main curriculum areas are identified as: Language and Literature, Mathematics, Natural and Social Environment, Arts (including Music), Physical Education, Religion (which all schools must offer, but which is voluntary for students). A foreign language is to be introduced as an obligatory feature from the second cycle (i.e. at the age of 8). Each school is to benefit from at least one additional support teacher. (Provision was already being made in 1989–90 for the appointment of specialist teachers in Physical Education and Music.) A child who does not make satisfactory progress during any cycle can be required to repeat a year, but this is to be regarded as unusual, and no child should be allowed to repeat more than two years across the whole of his or her education, primary or secondary. It is stressed that the decision to require a child to repeat a year should be a participative one, involving all persons concerned. The maximum teacher–pupil ratio is established at between 1:25 and 1:30. At the end of primary education all students will obtain a certificate of primary studies which will give them access to secondary education. The certificate will state how far the student has reached the objectives of the primary stage, and what help may be needed to facilitate the transition to secondary education.

Bachillerato Unificando y Polivolente (BUP)

The *Bachillerato* structure established in 1970 has been subject to continuing criticism. The 1984 *Libro Blanco* of the Comunidad Valenciana argued that BUP lacked its own independent *raison d'être*, subordinated as it was to university preparation. BUP studies were found to be abstract, excessively verbal, and élitist as well as overcrowded. School subjects were like 'independent kingdoms', insufficiently relevant to the 'necessities of geographical, social and cultural reality'. Writing in *Comunidad Escolar* (9 September 1987), a group of secondary teachers complained that the system was geared to monotonous oral expositions requiring little student participation and which were out of touch with real-life daily problems. The curriculum programmes of study were too rigid, over-charged with factual information of greatly varying significance and left little room for innovation. The timetables were drawn up more to suit the administration than the educational requirements of students, and they repressed opportunities for creative teaching. Knowledge was compartmentalized into subjects with little or no inter-disciplinarity. This system of teaching promoted passivity in the student, reducing his/her role to that of mere receiver, restricting creativity and critical thought, and depriving the student of any motivation to learn. There continued to be an emphasis on memorizing rather than on the development of study habits, techniques of work and organization of thought. A general lack of historical perspective impeded the students' understanding of epistemological and methodological aspects of science.

The general drift of these criticisms is not far removed from those of the 1968 *Libro Blanco* (MEC, 1968) twenty years previously. They certainly highlight the limitation of law and regulation as a guide to practice, especially perhaps with respect to teaching methodology in the classroom. Such criticisms may underestimate certain improvements. They do not take sufficient account of the curricular implications of such changes as have occurred in the basic guiding philosophy of education, the move towards more democratic community participation in and control over management and provision, and the introduction of community languages both as subjects of study and as vehicles for education. While progressive Spanish teachers are generally critical of the pervasive importance of textbooks in Spanish education, it has to be said that the quality of these has improved beyond recognition over the past twenty years.

In the reform proposals introduced in 1987, the *Bachillerato* becomes the second but non-compulsory phase of secondary education, spanning only the age range 16 to 18. The pre-university COU course which had served in effect as the fourth year of the old *Bachillerato* is to be abandoned altogether. This then considerably reduces the period of post-compulsory pre-university education. Critics fear that the *Bachillerato* will no longer carry sufficient weight on its own and will be squashed between the ambitions of compulsory secondary education and the demands of the universities.

Reform: secondary education

In the reform model, therefore, the 12 to 16 age range becomes the first and compulsory stage of secondary education, extending over two cycles. The main objectives of this new structure of secondary education are to combine general formation with progressive specialization, a common curriculum for all with progressive diversity geared to individual needs and interests and supplied by a range of specialized teachers. The curriculum is considered in terms of areas and their related disciplines. The *Proyecto Para Reforma* recognizes the value of inter-disciplinarity and informal learning. There is reference to the need to cater for fast and slow learners, and for different communities.

The weekly timetable will comprise twenty-seven hours in the first cycle, going up to thirty hours in the second. Common curriculum teaching is to take up 90 per cent of the time to begin with, but reducing progressively to 65–75 per cent at the end of the second stage. Optional hours may be used for compensatory or remedial purposes, for intensifying or going more deeply into one or more of the main subjects, or simply for extra subjects. As students progress through this stage of secondary education they will enjoy increasingly more choice. Schools are to benefit from counsellors, trained to advise and direct students in their paths of study.

As in the case of primary education, the 1989 *Libro Blanco* (MEC, 1989a) establishes the main aims and objectives for this stage of education. It identifies the principal common curriculum areas as Natural Sciences, Physical Education, Art, Geography, History and Social Science, Foreign Languages, Language and Literature (*castellano* and, where appropriate, the community language), Mathematics, Music, Religion (voluntary for students), and Technology. A minimum number of hours is attributed to each of these. The detailed curriculum content for each area is to be specified in the appropriate *Diseño Curricular Base*. But these will allow for flexible interpretation and adaptation within the communities, and will be further modified and adapted in the *proyecto curricular* adopted by each school. Exceptionally, and in the second cycle, the process of adaptation can even mean that particular students do not follow one or more parts of the curriculum but undertake alternative studies.

In the *Libro Blanco* it was proposed that on completion of their secondary education, students would receive a unified form of certificate comprising a historical record, a statement of overall achievement and specific subject achievements, and the future directions that it is recommended are appropriate for the individual student in his or her next phase of education or training. But in the 1990 *proyecto de ley* this was modified:

where students have achieved the objectives of secondary education they are to be awarded the title of *graduado en educación secundaria*, which will qualify them to go on either to the *Bachillerato* or the second grade of *educación técnico profesional*. Thus the 1990 *proyecto* (MEC, 1990) reintroduces the possibility of clear failure. There is relatively little discussion concerning the existence or adequacy of mechanisms to ensure nationwide consistency of standards. In practice, uniformity will be dependent on the combination of national curriculum, university entrance examinations, a more professionally orientated inspectorate, and a new national institute for educational evaluation set up by LOGSE.

While the proposed reform appears, on paper at least, to have removed the basis of a status differential between BUP and FP, it will very likely create a new and somewhat older generation of teenage scholastic 'failures'. If these are not to be lost to further education altogether, there will be two options for them: either to continue in secondary education free of charge to the age of 18 in order to qualify as *graduado* (which the proposed law allows) or to benefit from the specific compensatory programmes which were being discussed by Education Minister Javier Solana prior to final presentation of the bill to the Parliament.

The new *Bachillerato*, the second but non-compulsory stage of secondary education in the reformed system, is to comprise a common core, plus one of four modules within each of which students have a choice of options. The common core will comprise Language and Literature (*castellano* and, where appropriate, the regional language), a foreign language, Mathematics, History, Geography, Natural Sciences, Philosophy, and Physical Education. These will constitute 40 per cent of the timetable. Students will spend a further 40 per cent of their time following one of four modules, choosing from Arts, Natural and Health Sciences, Humanities and Social Sciences, and Technology. Alternative modules may be possible (e.g. the *Libro Blanco* mentions Science and Technology, and it is envisaged that there could be professionally related modules as well, forming part of *educación técnico profesional*.

The *Bachillerato* of Human and Social Sciences, to quote an example from one of the four, will include options in Latin and Greek, Epistemology, Economics and Sociology, History and Geography, and History of Art.

The remaining 20 per cent of available time after study of core and options is to create space for schools to provide their own options within the framework established by their respective autonomous communities. The aim is to allow schools to adapt the curriculum to their own special circumstances, and to correct or to accentuate specialist interests of individual students in the light, for example, of their intentions to go on to further education, training or work. All students are to have the opportunity of studying a second foreign language if they wish.

Curriculum specifications

During 1989–90 the Ministry published for debate its *Diseños Curriculares Bases* (DCB) (MEC, 1989b), a series of documents covering each area of the curriculum across primary and secondary education. Once formally approved these would then serve as the regulatory framework for the actual curriculum as such. It is here, in particular, that the scholar must look for evidence of change in the formal ideological infrastructure of Spanish education.

Many Europeans will find that the language of the DCB is familiar, albeit very fresh in a Spanish context. For example, the second of the overall features of primary education is to be 'a non-discriminatory education, orientated to equality of individuals and their potential, whatever their personal and social conditions, sex, capacity, race or social origin, attempting to eliminate sexual, racial and other stereotypes in our society' (MEC, 1989b). The principal goals of primary education are defined as: autonomy of action in the environment; socialization; and the acquisition of basic tools. The first of these tools is talked about in terms of developing the child's observation of reality, and 'a reflexive and critical thinking which favours the elaboration of personal judgements and creative ideas, on the basis of an adequate, effective and social equilibrium and of a positive self-image' (MEC, 1989b). There are thirteen objectives which specify what children should be able to do at the end of primary education. One of these, to pick an example, concerns collaboration in planning and realization of group activities, which involves among other things the children accepting the norms and democratic rules established, articulating their objectives and interests to the other members of the group, renouncing the exclusivity of their own point of view, and assuming their appropriate responsibilities.

The curriculum framework is seen as contributing to 'the autonomy of schools and teachers who, on the basis of the framework, can programme and establish their intentions in curricula adapted to their characteristics' (MEC, 1989b). Whether this mixture of central regulation and individual autonomy is actually possible remains to be seen.

The prologue to the DCB for primary education considers it is premature to offer terminal and stage objectives, and insists that the document is a proposal, albeit one which draws on the best of research and innovation of the past few years. Points of contrast with more *dirigiste* systems such as the UK's National Curriculum (1988–94) are that it is tentative in its approach, is a result of a long gestation, claims a foundation in research and development, is respectful of the teacher and the school's autonomy, and prefers biological to military analogies.

A DCB, says the prologue, must be open and flexible but at the same time serve to guide teachers, justifying its prescriptive character, and limit itself to statements of objectives and the basic building blocks of curriculum content. Each DCB has five basic elements:

- Statement of general objectives of the appropriate stage (*etapa*) of education, expressed in terms of the capacities which the student will have achieved at the end of that stage;
- Definition of the major areas of study;
- Statement of the general objectives of each particular area, derived from the objectives for that stage as a whole;
- Major blocks of content for each area in terms of its relevant facts and concepts, procedures, values and attitudes; and
- Relevant pedagogy and evaluation, where a series of principles is recommended for the design of teaching–learning activities and methods of evaluation consonant with the psycho-pedagogical options which underlie the rest of the DCB.

Evaluation is to be continuous, individualized and criterion-referenced. It is a matter for each school to decide in the context of its annually reviewed *proyecto curricular del centro* on the distribution, sequencing, treatment and organization of contents throughout each stage and cycle.

Pre-university year

The *Curso de Orientación Universitaria* (COU), introduced by the 1970 law, was perhaps one of its most spectacular flops (along with the first year of FP). It was intended to deepen student knowledge of the subjects they had previously studied for their *Bachillerato*, to guide them in their choice of course or career and to prepare them for university study. In practice the course was treated as just a fourth year of secondary education. Performance was assessed in pass/fail terms. Little or no real guidance was given, and any such guidance was of limited value anyhow, since basic subject choices had been made much earlier. The 1987 *Proyecto Para Reforma* made it clear that the Ministry did not wish to see the COU feature in a reformed system, but that it did want to retain a university entrance test separate from the *Bachillerato*. The new university test that is proposed will have a structure common to all universities, and two broad objectives: evaluation of academic maturity, and evaluation of skills and knowledge in each major subject area. The marks attained are to be averaged with the internal continuous assessment scores achieved in the *Bachillerato*. It will therefore combine the internally assessed *Bachillerato* with the external assessment of the university entrance test.

Formación Profesional (FP)

The reformers of the 1970 *Ley General de Educación* (MEC, 1970) envisioned a three-tier FP structure, although the 1976 regulations provided for only two: FP1 and FP2. Children who had failed to acquire their *certificado de graduado* on leaving EGB at age 14 were obliged by law to take FP at least to the first level. Although this obligation was not actually enforced it stamped the whole concept of such education with the mark of the second best and second rate.

Despite its vocational bias, the curriculum contained a substantial element (at least 50 per cent in FP1 and 40 per cent in FP2) of general education and applied sciences. FP1 was meant to provide a general introduction to work; FP2 (catering for students who had passed FP1 or were moving across after *Bachillerato*) was more specialized, leading directly to careers, and has enjoyed greater prestige than FP1.

Despite its name, the FP1 curriculum was still fairly general and academic, not suited to EGB 'failures'. As the 1984 *Libro Blanco* for the *Comunidad Valenciana* bitterly observed: 'The theoretical subjects of FP have been converted into a second-class *Bachillerato* into which are shipwrecked all EGB failures' (*Conselleria de Cultura, Educació I Ciencia*, 1984). FP was supposed to prepare for employment but there was no linking mechanism to adapt the range of courses offered to changes in the economy. Because some FP centres offered only a small number of specialisms, opportunities varied considerably, depending on their location or the student's home. Nor were employers particularly keen on FP1. While they were supposed to insist on an FP1 qualification for certain categories of employee, this was not much observed in practice. The continuity between FP1 and FP2 was disrupted in order to accommodate students moving into FP2 after passing their *Bachillerato*.

In his introduction to the 1988 *Proyecto Para la Reforma de la Educación Técnico Profesional* (MEC, 1988), the Education Minister, Maravall, noted that, apart from its own internal problems, FP had a negative impact on the rest of the educational structure, spoiling the last cycle of EGB, reinforcing the academicism of BUP and weighing down the universities with responsibilities in technical education which did not properly belong to them. He observed that enhancement of the system through work experience was difficult because most pupils in FP1 were still legally too young to work. While FP2, by contrast, had enjoyed something of a boom in recent years, it was still excessively rigid, regulated and academic. Training was conceived in a linear way, leaving few opportunities for intermediate exits. The offer of specialisms was considerably more diverse than at FP1 but some were obsolete, and there were insufficient specialisms relating to the new technologies.

The new system of *Educación Técnico Profesional* (ETP) proposed by the Ministry aims at greater system agility, flexibility, relevance and self-regulation. It is to be a system to which both the world of education and the world of employment contribute in equal measure. Its first or foundation level is *La Educación Profesional de Base*, starting in the first or compulsory part of secondary education. At this level it includes technology as a foundation subject for all students, as well as professionally related activities in some of the options at this level. ETP continues into the new *Bachillerato*, in the form of certain modules or options, which in turn serves to prepare students either for university and/or professional modules of the highest grade. Following from this foundation comes *La Formación Profesional Específica* (FPE). This relates to specific professions or 'families' of occupation. It is made up of professional modules which may be at any of three levels. Level 1 modules may be accessed upon completion of compulsory education; Level 2 modules require a year of ETP; and Level 3 modules require the possession of the *Bachillerato* or equivalent.

CONCLUSION

Education in Spain during the 1990s will increasingly be dominated by issues affecting the implementation and financing of the reform process. The period of consultation leading to this reform did not seem to take much explicit account of the experiences, positive or negative, of countries in which similar reforms had already been implemented. The progressive forces which have done much to inspire this legislation are likely to face disappointment and frustration in the same measure that reality (and the economy) proves resilient to their ideals. In a period where the supply of teachers still far exceeds demand there is an expectation that highly talented and qualified young people will continue to be attracted into the profession in the medium term until recruitment is affected towards the end of the decade. The challenge to government will be to develop and maintain a professional and working environment in which teachers will feel motivated and esteemed. There will be continuing pressure on the Government to commit itself to free education below the age of 6 years (and some other European countries, the UK included, might watch with interest the development of Spain's commitment to satisfying the demand for places in pre-school education). Great attention will be paid to Spain's new approach to technical education, and its intention to involve industry as an equal partner with education in this process.

NOTE

1 *Comunidad Escolar* is a weekly educational newspaper published by the Ministerio de Educación y Ciencia, Madrid.

REFERENCES

Bolivar, A. (1994) Dirección y organización de centros, *Comunidad Escolar*, 2 March.
Boyd-Barrett, O. (1990) Structural change and curriculum reform in democratic Spain, *The Curriculum Journal*, vol. 1, no. 3, pp. 291–306.

Boyd-Barrett, O. (1991) State and Church in Spanish education, *Compare*, vol. 21, no. 2, pp. 179–97.

Conselleria de Cultura, Educación I Ciencia (1984) *Libro Blanco de la Educación en la Comunidad Valenciana*. Valencia: Generalitat Valenciana.

Fernández-Enguita, M. (1993) *La profesión docente y la comunidad escolar*. Crónica de un desencuentro. Madrid: Ediciones Morata, SL.

Jímenez, J. (1992) Editorial, *Heraldo de Aragon*, 6 May.

McNair, J. (1984) *Education for a Changing Spain*. Manchester: Manchester University Press.

Maravall, J. M. (1984) *La Reforma de la Enseñanza*. Barcelona: Editorial Laia.

Maravall, J. M. (1985) (Prologue to) *Cuadernos Legislativos: Ley Orgánica del Derecho a la Educación y Reglamientos*. Madrid: MEC.

Ministerio de Educación (1970) *Orientaciones Pedagógicas para la Educación General Básica*. Madrid: Centro de Publicaciones, MEC.

Ministerio de Educación (1981) *Programa Renovadas para Preescolar, Ciclo Inicial, Media y Superior de EGB*. Madrid: Centro de Publicaciones, MEC.

Ministerio de Educación y Ciencia (1985) *Ley Orgánica del Derecho a la Educación* (LODE). Madrid: Centro de Publicaciones, MEC.

Ministerio de Educación (1987) *Proyecto para la Reforma de la Enseñanza: Propuesta para Debate*. Madrid: Centro de Publicaciones, MEC.

Ministerio de Educación (1988) *Formación profesional: Proyecto para la Reforma de la Educación Técnico Profesional*. Madrid: MEC.

Ministerio de Educación (1989a) *Libro Blanco para la Reforma del Sistema Educativo*. Madrid: Centro de Publicaciones, MEC.

Ministerio de Educación (1989b) *Diseños Curriculares Bases: Educación Infantil: Educación Primaria; Educación Secundaria Obligatoria*. Madrid: Centro de Publicaciones, MEC.

Ministerio de Educación (1990) *Proyecto de Ley Orgánica de Ordenación General del Sistema Educativo*. Madrid: Centro de Publicaciones, MEC.

O'Malley, P. (1990) Reservoirs of dignity and pride: schoolteachers and the creation of an educational alternative in Franco's Spain, PhD thesis, Open University School of Education.

Puelles, M. de (1980) *Educación e ideologia en la España Contemporánea (1767–1975)*. Barcelona: Editorial Labor Politeia.

2 Turning point: the 1970 Education Act

Pamela O'Malley

The 1970 Ley General de Educación (LGE) is generally regarded as marking an important watershed in the history of Spanish education, similar in significance to if less effective than, say, the 1944 Education Act in England and Wales. Its major provisions are outlined in the previous chapter. Saying that it signified the beginning of a 'modern' conception of education even in the final years of the Franco regime is perhaps to run the risk of undervaluing earlier periods of educational innovation, as during the pre-Franco Second Republic. The 1970 Act is sometimes regarded as a good illustration of the 'technocratic' period of late Francoism, an attempt to adapt social institutions to the demands of a more advanced and competitive industrial economy within an authoritarian framework of government. On the other hand, there was much in the legislation that still seems educationally sound in the 1990s. While certain of its measures were flawed – the continuing division between academic and vocational education, the conception of a 'pre-university' year of secondary education – by far the most debilitating feature of the reform was the failure of the Cortes to vote through necessary finance for its full implementation. The memory of that failure continues to inform much of the educational critique of the 1990 successor to LGE, namely LOGSE. This article was originally written in the context of a doctoral dissertation (O'Malley, 1990) which examined the political antecedents of the 1970 Act.

In contemplating the present reform movement in education, expressed in important education Acts such as LODE, LRU and LOGSE, one is inevitably drawn back to another very different moment of reform – the 1970 Education Act introduced during the dictatorship of Franco. It is useful to analyse that moment and the reasons for that reform in order to understand better the situation of education in Spain at the advent of democracy after the Dictator's death and why the present reform is seen as necessary for a new democratic society.

The decade of the 1960s represented a period of rapid economic growth in Spain. Income per capita increased by 350 per cent and the distribution of the working population underwent a radical transformation. The agricultural sector which had represented 41.7 per cent of GNP in 1960 fell to 29.1 per cent by 1970. GNP grew at a rate of over 8 per cent per annum between 1960 and 1968.

The period of autarky which lasted from the end of the Civil War in 1939 up to 1959 could not have been avoided before the end of the Second World War because of Spain's total isolation, and was later artificially maintained by Franco until 1956. As a consequence, economic growth was considerably slower than in the rest of Europe. Per capita income revived only very slowly and did not even recover to the level of 1929 until 1954. Investment figures were also the lowest in Europe, with the single exception of Portugal. Rationing of essential commodities was maintained throughout the decade of the 1940s. This period is still referred to as the post-war years of hunger.

This situation began to change during the following decade and in the 1950s nearly a million under-employed agricultural workers left the land. About half of these emigrated to South America and the rest found employment in the timidly expanding industrial sector, especially in areas like Barcelona. Adding to this migration from the land, the incorporation of women into the work force began a gradual ascent from 12 per cent of the total female population in 1950 to 15 per cent in 1960, further accentuating the shift towards industrialization and modernism.

Spain's isolation began to break down as diplomatic relations were renewed with the United States, followed by American aid in return for accepting American military bases on Spanish soil. The acquisition of foreign currency through the incipient tourist trade, together with the American aid, enabled the industrial sector to import equipment. However, it was still incapable of competing in an exterior market.

By 1959 the economic situation had reached breaking point and a change in government in 1957 showed that the dominant class was beginning to wake up from its autarkic lethargy and to recognize the existence and possible relevance of European capitalism. The new ministers were in favour of liberalizing the economy. Prices were rising and, in spite of severe repression, increasing labour conflicts were successful in pushing up salaries in industry, all of which added to the alarming deficit, and pressurized the Government to introduce measures referred to as the Stabilization Plan. The peseta was drastically devalued, controls were removed and the economy was partially liberalized.

Two factors in particular contributed towards the spectacular economic growth of the 1960s. One was the advent of tourism, which rose from 2.5 million tourists in 1955 to 6.1 million in 1960, reaching 24.1 million by the end of the decade. The other was the emigration of workers to Europe. The figures rose from 40,189 in 1960 to 181,278 in 1965. It is estimated that one million workers emigrated to Europe in all. In this way unemployment was reduced and the flow of emigrants' savings back to the mother country helped to reduce the negative balance of payments and provided the foreign exchange necessary to import foreign technology.

The rural population which flocked into the industrialized areas of the country provided an abundant labour force at relatively low cost, as in 1958 the salaries had still not recovered to the level of 1936. The conditions for economic boom, albeit of a dependent economic nature, were in place.

Politically there was no change. The Regime continued to deny all political freedom. Political parties and trade unions were banned and any activity attempting to restore such institutions or their functions was considered an offence against the State and severely punished.

That the economic transformation took place with almost no attempt to help the population adjust to their new conditions of life created enormous social problems. These included poor living conditions, lack of urban planning, and low standards of construction and services in new working-class areas, where only the imperative of the most blatant speculation prevailed. The process of converting a rural population into an urban, industrialized work force was brutal and cruel.

In 1965 a study of levels of education among the working population gave the following results (and see Table 2.1):

* Five per cent had no education;
* Ninety per cent had been to primary school;
* Three per cent had been to secondary school; and
* Two per cent had been to university.

In the same year the student population was distributed in the following manner:

* Twenty-five per cent had not completed primary studies;
* Fifty per cent had completed primary studies;
* Seventeen per cent had completed secondary studies; and
* Eight per cent had completed university studies.

(Castro, 1973, p. 172)

Table 2.1 Distribution of the levels of education in the over-14 population in 1969

Education	Total population		Working population	
Degree	253,300	(1%)	187,900	(1.5%)
Secondary diploma	898,200	(3.7%)	425,000	(4%)
Vocational training without diploma	1,836,700	(4.2%)	499,100	(4%)
No vocational training	20,356,200	(82.9%)	10,756,300	(87%)
No education	2,022,600	(8.2%)	486,200	(3.9%)
Total	24,566,100	(100%)	12,363,500	(100%)

Source: Castro, 1973, p. 173

The deficiencies demonstrated here show that the school system had almost completely failed to provide a relevantly skilled labour force during all this period of industrial expansion. The fact that 87 per cent of the working population had no vocational training is sufficiently illustrative. Learning on the job was a costly process from the employers' point of view, especially when the general educational level from which these workers had to start is taken into account – 96.6 per cent of agricultural workers, from which sector the migration was produced, were either uneducated (13.4 per cent) or had not finished primary studies (Castro, 1973, p. 166). Low salaries, the legal prohibition of trade unions and a police force as a readily available instrument of repression for any labour unrest, helped alleviate the cost, notwithstanding the low productivity rate which such a labour force implied. In this way approximately 3 million agricultural workers were transformed into unskilled and subsequently skilled workers for the other sectors. From the employer's point of view, the process took place with little or no contribution on his part. The school system had at most contributed a few years of primary studies, generally without completion and therefore without a certificated qualification. The economic boom was achieved with an unskilled labour force and the extension of manufacturing without requiring technical and organizational resources, or the creation of highly skilled specialists.

In response to the experience of migration and the promise of upward mobility, the number of people who completed secondary education increased from 600,000 in 1950 to two million in 1970; that is to say, it went from 3 per cent of the young adult population to 8.4 per cent in twenty years.

It is true therefore that social pressure, an awareness of the importance of schooling in a society undergoing a process of modernization (albeit within a police state), existed, especially among the middle classes who could reasonably aspire to access to higher education for their children. This demand stretched the existing school system to the limit and is reflected in the increase in the number of pupils in secondary schools. At the same time, children of workers and peasants who joined the working population, and represented much of the 43.1 per cent of workers without any vocational training, plus the 4 per cent possessing vocational training but no diploma, and the 3.9 per cent of illiterates or those without education show that the education system had done very little to prepare these young people for their entry into the work force.

That this occupational transformation was possible without the back-up of an organized educational programme reinforced a secular attitude on the part of the conservative right, which had traditionally seen no necessity to educate the masses. Promotion of popular education had always been exclusively a matter which interested the liberals of the eighteenth and nineteenth centuries and the left. This indifference on the part of the dominant capitalist class to what, in a more general

European context would seem to be their own interests, had few exceptions. Thus, when finally at the end of the decade of the 1960s the necessity for educational reform became manifest through popular demand, the process of reform was arduous and achieved only in the midst of constant internal opposition.

The social changes which industrialization had brought about – migration, population explosion in the cities and towns, and growing dissatisfaction with the Franco Regime – also ensured that opposition was expressed more openly and with greater articulation. The workers' movement led the process with struggles for better pay and conditions which, upon being severely repressed, were converted into more political demands for democratic rights. The university students followed their example, linking their criticism of academic conditions to the workers' demands. On a popular level, the families newly installed in cities began to demand more humane surroundings and, in particular, schools for their children. The middle classes were also becoming impatient with the lack of services and the terrible restrictions which the Regime imposed on society. They, too, demanded better educational facilities.

As a result of this complex situation, the need to modernize the education system so that it could supply the kind of work force that would be required in the newly emerging industrialized society was recognized by some of the dominant classes and their representatives in the Franco Government, the *Opus Dei*, and by the so-called 'technocratic' ministers. Yet other elements of the Regime remained exclusively anchored to the past and to the fascist origins of the system. Added to this was the pressure exerted by the opposition to the Regime, now expressing its demands with greater confidence. In response, the 'technocrats' in government decided to embark on a process of educational reform and formed a team composed of experts who were recalled from posts they held in UNESCO.

The instigators of the Reform Bill published a White Paper (ironically published during a state of emergency, when the few existing rights and freedoms were suspended) which had considerable impact. It was an unusually frank and critical report on the state of education. Undoubtedly, the possibility of educational reform raised expectations and attracted considerable interest. The opposition to the Regime, while demanding reform, none the less remained very sceptical as to the capability of the Regime to implement it.

The White Paper presented a reasonably accurate picture of education in Spain at the end of the 1960s, drawing on data which hitherto had never been made available by the administration. The tone, language and style of the publication marked a refreshing change, being neither rhetorical nor triumphalist. All the statistics provided in the report were of enormous interest and were especially illuminating in view of the difficulties experienced hitherto in obtaining almost any information. They demonstrated the effects of rising school rolls, the effects of migration, overcrowding, of a teaching profession poorly paid and deprived of adequate initial or in-service training, the desolation of the rural areas and excessive illiteracy, admitting the unreliability of available figures and the false picture which had attended previous literacy campaigns. However, the analysis desisted from any attempt to investigate the causes of the dramatic educational scenario which it had unfolded.

The proposals of reform promoted by this document, from the initial definition of aims and objectives to the more concrete delineation of a new structure and content, suffered from considerable ambiguity and nebulousness. There were many positive elements which floated in the air without ever being brought down to earth by the weight of a realistic programme of ways and means, lists of priorities, calendar of application or an explanation of the economic and administrative support the proposals would require.

The contradictions which were themselves forcing the issue of educational reform were reflected in the timidity with which the reform was presented. Those sections of government who proposed the reform, the 'technocratic' ministers, were gravely inhibited by the fact that they could never set themselves against the nature of the Regime, nor cease to protect the interests of the ruling classes. They produced a proposal based on the UNESCO model for developing countries. The strength of its critique of Spanish education (while it never examined the causes of the situation it described) contrasted sharply with the vagueness of the proposals, their timidity and lack of concrete commitments. The reformers were very isolated within the Government and conscious of the limitations and obstacles they were bound to encounter, as well as the hostility they were to provoke.

The 1970 bill was an attempt to modernize the structure of schools, which had remained basically unchanged since the Education Act of 1857, known as the Moyano Law. The proposed new structure comprised a pre-school cycle divided into two phases, one for 2- and 3-year-olds and another for 4- and 5-year-olds, followed by a period of compulsory education from ages 6 to 14, known as EGB, after which students had different possibilities depending on their EGB results: *Bachillerato* from ages 14 to 16 and then COU (a pre-university course) at age 17 for the more successful; and vocational training (FP) from ages 14 to 16 for the less successful.

The teacher training courses and colleges were elevated to higher education status, requiring the completion of secondary education (BUP at first, and subsequently COU) as entrance qualification. Students were awarded a diploma, inferior to a degree, on completion of these studies. There was a prolonged period of adaptation to the new EGB (the last three years of which had formerly been divided between primary as terminal cycle and the beginning of the *Bachillerato*) for practising primary teachers, and new specializations were introduced.

In secondary education, the various *Bachilleratos* of the previous era were unified.

The vernacular languages (*euskera, catalán and gallego*), as they were called, were to be permitted to be taught as subjects, while the subject known as *Formación Pólitica Nacional* (a form of nationalist civic indoctrination) was to be eliminated. However, in the debate in the *Cortes* these provisions were removed.

The general pedagogic orientation for both primary and secondary was towards active, pupil-centred teaching which would take into account the pupils' environment and help to promote pupil participation. A certain degree of limited school autonomy was also introduced. In these respects the proposals went beyond the 'merely technocratic' label which has often been used to describe them.

After a period of intense controversy, with constant attacks from the more fundamentalist fascist elements of the Government and the *Cortes*, the so-called Parliament of the epoch, the Education Bill was finally approved. But its opponents had succeeded in removing the bill's financial support, thus rendering it relatively sterile and inoperative. Originally, the bill was to have been accompanied by a tax reform in order to underwrite its application. This was a realistic measure on the part of the legislators, given the deplorable state of education at the time. Yet the Regime as a whole was not prepared to dedicate the necessary funds to the task of modernizing the education system.

Notwithstanding these difficulties, the 1970 Education Act was slowly, while never completely, implemented and it did indeed transform the terrible reality of Spain's schooling system, with all the defects embedded within its initial framework and the subsequent curtailment of funds. It is to this slow transformation which took place in the 1970s that today LOGSE is applying the reforms deemed appropriate by a socialist government for a free and democratic society.

REFERENCES

Castro, F. de (1973) La fuerza de trabajo en España, Madrid, Cuadernos para el diálogo.
O'Malley, P. (1990) Reservoirs of dignity and pride: schoolteachers and the creation of an educational alternative in Franco's Spain, PhD thesis, Open University School of Education.

3 Education as resistance: the 'Alternativa'

Pamela O'Malley

Operating sometimes in clandestine conditions and at risk of severe repression, a movement for educational reform that came to be known as the Alternativa *was sustained within the educational profession as part of a more general resistance to the Franco Regime. This extremely formative period in the 1960s and 1970s contributed directly to ideas that would later inform the legislative programme of the Socialist Government from 1982, although the author argues that many proposals of the* Alternativa *have been lost, watered down, or inadequately supported. Study of this period offers further insight into the politicization of the teaching profession and the critical experiences of leading educators who later became influential in politics. Many teachers who were politically active in this period were later to be involved in the progressive 'movements for pedagogic reform' which have represented the cutting edge of reform over a period of two decades, even if they are now in danger of being absorbed within the political and administrative establishment. The chapter draws upon the first-hand experiences of the author, who wrote the original version for a 1992 scholarly retrospective of the 1970 Education Act (O'Malley, 1992).*

The blueprint for an alternative conception to the prevailing education system, which was developed in the 1960s and 1970s, during Franco's dictatorship, was yet another milestone in the eventful history of education in Spain. It is not by chance that this reform project emerged from a movement of opposition to the authoritarian regime. Education had been at the centre of the political preoccupations of both the 'two Spains' for more than a century.

Education in Spain during the nineteenth and early twentieth centuries was characterized by a grossly neglected primary school system. The private sector predominated in secondary education and the university system was totally élitist. During this period the dominant forces in education were the most conservative elements of society, allied with the established Church. However, as the opposing liberal and progressive forces consistently rallied behind the banner of education, given their belief in education and in the necessity for an improvement in the general cultural level of the population as an effective means of regenerating society, there was considerable social and political tension, at all times, revolving around education. Indeed, it became an explicit arena of struggle between these two forces of conservatism and liberalism, and frequently served as the spark that ignited conflict and struggle.

The one real period of advance, the Second Republic, was enthusiastically supported by teachers and the severe fascist repression that followed upon the Republic's defeat brought with it terrible recrimination. The very emphasis given to education by progressive forces ensured that the repression was all the more fierce, and the initial remodelling of the school system along fascist lines all the more restrictive.

From the decade of the 1950s, and even more so from the 1960s, initial opposition by teachers to the Regime became manifest. The politicization of anti-Regime sentiments which remained with many teachers from their experiences of student struggle in the universities and, to a much lesser degree, in the teacher training colleges, meant that sections of the new generation of primary and secondary teachers were already conscious of the social inequalities all around them, and were disposed to participate in the growing opposition movement. Once they became part of this professional group, which carried with it an important social responsibility, and established contact with their pupils' parents, their political awareness deepened. The movement which developed had its roots in the popular workers' and citizens' struggles, but was integrated with the intellectual convictions which teachers, many of whom had university qualifications, had developed in their situation as professionals.

In spite of their middle-class origins, rigid controls and their depressing professional and labour conditions (or rather, because of these), many teachers sought greater democratic participation and an alternative to the impoverished school environments in which they were obliged to conduct their professional duties. Given the nature of the regime, this professional awakening became rapidly politicized and led to more militant attitudes of confrontation. As a result, the teachers' movement became increasingly open to the influence of workers' and students' struggles and to the programmes of the different clandestine political groups which were functioning in the 1960s. The varying conditions suffered by teachers, in the state and private sector, at primary and secondary levels, and in religious schools led them to adopt, with different rhythms, anti-Regime attitudes and to enter into contact with activist groups.

A vital necessity for the expansion of any professional movement is the establishment of legitimacy. The teachers' movement stimulated considerable imagination and inventiveness for this task, taking advantage of existing institutions such as the *Colegios de Licenciados*[1] or the State Vertical Trade Union, and creating new institutions (such as the old pupils' associations in teacher training colleges, GOES,[2] pedagogic associations, etc.). Through such platforms a more open confrontation with the

Regime was established and, in spite of repression, a certain space was created for this confrontation.

The teachers' movement created flexible, pluralist structures which allowed it to analyse the experiences of struggle and to elevate them to a higher theoretical level of consciousness. In this way it achieved a really remarkable political unity among the anti-Regime forces which meant that the alternative programme which finally emerged was, in its general lines, shared by the different parties of the left and by an important number of democratic teachers.

The White Paper and the 1970 Education Act provoked a considerable social reaction and the criticisms published, both legally and clandestinely, in themselves created the need for the development of alternative solutions. In fact, they stimulated the spreading of the movement throughout the country, and increased both the quantity and level of teacher participation in the various clandestine organizations and gained them public support through the legal platforms.

Whatever the members of the anti-Franco teachers' movement had learnt through their sterile professional experience in the schools of the Regime and through the more enriching if arduous experience of their struggle for better professional conditions and for political freedom, they put it to use in formulating an alternative conception of education for Spain. Their conclusions were in no way limited to a study of their own professional and labour problems, although these had been the starting point for their reflections, but they were carried through to represent a formulation of what they considered to be the best way of meeting society's needs in the field of education.

The socialist ideological inheritance, drawing from the experiences of the nineteenth and early twentieth centuries, included reformist ideas and even more radical positions. These were divided into two trends, those which supported a state system and those which supported an autonomous, alternative, class-orientated school. Although in the 1960s, the events of the Spanish Civil War and the dictatorship conditioned educational proposals, nevertheless these two tendencies emerged once again. The first trend was supported by the clandestine Communist and Socialist parties and prevailed in the teachers' movement. The other trend lacked the support of the active anarchist organization which had existed before the Civil War, but found expression in nuclei of teachers who were influenced by their professional conditions. These ideas frequently found expression through pedagogic groups which were spontaneously formed and which connected especially with the anti-authoritarian educational ideas of Neil, Rogers, Illich, etc., imported from abroad.

Other authors who had a significant influence on teachers active in the movement were Freinet (especially among primary teachers), Marx, Engels, Lenin and Gramsci (their studies on education) and, in a very special way, Langevin, Wallon and Merani. The Langevin–Wallon Plan coincided in many respects with the 'Alternative' which the teachers' movement was developing. Luria, Leontiev and Vigotsky were also read by many teachers. The books of the Polish author Bogdan Suchodolwski were very popular, as were the Italians, Manacorda and Lombardo Radice. Piaget was, of course, a prominent influence, among primary teachers especially. Another important influence was Freire, introduced especially by progressive Catholics of the movement. The social doctrine of Vatican II, with its forward-looking ideas on education, served as an inspiration.

From 1969 or 1970 onwards, a series of progressive ideas, proposals and principles, which emerged almost simultaneously in various parts of the country, concerning what should be the most appropriate system of education in a future, democratic Spain, came to be known as the 'Alternative'. At first it was expressed almost as a slogan or a long-term utopian proposal, but little by little a theory was developed about the type of education which should replace the grim reality of Francoist schools.

Up until the first legal publication of a draft of the 'Alternative' in January 1977, in the Madrid *Colegio de Licenciados*, the process of elaboration had been lengthy and collective. In various illegal pamphlets different aspects of it were developed. In No. 3 of *Enseñanza Democrática*, the clandestine publication of Madrid's Teachers' Commissions (published some time in 1971 although it bears no date) there appeared perhaps the first more developed version of the 'Alternative', *Cuerpo Unico–Ciclo Unico* (One Body of Teachers–One Cycle of Education). The term *Escuela Pública* was not used until 1974, when the 'Alternative' began to be discussed in the Madrid *Colegio de Licenciados*.

This plural expression began with a design for teachers who would enjoy equal status, at whatever level they were employed. This meant that their initial preparation should be equal in length and category, although differentiated in its content. This was a constant refrain throughout all versions of the 'Alternative'.

Some differences arose with respect to the management of schools as decentralization, a factor common to all the proposals, was accentuated to different degrees in different versions. The degree of autonomy for schools – the freedom to select curriculum and activities and to adapt the learning process to the environment of individual schools - was another of the dimensions which distinguished various versions of the 'Alternative'. There was complete agreement on parents' role in education and their right to participate in school management.

More polemical were the different attitudes towards private schools and to teachers' trade unions. In the first case, most versions of the 'Alternative' adopted a pragmatic, realistic view, conditioned by the quantitative importance of the private sector, in which special emphasis was laid on teachers' rights of expression and freedom to carry out their professional tasks in accordance with their personal values, while accepting the possibility of private schools of different hues entering into the public network. This feature led to a more flexible and enriching definition of the public school. On the other hand there was a more orthodox, rigid viewpoint which advocated nationalization of the school system and the prohibition of private schools.

In relation to a future independent, democratic trade union, most versions opted for a single union of teachers connected to a central trades council. However, in some versions the establishment of different trade unions which should work towards this unity was advocated.

The first element of the 'Alternative' commenced with the *Cuerpo Unico*, the single body of teachers, which was aimed at eliminating both labour and professional discrimination among teachers. Sources of discrimination to be eliminated, in terms of salary, working hours, initial training and so on, were seen both from the point of view of social justice for this professional group and from the impact this would have on the process of education itself. Teachers who were better paid, better trained, less divided and enjoying greater social esteem would be more efficient and creative in their work. Obviously this first element developed out of teachers' analysis of their extraordinarily divided situation, which had been one of their earliest preoccupations, as the different pamphlets of the epoch show.

The next element, *Ciclo Unico*, one cycle of education, again rose from the study of discrimination, this time among pupils, and was aimed at achieving equal education and opportunities for all, without internal selection processes, until the age of 18. Some optional divisions were seen to be necessary from the age of 16, but not before that. The very obvious differences between the educational opportunities of the working-class and peasant children, as compared to the more prosperous classes, were scandalously apparent in society. Besides, this discrimination had a long history, since the school itself had served as an instrument of reproduction of social inequality. Hence the desire of the authors of the 'Alternative' to convert the school into its opposite, that is, an instrument for readjusting social injustice and for developing a spirit of freedom and egalitarianism among citizens.

The idea of *Escuela Pública*, public school, emerged from the study of the chaotic situation of the Spanish system where over 40 per cent of all pupils of different age groups attended private schools. The private schools themselves ranged from the *colegio de piso* (schools set up in flats, of a more or less pirate nature) to well-appointed, expensive religious schools, such as the Jesuit schools for boys, or the Sacred Heart Convents for girls. It was obvious that the problem of state subsidization of private schools was going to become a political issue of major importance and solutions would have to be thought out, in order to bring as much of this sector into the public service as possible, by gradual means.

On the other hand, the existing model of state schools did not satisfy, in any way, the aspirations of progressive teachers who were drawing up the 'Alternative'. They wished to introduce aspects of social participation into the running of schools, through the participation of parents, teachers and pupils, as well as local government, neighbourhood associations, etc., and to take the school out of its isolation and relate it to its environment. This led to what became known as the *Escuela Pública*, which finally was the name by which the many versions of the 'Alternative' were identified.

We have already stated that an unusual degree of political unity was achieved in defence of the essence of this 'Alternative', despite differences over certain questions. It is fair to say that in the first legal elections held in 1977, the political programmes of all left-wing parties reflected this unity. The first democratic governments of UCD, and the debate which took place about those articles of the 1978 Constitution that related to education saw the parties of the left united in their attempts to establish guarantees for a democratic school system, following the orientations laid down in the original 'Alternative'. Other important legislation was presented and debated in Parliament: the Statute of Schools was intended to regulate the content and government of the institution and to take the first steps towards its democratization, and once again there was considerable identification of criteria in amendments presented by the parties of the left.

Since the socialist party (PSOE) came to power in 1982, they, too, have introduced important reform Acts in education, including LRU, LODE and finally LOGSE. To what extent have these followed the same orientation as the original 'Alternative'? Does the fact that the left-wing party *Izquierda Unida* (IU) supported LOGSE in Parliament after pacts which guaranteed the introduction of a series of amendments in the original draft of the Bill, as well as parliamentary support from PSOE for other amendments, signify that this unity was maintained and that the spirit of the 'Alternative' was expressed through these measures?

The 'Alternative' was a generic programme establishing the objectives of education and the school system in terms of a universal, free public service, in which citizens should be able to participate and which should aim at establishing a curriculum which guaranteed equal opportunities for all pupils, a development of their critical capacity and ability to participate in a future democratic society. The unification of teachers' conditions and training and of the content of educational cycles for pupils, plus the opening up of schools to their environment, were the main characteristics of the future *Escuela Pública* as envisaged in the 'Alternative'. The problem of the preponderance of the private sector was taken into account with proposals for the transformation of many such schools into participants in a flexible, plural network of public schools. These proposals were drawn up without the benefit of concrete experience of government or even of political freedom, and inevitably they suffer from a degree of excessive generality. Such clarity as they achieved can only be hailed as a notable achievement in an area as complex as that of education and in such a politically difficult epoch.

While it can be said that to an extent all the elements of the 'Alternative' have been reflected in the various legislative initiatives introduced by the Socialist Government, the priority of such legislation has been the modernization of the school system to bring it into step with the requirements of present-day European capitalism, and the socialist values which had imbued the original documents have been much watered down.

In LODE, which determined the organization and management of schools, the principles of internal democracy were respected. But the regulations which followed the original Act did not provide sufficient means to facilitate such internal democracy, and there is some justification in the accusation that it signified changes in vocabulary rather than in the day-to-day practice of schools. It is certainly true that APAs (parents' associations) for the first time were assigned a meaningful role, but the measures and means which should have helped them to carry out this role have been sadly lacking. The previous authoritarian, closed system of management was roundly banished, but its replacement with a new system of democratic participation involving all sections of the school community has lacked adequate support, means and encouragement from the Administration and, indeed, from society generally.

Equally, with respect to the most political aspect of LODE – that of public financing of private schools – most teachers, the trade unions and left opinion generally have felt that the Government conceded far too much to the religious schools who, with the backing of the hierarchy (on whose support in former epochs they had not always been able to count), conducted a full-scale offensive in an attempt to retain their privileges and, to a large extent, succeeded in doing so. Gradually, and through subsequent regulations, the sustained opposition of teachers' trade unions and the changing character of state schools, more effective pressure has exerted, and control has now been exercised to compel those private schools in receipt of full grants to meet the same requirements as the state schools. But the original proposal in the 'Alternative' for one network, to include all schools financed from public funds, is still far from a reality.

In LOGSE, the most important, progressive elements – the extension of compulsory education to the age of 16, the division of primary and secondary education to take place at 12 years, the creation of a comprehensive secondary cycle up to age 16 and the recognition of the period 0 to six years as a cycle of education – are all genuinely in the spirit of the 'Alternative'. However, it remains to be seen if the necessary means to make such proposals a reality are going to be forthcoming. Up to the present the initial application of LOGSE has fallen very far short of expectations. Fears that it will end up like the 1970 Act, producing purely nominal changes, are to this extent entirely justified.

In relation to the content of education, the introduction of open curricula with teacher participation in curriculum design were positive elements of the early stages of the reform. However, the necessary support and universalized in-service training for teachers which such a change demands have not been implemented to the extent and depth which were expected. Consequently, a growing scepticism among teachers – especially secondary teachers who are to be faced with the most dramatic changes – means that their collaboration and enthusiasm cannot be counted upon to ensure successful application of the reforms. Added to teachers' insecurity in facing what for secondary teachers is a totally new experience, i.e. mixed-ability teaching in a compulsory cycle, there is considerable confusion as to the type of schools they are going to be teaching in. Considerable reorganization of schools is required, with many options possible for the future character of existing EGB schools, and centres for BUP and FP education. The Administration has not clarified its intentions. This adds to teachers' uncertainty and has a corrosive effect on their initial enthusiasm for the reform.

With respect to the original aspiration for a single professional body of teachers as expressed in the 'Alternative', this has never been contemplated by the Ministry nor by the reformers, who have tended on the contrary to crystallize the separation between primary and secondary teachers, in their initial training and in terms of salaries and conditions of work. There is a considerable problem with respect to teachers' initial training, as neither the pending elevation of primary teachers' qualifications has been dealt with (although in some universities a new degree in education is being set up) nor has the need for adequate pedagogic preparation of graduate teachers been resolved. In this respect the 'Alternative' proposals have been relegated to a distant utopia.

In summary, it is impossible to deny that the original 'Alternative' has had a certain influence on the contents of the reform but, equally, certain aspects of its proposals have been totally abandoned and in the case of others, an alarming shortage of resources to support the implementation of reform measures may indeed reduce them to purely nominal changes.

NOTES

1. Graduate associations which were introduced in the nineteenth century to prevent the entry of unqualified persons into the professions. All professions have such *Colegios*. Several were active in the opposition to the Franco Regime.
2. Associations set up by Catholic Action, concerning different social problems. They were also active in the opposition.

REFERENCE

O'Malley, P. (1992) La Alternativa, in *La Ley General de Educación Veinte Años Después*, Revista de Educación, Número Extraordinario, Madrid: MEC, pp. 325–40.

4 The pre-history of educational reform in Spain*

José María Maravall

José María Maravall was the first Minister for Education and Science in the ruling government of Partido Socialista Obrero Español *(PSOE) which came to power in 1982. His period in office lasted from 1982 to 1988. This chapter provides an important insight into PSOE's approach to education in the early 1980s.*[1] *Maravall is most of all preoccupied in this period by the continuing quantitative deficiencies of state provision for education, and by the historical circumstances which accounted for these, and, in particular, the powerful and socially divisive role of private providers (most important of whom was the Catholic Church) during the dictatorship and the 'subsidiary' role adopted by the State. In spite of the watershed represented by the 1970* Ley General de Educación *(LGE), private education continued to enjoy considerable financial subsidy during the last years of the Franco Regime and the succeeding government of Adolfo Suaréz. The 1978 Constitution, to which PSOE was strongly committed, guaranteed a system of mixed provision and the right of private providers of compulsory education to state subsidy, provided certain conditions were fulfilled. Maravall argues that the educational policies of the Suaréz Government, as represented in legislation which it introduced only shortly before falling from power in 1982, adopted a very partial interpretation of the Constitution and of the concept of 'freedom of education', one which privileged the proprietors of private establishments, even where these were almost wholly state subsidized, and which neglected the interests of the other partners of the educational community. It was to correct this imbalance that the PSOE introduced in 1984 the* Ley Orgánica Reguladora del Derecho a la Educación *(LODE) which, among other things, established the right of teachers, parents and children to participation in school management and control.*

* This chapter translated by Oliver Boyd-Barrett

A HISTORY OF FRUSTRATION

Just as in other areas of our collective life, our country has enjoyed only very brief periods of freedom in the field of education. Inequality and scarcity have constituted the other significant characteristics of education in Spain. It is still not so long ago that Spain managed to reduce its deficit in the provision of state school places to less than a million. From the very origins of the modern Spanish State, thousands of children have been deprived of the possibility of going to school. Unlike other countries, the Spanish State long delayed assuming responsibility for public instruction. In very large measure, education thus remained in the hands of private initiative, mainly religious, which has regarded the public authorities as having claim to only a subsidiary, supporting role in relation to private providers. The consequences of this reticence of the State endure even up to the present time although, naturally, they are mitigated by recent and welcome transformations in Spanish society.

The reason for this fundamental theme (of state subsidiarity) in the history of education in Spain must be sought above all in the intrinsic weakness of the modern Spanish State, and its consequent incapacity to provide, in due time and as a public service, a system of education that is obligatory, free and comprehensive. A similar phenomenon can be seen in the field of social welfare.

The social consequences, so far as they affected education, were particularly grave, not simply in terms of the thousands of children who remained without schooling but because that same weakness (of the State) predictably turned education into a site for the confrontation of opposed interest groups, manifested in spectacular, passionate, ideological debates. The scarcity of school places was thus linked to an ideological struggle to determine who should prevail over the system, and whose leadership should be imprinted upon it.

Even today, when the economic conditions of Spanish society have changed so much, and when the educational system has been extended considerably, the debates and discussions around the alternatives for educational provision continue to be dominated by the imaginative ideological expression of supposedly eternal principles or supposedly inalienable rights on the part of those sectors who strive to defend to the death any privileges they have acquired, no matter how precarious their legitimacy in historical terms.

Those great ideological battles, not always unbloody, which have been waged on the field of compulsory education in Spain have in turn, and with considerable frequency, stood in the way of all attempts at a just resolution. In effect, these battles have been waged to defend the principle that education is the bedrock for the 'regeneration' of Spain, or the principle that education represents the strongest foundation of the established order. The more incompatible, politically, the opposing factions, the more profound the confrontation. It was not always an uneasy confrontation: persecutions, purges, killings, the destruction of libraries are counted among the results of this inhibition of the State, this scarcity of places, politicization and ideological passion.

While the observation is out of sequence here, strictly speaking, it is relevant to note that the scarcity of schools would not have been so prolonged, nor the ideological struggle so inflamed, had Spain found some other way to resolve the contradictions inherent in the creation of a modern liberal State. The liberal State finally arrived in the 1830s after the attempt of 1812 had failed to overturn the various, important legacies of the previous nation of Estates, and despite the legislative attempts that had been undertaken in that direction.

Social welfare and education were two of the fields in which the Church maintained its traditional role and influence, thus sustaining key features of what was otherwise already, at least politically, a modern society. Thus Spanish society and the State arrived at the 1930s with a deficient educational system and without an effective system of social security. The State had virtually renounced a modern administrative role in these two areas of social life. Nor were the problems resolved by the initiative of the most powerful social groups. By the 1930s, Spain was not only a poor country, it was an uneducated country. For example, while the majority of civilized nations were laying the foundations of their public administrations, the Spanish were organizing an army on the basis of compulsory conscription and recruitment from outside the aristocracy. While the other European States were giving shape to the constitution of modern citizenship by means of basic, compulsory education and incipient forms of social security, the Spanish State was declining the responsibilities which governments of other countries were willing to shoulder.

With respect to the educational system, this weakness of the State – itself a clear expression of the influence over it of the most narrow and conservative interests – was manifested in a secular neglect at the primary levels, in the early discrimination which the system imposed between those who followed the privileged road towards the *Bachillerato* and those who could not hope to pass beyond primary, and in its general abandonment of secondary levels (to market forces). Conservative interests always responded harshly to any liberal attempt to dismantle the barriers of injustice and inequality in education. Thus, even in the levels which were theoretically regarded as compulsory, the Spanish educational system did not acquire the essential features of a free and unitary system. To put it another way, the long period of conservative hold on power produced a system of schooling to which many children did not even have access and from which the immense majority were quickly ejected.

The liberals, and with them many other groups in society, tended for their part to think that all the evils of the country stemmed from the deficient organization of the educational system and the enormous power over it exercised by the Catholic Church. To educate, to extend education, to ensure that all children had a school place and that no potential for the fostering of intelligence should be wasted – these were the corner-stones of the liberal project for regeneration. Francisco Giner de los Rios summed up this view with the telling words: 'Of all the problems faced on the way towards the political–social regeneration of our community, I know of none so under-rated as that of national education.'

In education, therefore, Spain had to lay the foundation of its redemp-tion and regeneration, and only by means of education would she manage to escape her age-old backwardness. In order for this to happen there was an inevitable demand for the universalization of education, for equality of provision as a public service, and within a unitary structure.

To maintain the existing social order, or to regenerate society: the convergence of conservative and liberal principles, which had been one of the characteristic features of the political development of other European societies, was not possible in Spain. Conservative power, which assumed positions opposed to any change whatsoever, was organized by means of a network of local political rulers with which any attempt to introduce significant political or social reform had to contend.

This solidarity was crystallized in the form of an ideology of the domi-nant social classes. When Menéndez Reigada claimed that the worst enemies of Spain were 'liberalism, democracy and judaism', the words used by Macías Picavea (in *El Problema Nacional* in 1891) to describe primary instruction were still resonating:

> What schools we have! No resources, no functions, no personnel. The mass of the people for whom this level of education is principally intended emerge (i.e. those who had entered in the first place) as unskilled, uncultured and undistinguished as when they went in.

Liberalism could find no routes towards alliance with conservatism and was obliged to place itself beyond its own political system: in other words, to become republican, a new territory where it could find different allies, namely the socialists. While the socialist philosophy of education did not differ substantially from that of the liberals, it placed greater emphasis on strong state commitment to 'equality of educational opportunity' and it married the 'redemptive' character of education with the view that 'the evils of Spain stem above all from the unjust distribution of wealth'.

The encounter of this liberalism which had become republican – that is, which advocated a change of political regime – with a socialism of deeply reformist roots constituted the basis on which had to be built the first global reform project for the educational system of contemporary Spain. The urgent construction of schools, the dignification of the school teacher and a substantial increase in teacher pay, the establishment of a unitary system of three levels, the development of an active and particip-ative pedagogy – these were some of their premises, which they combined

with a distinctly secular attitude and an interpretation of the social function of education as the 'shield and defence' of the Republic. The old
echoes of liberalism were mixed here with the humanist tradition of
socialism and with a radical attitude whose goal was to suppress the
strong Catholic involvement in education by means of administrative
controls.

The reform provoked hostility among substantial sectors of Spanish
society. The 1930s were years in which education was regarded as an
ideological arm, whether as a foundation of a modern and secular State
or as a defence of a traditional and confessional social order. The Civil
War which divided Spanish society in 1936 completely changed the terms
in which historically the confrontation between the supporters of one or
other conception was realized.

The defeat of the Republican sectors in the Civil War was translated
in the fields of education and culture as an annihilation of the humanist,
liberal and reformist tradition. In place of that tradition the ideas of the
dictatorship were presented, with more strength or emphasis than ever,
as the unique and exclusive foundation of a 'new' social and political
order – 'new' in name, traditional in its source of inspiration. Within the
realm of education the new State proceeded to persecute all pluralist
ideas that challenged the national Catholic monopoly.

Where the Republican State had promoted the construction of schools,
dignification of the teacher, equality, secularism and coeducation, the
national Catholic State followed exactly the opposite course. It paralysed
the building of schools, decimated the ranks of the teaching profession,
abused public education in which it saw the germs of a secular evil,
promoted inequality between schools and students, pitilessly indoctrinated
its students and regressed to rancid pedagogies inspired, for example, by
the rantings of Onésimo Redondo who condemned coeducation as a
'crime against the honour of decent women, for which the traitors responsible will pay with their heads'.

Thus, the real freedom of education was roundly condemned and persecuted. Recall the words of the Ripalda catechism: 'Are there other
pernicious liberties?' 'Yes, Señor, the freedom of education, of propa-
ganda, and of assembly.' 'Why are these liberties pernicious?' 'Because
they serve to teach error and propagate vice.'

We cannot allow the useful social service which many private institutions do provide to obscure the historical opportunity which they
exploited in order to develop their school networks.

State policy of non-involvement in education, dramatic scarcity of
school places, ideologization, extreme indoctrination of pupils: it would
have been comical were it not so tragic that on premises such as these
did the parties of the right seize their opportunity in the name of a
peculiar interpretation of 'freedom of teaching' and of private education.
The decades of the 1940s, 1950s and 1960s were, without a shadow of

doubt, the most favourable period for private education. While the State was at once attentive to and compliant with every suggestion of the private sector, the pathetic situation of the public system robbed it of all esteem. The splendour of private education, therefore, was developed not only upon the annihilation of all previous liberal experience but also on the deterioration and abandonment of state education.

Inevitably the triumph of this new 'model of society' meant that for many Spaniards it was practically impossible to send their children to any school, especially if they lived in rural areas. Private education preferred to serve the urban areas, the only areas which could guarantee the economic viability of its schools, thus abandoning the rural areas where to start up a private school was only one step short of ruinous. For many other Spaniards, the city dwellers, freedom of choice of school meant sending their children to colleges presided over by any of the various religious orders dedicated to education.

The splendour of confessional and private education reached its pinnacle towards the end of the 1950s, and then from the beginning of the following decade it slowly but gradually began to lose ground to state education. Why?

For one thing, its capacity to deploy sufficient human resources to respond to the tremendous expansion of the post-war decades seemed to falter: the huge buildings which had been constructed to take in religious vocations began to show worrying vacancies. In order to staff their schools the religious orders had to recruit a growing proportion of non-religious staff to make good the incipient 'crisis of vocations'. It followed, logically, that the real cost of teaching dragged very heavily on the economies of such schools which until then had depended on the fictitious saving which assumes that it is not necessary to pay real salaries to religious teachers.

Simultaneously, the very transformation experienced by Spain with the ending of the dictatorship and the subsequent period of development forced governments to compensate for what had become a huge deficit in available school places, which has been estimated as affecting close to a million children (including in the concept of 'deficit' both those children without a school place and those whose schools were very antiquated).

Given the accelerating pace of industrialization, which created pressure for the expansion of education and an improvement in its quality, there was no alternative for the State other than to assume, decisively, its powers and responsibilities for this sector. At the very time that the theory of 'human capital' had become internationally fashionable as a key-stone to the process of economic growth, the insufficiency of educational resources in Spain constituted a distinct hindrance to the country's ambition for economic take-off.

More than it needed a change in educational policies, the transformation of Spanish society favoured a change in the balance of advantage between the State and private initiative in the provision of education, without the interruption of ideological confrontation. While the Church maintained its hegemonic situation within the private sector, this sector began to lose position, quantitatively, relative to the State. Not that there was a decline in the number of children receiving private education: in absolute terms there was considerable stability. But the volume of state provision grew decisively, increasing the rate of participation in schooling, especially in the social and geographic areas which had been most neglected by private initiative.

In the twenty-five years from 1939 to 1964, the number of children receiving pre-school education and compulsory basic education in state schools remained roughly constant at two and a half million children. By the end of the 1960s the number had climbed to three million. At the end of the 1970s it surpassed four million. At the level of *Bachillerato*, children in official state schools numbered 82,000 in 1960–1; ten years later, in 1970–1, the number was 530,000, and had reached 700,000 a decade later in 1980–1.

The 1970 *Ley General de Educación* (General Law of Education) introduced a unitary, free system of *Educación General Básica* (General Basic Education) which emphasized the public service character of education. In reaction to this reorientation of the State's role in education, the private sector centred all its energy and influence in extracting from the State a legal, financial agreement which would guarantee the survival and continuity of private education. To the difficulties already faced by this sector were now added others, no less serious. The fact that the State had extended its involvement in teaching led to a significant increase in teacher pay, which put private schools in great difficulty. On the one hand, improvement in teacher remuneration signified the potential for a start to improving the status of state-school teachers, which had fallen very low as a result of a history of neglect. On the other hand, the increase in salary levels also placed intense upward pressure on the salaries of teachers in private schools.

In response to this challenge of increased costs for a teaching force which was already mainly secular, the private colleges lobbied the State for recognition as deserving beneficiaries of state grants. The principle of 'freedom of teaching' was exhumed for the occasion in order to support the demand to be financed by the State. In other words, 'freedom of teaching' was a pure fiction, a freedom with no real content, or which would be exclusively reserved for the higher social classes. This consideration was of concern, doubtless, to the campaigners for grant-aid. Despite the egalitarian appearance of the argument, it contrived to obscure the demographic reality that the birth rate of the better-off social classes was not sufficiently high to warrant a free-market regime for the two million places represented by private provision in the early 1970s. The complementary objective of private education was to limit the rate of state expansion, for which it dusted off the old argument according to which the State should be accorded a merely subsidiary role in the field of education.

Over the past ten years (i.e. 1972–82) most of the financing for private education has fallen upon the State which, during the same period, has increased its direct participation in the overall educational system. Thus, for the first time in the history of Spanish education, the cost of compulsory education falls, both directly and indirectly, almost entirely on the State.

But two explicit objectives of the 1970 *Ley General de Educación* were not fulfilled: firstly, the establishment of a system of criteria agreed between the State and private schools for the channelling of subsidies, as provided for under article 96 of the law; and secondly, the rationalization of the school network, as provided for both in the preamble to the 1970 legislation and in the first chapter of the fifth section. What in fact has happened has been a generalized and indiscriminate extension of subsidies without the State having used its budget effectively to overcome the deficiencies of the educational system and to correct its inequalities.

Thus, even though the number of students in private education has fallen slightly but consistently over the past decade, subsidies have increased ceaselessly: from 1,385 million pesetas in 1973 to 14,612 million in 1976 to 70,000 million in 1982. In these ten years, from 1973 to 1982, the budget of the Ministry for Education and Science multiplied by a factor of seven, while subsidies directed to private EGB schools have multiplied by fifty and those to private colleges of *Formación Profesional* (vocational training) by ninety-five. Over the decade, subsidies have grown eight times faster than the annual education budget and sixteen times faster than investment in public education.

Various reports, the most recent of them conducted by the *Inspección General de Educación Básica* (General School Inspectorate), entitled *Subvenciones en La Educación General Básica. Análisis de un Decenio* (Subsidies for basic education. Analysis of a decade), have exposed the irregularities which have accompanied the grant-aid system. What was born as an exceptional procedure has continued year after year, despite the repeated protests of specially appointed internal ministry commissions. The increase in grants has had more to do with the excessive demand for generalization of the grant-aid system (or extension of its 'protection', in the words of the private sector) than with the effective implementation of the principle of free education, which has hardly even been achieved.

Regulations established in 1972 have not been observed. These limited grant aid to schools located in rural zones or in deprived urban areas, or where pupils are selected among residents living in the zone in which the school is located. Requirements in 1976 and 1978 that there should be control committees in schools and regional monitoring committees have been overlooked. Norms governing teacher qualifications, complementary charges to students, classroom capacity and school equipment have been transgressed. A meagre judicial instrument – the Ministerial Order – has been exploited in order to transfer more than half a billion pesetas of State Treasury funds to the private sector.

The consequences of these policies for the rest of the decade do not rest there. In 1970 there were 2,634,394 pupils in private schools. There were approximately the same in 1980 or, to be exact, a slightly higher number. All were dutifully paying for their studies. Today, the public treasury pays for the large majority. Rather more precisely, 90 per cent of students in private sector EGB are subsidized. Over the past ten years the educational establishment has concentrated its energies on alleviating the economic weight that is borne by the families of these students. Less effort was spent in attending to the deficiencies of the educational system. The geographical distribution of public funds for education is revealing – a high concentration in urban zones which enjoy abundant provision and, by contrast, grave inadequacies in rural and suburban zones where private education was and continues to be in scarce supply.

THE 1978 CONSTITUTION AND THE EDUCATION PACT

The Spanish Constitution of 1978 resolved this long historical struggle over education which had degenerated into a confrontation that was as frequent as it was pitiful. The Constitution was the outcome of a process whose intention was to furnish an enduring stability independent of the particular political party in power. Political commitment to the Constitution secured a convergence of differences and the willingness of the different political parties to work collaboratively. The result was a system of checks and balances which is a fundamental characteristic of our Constitution. It is the only way to guarantee political stability for the future, as has occurred in the other civilized nations. It is the only formula capable of ensuring that conflicts of interest will not be unleashed destructively.

The constitutional pact embraced the field of education with an agreement not so very different, for example, from that to which the principal political parties in Belgium subscribed in 1959. But being sanctioned by the Constitution, the agreement acquired a more profound and a more robust consensus. The pact removed many uncertainties about the future of education in Spain.

Article 27 of the Spanish Constitution in its various paragraphs, together with articles 16, 20 and 44, form the basis of our system of schooling. I shall list the components of this balanced system of constitutional checks and balances in the field of education: the right to establish private teaching institutions, the right to state aid or subsidy for private educational providers who fulfil certain requirements, the right of parents to have their children receive a religious and moral upbringing which accords with their own beliefs, the freedom of teaching and, at the same time, the right of all to education, the liberty of conscience, the freedom of the teacher, and the right of parents, teachers and, where appropriate, students, to participation in both the general teaching arrangements and in the control and organization of all schools that are sustained by public funds.

In this way an educational system was designed, thanks to the constitutional consensus, that had a mixed character in which public or state-owned schools coexisted with schools belonging to private persons or enterprises exercising their right to establish schools. The possibility was simultaneously established of state provision of financial or other means of support to those private schools which met certain legally defined prerequisites.

Such schools were required to adopt a system of management and control equivalent to those of state schools; their resources were to be pegged to a level equivalent to those of state schools in fulfilment of their duty to guarantee the right of all to an education. Finally, throughout the education system there were safeguards for the constitutional principles of liberty of conscience and freedom of teacher expression, as well as the right of parents to choose any school among those established by the state authorities, and to provide for their children the moral or religious education of their choice.

In opposition to this set of principles which integrate and standardize the constitutional mandate in the field of education, sectors of the educational and of the political establishment exercised pressure to substitute three alternative principles: firstly, freedom of education, interpreted in its narrowest sense as the freedom to set up new schools; secondly, the subsidiary role of the State, whose duty is to finance private initiative generously; thirdly, the right of each private school to its so-called 'unique philosophy' without intervention by the State in its regulation and, despite full finance by public money, without any monitoring by the State to ensure the fulfilment in any such schools of constitutional rights as basic as those of non-discrimination or freedom of conscience.

In this way the *Ley Orgánica por la que se regula el Estatuto de Centros Escolares* (LOECE), which claimed to develop article 27 of the Constitution, ruptured the balance of the constitutional pact. The law was intended mainly to guarantee to private initiative the right to create and to direct schools, and the right of owners of such schools to establish their own 'philosophy'. Principles such as the participation of the school community in state-financed schools, freedom of conscience, freedom of the teacher or control of grants to the private sector, which were an essential part of the constitutional mandate for education, were negated in LOECE.

LOECE therefore radically restricted the framework of options in educational politics. This framework may have made for an easy life for some political interests, but it blocked any chance of a socialist educational policy, given that it failed to comply with the obligation to develop all the requirements of article 27 of the Constitution, and favoured only those that were to the liking of the government of the day. For example, the provisions of LOECE played down the involvement of teachers, parents and students in the control and management of those schools supported by public funds, delegating this, instead, to the internal rules of each school. The law thus protected the rights and interests of school proprietors; it did not consider or protect the interests of the other members of the school community including parents, teachers and students. For this very reason it was declared, in part, unconstitutional in the judgment of the Constitutional Tribunal of 13 February 1981.

The history of compulsory education in Spain, especially the form in which that history has taken shape over the past twenty years, has brought about a situation which is probably very different from the intentions of the public authorities during that period. In taking on such extensive responsibility for the financing of private education, the State has considerably lessened the classic opposition between public and private education. In EGB, approximately three and a half million students a year were registered in state schools and a little more than two million in private schools. Yet the State now finances around 90 per cent of all places in private schools at this level. Thus, the State has secured the right to free or very nearly free education of 5.3 million children aged between 6 and 14. Only 200,000 youngsters at EGB, somewhat less than 4 per cent, were studying at private schools which received no economic support from the State.

It is the State, therefore, which currently finances almost all compulsory education. This has brought about a degree of standardization of the total educational system far greater than any political attempt to destroy private education. It is now technically incorrect to speak of a state education and a private education as though these were distinct compartments at this level (EGB) of education for the simple and obvious reason that practically the entire system functions as it does thanks to finance from the State. There is no doubt that in a free market and entrepreneurial society such as Spain the private sector is not truly private where its existence and operation depend completely on public finance.

A significant part of the current educational system, therefore, is private only in the sense that this refers to ownership, but not with respect to its sources of finance. A more exact definition of the system, which includes both the aspects of ownership and of finance, would distinguish between state schools (state-owned and state-financed), grant-maintained schools (privately owned and publicly financed) and private schools (privately owned and privately financed), with a clear predominance of the first over the second, and of the second over the third (which constitutes a tiny exception in the range of Spanish education).

None the less, this social reality has not had the benefit of a legal framework to organize the relationships between schools. Up until the approval of the *Ley Orgánica Reguladora del Derecho a la Educación* (LODE), the State limited itself to timid proclamations of the necessity for harmonization of its procedures with those of the grant-maintained schools, while these continued to view their relations with the State solely from the perspective of beneficiaries of state grants.

Spain can be considered as a mixed educational system in terms of ownership, but practically homogeneous in terms of financing for compulsory levels of education. But the situation presents other problems: problems of scarcity, many of them serious (which certainly cannot be attributed to history). The deficit of usable school places in public education is estimated at about one million classrooms with respect to equipment, and 400,000 classes in need of replacement. At the pre-compulsory and post-compulsory levels (i.e. ages 4 to 5 years and 14 to 15 years) there existed in 1982 a combined deficit of half a million school places.

Shortages are not equally distributed. They distinctly reflect patterns of public and private provision. In 1983, 45 per cent of state schools, as against 94 per cent private, had a laboratory; 68 per cent of state schools and 95 per cent of private schools had a library; 51 per cent of state schools and 78 per cent of private schools had functioning sports centres. What is the significance of these figures? That if the school network is homogeneous in terms of finance, there is still a long way to go with respect to equipment. The state schools, which serve rural as well as densely populated areas, have suffered evident discrimination.

NOTE

1 José M. Maravall, *La Reforma de la Enseñanza*, Laia/Divergencias, Editorial Laia/Barcelona, 1984.

5 Preamble to LOGSE*

Ministerio de Educación y Ciencia, 1990

The prologue to the 1990 Ley Orgánica de Ordenación Géneral del Sistema Educativo *(LOGSE) (MEC, 1990) provides an official rationale for the law, summarizes its main provisions and gives expression to its underlying values. The reform is dedicated above all else to the needs and aspirations of individual citizens within the framework of a democratic, participative, consensual, pluralist, non-discriminatory society that is part of a wider Europe, and of a world of increasingly rapid change. The law facilitates the further realization of aspirations embedded within the Constitution. It is fully compatible with the sharing of responsibilities between the State and the autonomous communities. It is a logical development from previous legislation introduced by the Socialist Government during the 1980s, and directs itself to the need to overcome a number of pressing, specified deficiencies of existing provision. It is an unusual law in the history of Spain, in that it has been preceded by extensive piloting, research and debate. Moreover, the law itself is contextualized by recognition that reform cannot be implemented through legislation alone but grows from initiatives that have already been taken, requiring resources, commitment, consensus and participation of all sectors involved, and which is not implemented all at once but, like the concept of education which it wishes to establish, is a continuous process. Because it must endure, adapt to change and remain embedded in a framework of consensus and participation, it must not be over-prescriptive.*

Educational systems fulfil essential functions in the lives of individuals and of societies. The potential for the harmonious development of all citizens resides in the education which these systems provide.

The first and fundamental objective of education is to provide for all boys and girls, young persons of either sex, a holistic preparation which will enable them to realize their own, essential identity, and to develop an outlook on life which integrates knowledge with ethical and moral values. Such preparation must be directed to the development of their

* This chapter translated by Oliver Boyd-Barrett

capacity to exercise – in a reflective manner and within the context of a society which is axiomatically plural – freedom, tolerance and solidarity.

Education transmits and exercises the values which make social life possible, in particular the value of respect for all fundamental rights and liberties. It develops the habit of democratic living with others in mutual respect. It prepares for responsible participation in various social activities and movements. The maturity of societies derives in good measure from their capacity to integrate the dimensions of individuality and community, a process which starts with and is fostered by education.

Lastly, education facilitates progress in the struggle against discrimination and inequality, whether by reason of birth, race, sex, religion or opinion, whether these have a family or social origin, and whether they arise from tradition or emerge continuously with processes of social change.

For all these reasons, different societies throughout history have concerned themselves with the provision of education, aware that through education they shape their own futures, a concern that has too often culminated in systems of privilege, of closed, élitist propagation of exclusive orthodoxies. None the less, every transformation, whether large or small, has been accompanied by or has originated out of a revitalization and advance in education. The conceptualization of education as a basic social right and its extension to all citizens is one of the most profound achievements of modern societies.

Ours is a society in a process of accelerated modernization which leads ever more certainly towards a common horizon with Europe. When incorporating the citizens of the next century into the schools of today, the countries with which we are attempting to construct the European project, which will offer a new dimension to our youth, place great confidence in the relevance of education and training, and are endeavouring to adapt these to the widening of individual, political, cultural and productive opportunities, to the greater rapidity and complexity of change of every kind, offering a longer period of education to a greater number of citizens, promoting the best means in order to guarantee its quality and putting into motion processes of reform of their respective systems.

The same necessity for adaptation has been strongly experienced in our country. Spanish society overall, and the educational community in particular, has expressed itself in favour of fundamental reform of our educational system.

The design of the current system goes back to 1970. In the last two decades, lived for the most part in democracy, Spanish society has experienced a notable momentum and has put behind it the damaging shortages of the past. It has accomplished schooling for all children through basic general education (EGB), creating for that purpose a large number of school places and improving the condition of those places already in existence, achieving important advances towards equality of opportunity, as much by the increase of grants and support as by establishing schools and places in zones which were previously deficient in these, and making various adaptations of educational content and materials. The professional conditions in which teachers now exercise their functions differ qualitatively from those which prevailed then.

The application of appropriate political and judicial mechanisms for the transition to democracy helped overcome residual authoritarian elements which had persisted in the 1970 regulations, and opened the educational system to the new dynamism that had been generated in various fields, in particular to that which came about as a result of the restructuring of the State into autonomous communities, which acknowledged the diversity of these communities, their specific characteristics and, in some cases, their own languages, all of which constitute a common cultural heritage.

In legislative terms the process of reform proceeded with the *Ley de Reforma Universitaria* (Law of University Reform) (MEC, 1983) for the reform of university education. The *Ley Orgánica del Derecho a la Educación* (LODE) (National Law of the Right to Education) (MEC, 1985), which replaced the *Ley Orgánica del Estatuto de Centros Escolares* (National Law of School Regulation) (MEC, 1980), regulated the simultaneous exercise of the various rights and freedoms related to education realizing, through its arrangements for education, the constitutional mandate governing these.

Legislation had not yet tackled the global reform which would regulate the totality of the system, which would adapt its structure and functioning to the great transformations of the past twenty years. In this period of our recent history the changes in our cultural, technological and productive environment have accelerated and Spanish society, organized democratically according to the 1978 Constitution, has achieved complete incorporation within the European Community.

The Constitution has guaranteed for all Spaniards the right to education. It has guaranteed the freedoms of teaching, of the teacher, of the establishment of schools, and the right to receive a religious and moral education in accordance with personal convictions. It has recognized the participation of parents, teachers and students in the control and management of all those schools financed from public funds. The Constitution has entrusted to the public authorities responsibility for providing the conditions for, and removing obstacles to, enjoyment of the right to education on the basis of freedom and equality. It has established the compulsory and free character of basic education and it has redistributed territorially the exercise of powers in education. All these dimensions, demonstrating a capacity to respond to the educational aspirations of society, go to make up the new educational system.

The extension of basic education to the total population, the expansion of opportunities of access to other branches of education, united with the growth in demand for education in the social and productive environment, have activated the legitimate aspirations of Spaniards for a longer and qualitatively improved education.

The progressive integration of our society within the framework of the European Community positions us, in an educational context, for a future of competition, mobility and free circulation which requires that our courses and qualifications should share a common point of reference and currency with the European Community, so that the opportunities for the citizens of today and tomorrow are not compromised.

The pace of the accelerated rate of change in knowledge and in cultural and economic processes requires a basic education which is longer, more versatile, capable of being adapted to novel situations through processes of continuing education, and capable of responding to the specific necessities of each citizen in order that each can achieve the maximum possible development.

All these transformations profoundly favour the need for reform of the educational system, to make it capable not only of adapting to changes that have already occurred but also of preparing itself for those which are to come, relying on a better structure, better qualitative means and on a philosophy which is more participative and responsive to the environment.

But these same transformations also strongly underline the need to find through reform an appropriate solution to structural problems, especially in education, to errors of philosophy, insufficiencies and dysfunctions which have become manifest or which have grown more serious over time.

These include, to cite a few, the lack of an educational framework for pre-compulsory education; the mismatch between the end of compulsory education and the minimum working age; the existence of a dual structure of qualifications at the end of EGB which, besides being discriminatory in its results, channels into FP (vocational education) those who have not satisfactorily completed compulsory education; the structure of FP as an inferior route which at the same time is excessively academic and far too out of touch with the world of work; the excessively propaedeutic design of BUP, which in practice is conceived of as a course of preparation for university; the relative mismatch in access to university between the character of demand and the conditions of supply, in the context of university autonomy.

However necessary the reforms are considered to be, there are very good reasons why they should be confronted calmly, maturely and thoughtfully. The comparative experience of the most advanced countries of our surrounding region shows us that relevant changes require ample periods for maturation and consensus in the educational community and in society at large. This is even more important where, rather than dealing with ephemeral arrangements, we are establishing foundations which will be capable of sustaining robust support for decades to come. For these reasons the calendar for the implementation of reform should be generous.

Equally, the same comparative analysis reveals the high risk of error and inefficiency that is threatened when reform is undertaken from a merely theoretical, abstract and conceptual basis. Our own history is replete with innovations which were conceived with the best intentions, which had solid intellectual support, but which could never be integrated into the world which they were designed to modify, precisely because in realizing their desired ideal model they took the present reality into account only as something to be rejected rather than as an inevitable point of departure. In truth, throughout the history of our education it has been unusual to engage in prior piloting as a process of analysis and in the testing of innovations considered to be desirable.

The conviction that a reform of this order, which it is desired should provide for Spanish education well into the next century, and which cannot reap all its benefits other than by being supported on the basis of a broad consensus, counsels, finally, that the widest possible debate should be facilitated with a view to developing reform on the basis of an essential and lasting consensus as to its fundamental objectives.

These considerations lead to the conviction that what is needed first of all is a rigorous process of research as the basis for profound reflection at the heart of the educational community and of society as a whole. Over recent years, both in the territory managed directly by the Ministry and in the autonomous communities which enjoy full educational competencies, there have been, with distinctive emphases and depths but with the same benefits and usefulness, different innovative experiments, methodological and curricular, carried out at the levels of infant education, at the higher level of basic education and at secondary level. Critical and analytical reflection upon such experiments has provided a more precise understanding of the real effects which the eventual extension of reform would bring about.

With the purpose of stimulating a broad debate, in 1987 the Government published the *Proyecto para La Reforma de la Enseñanza: Propuesta para debate* (Plan for the Reform of Education: A Proposal for Debate) (MEC, 1987), complementing it in 1988 with a document specifically about vocational education (MEC, 1988). Over a period of almost two years the debate attracted comment on the initial proposals and various related issues, from the public administrations, employers and unions, professional bodies, educational centres, recognized experts and people with experience, political parties, religious institutions and, above all, the different sectors of the educational community.

These very numerous and diverse contributions have facilitated a better understanding of the reform and have underlined at the same time its inevitability. From the basis of a broad understanding of essential objectives, expressing general support for the most significant innovations that must be introduced and incorporating quite a number of contributions which required variation from or modification of the original proposals, the Government in 1989 presented the *Libro Blanco para La Reforma del Sistema Educativo* (White Paper on the Reform of the Educational System) (MEC, 1989).

The *Libro Blanco* not only presented the reform proposal, already well formulated, but it also incorporated an arduous schedule of planning and development, to be executed in parallel with the debate and eventually adjusted according to the outcomes of that debate. The effort expended has yielded a very detailed knowledge of the present state of education, our starting-point, and makes possible a greater degree of precision in introducing necessary changes in order to improve the current situation within the terms of the reform. The *Libro Blanco* both proposes a broad and realistic calendar for application of reform, and considers in economic terms the anticipated cost of its implementation.

LOGSE gives judicial form to the proposals (of the *Libro Blanco*) and converts them into an essential instrument of reform. The fundamental objectives to be achieved include the broadening of basic education; raising the age of free and compulsory education to 16 years (the minimum legal age for starting work); the restructuring of education into the major phases of infant, primary and secondary – to include compulsory secondary education, *Bachillerato* and FP of middle grade – FP of higher grade and university education; giving the benefit of a secondary education to all Spaniards; profound reform of FP; and improvement in the quality of teaching. By these means the law attempts not only to overcome the deficiencies of the past and of the present but also, and above all, it provides a satisfactory and ambitious response to the demands of the present and of the future.

In this society of the future, progressively fashioned as a knowledge society, education will share with other social agencies the transmission of information and knowledge, but these will acquire ever greater relevance for education, given its capacity to order them critically, to infuse them with a personal and a moral dimension, to generate attitudes and individual habits, to develop skills and to preserve in their essence the values with which we identify individually and collectively, while adapting them to emerging situations.

These are the goals which will orientate the Spanish educational system in accordance with the preliminary title of this law and, within their compass, education can and must be converted into a decisive tool for overcoming – through the introduction of appropriate construction and use of language – pervasive social stereotypes that discriminate between the sexes.

The right to education has a social dimension. Above all, it demands from the public authorities the necessary, positive actions for its effective enjoyment. It is a right capable of being enriched in the process of its development, reaching ever more citizens, and of offering an extended education. In the opening chapter, basic education is shaped according to article 27.4 of the Constitution, which establishes its duration as ten years, consequently extending the previous range by two years so that it runs from the age of 6 to 16 years. Equally, the commitment to satisfy social demand for infant education contributes to the fulfilment of this right in practice.

The equality of all Spaniards in the light of this basic entitlement, the necessity that studies leading to the attainment of universally valid academic and professional qualifications should meet certain minimum fixed prerequisites, provides a rationale for why the education of all students should have a common content, and in order to guarantee this, the Government is assigned the responsibility for establishing the minimum standards of education, constituted as the basic components of the curriculum. In turn, the competent educational administrations, respecting such minimum requirements, will establish the curriculum for the various levels, phases, cycles, grades and modalities of the educational system. The law is founded both on the essential right to education and on the competencies which the Spanish Constitution attributes to the State, particularly clauses 1.1, 1.8 and 1.30 of article 149. Equally, it favours and facilitates a broad and rich exercise of the competencies which are reserved for the autonomous communities.

The dizzy pace of cultural, technological and economic change positions us for a future of frequent readjustment, updating and new qualifications. Education and training will acquire a more expansive role than they have had traditionally. They will continue beyond the basic period to which until now they have been limited. They will be extended to sectors of the population which have had previous employment experience. They will alternate with working activity. Education will be continuous. The law proclaims its determination that these will be the basic principles of the educational system.

That same perspective pronounces itself in favour of providing a broader, more general and more versatile preparation, a firmer foundation on which to establish future adaptations. The law guarantees a common educational period of ten years, which includes primary education and compulsory secondary education, regulated for in the second chapter of the first section (of LOGSE) and in the first part of the third chapter of the same section, respectively. Throughout basic education, which comprises both phases, boys and girls, young Spaniards without discrimination by sex, will develop a personal autonomy which will enable them to operate in their own way. They will acquire learning of a basic character and they will be prepared for incorporation into active life or to go on to further education through vocational education of middle grade or to the *Bachillerato*. With appropriate knowledge of the body of principles and values contained in our Constitution and of the institutional structure of our society, they will receive the education which will enable them to assume their duties and exercise their rights as citizens.

The period of common education for all Spaniards will be organized in a comprehensive manner, compatible with progressive diversification. In compulsory secondary education, such diversification will grow progressively, accommodating the different interests of students, adapting at the same time to the plurality of their needs and aptitudes, with the objective that they all should be empowered to achieve the common goals of this phase.

The creation of a diversity of modes – Arts, Natural Sciences and Health, Humanities and Social Sciences, Technology – characterizes the new *Bachillerato* which is assessed after four years of secondary education and which prepares students for employment or for continuation of studies, whether in vocational education at higher level or university studies.

For access to university it will be necessary to pass an entrance examination which will assess, objectively, the academic maturity of the student and the knowledge acquired in the *Bachillerato*.

In Chapter 4 of the first volume the law brings about a profound reform of vocational education, aware that this touches on one of the problems of the current educational system, one in need of radical and urgent reform, and which is an area of great relevance to the future of our economy.

This reform will comprise both the basic vocational education acquired by all students in secondary education, and specific vocational training, which will be organized in training cycles at medium and higher levels. To access medium grade it will be necessary to have completed basic education and to be in possession, consequently, of the award of *Graduado en Educación Secundaria*, the same requirement as for access to the *Bachillerato*.

Thus, the dual certification which has existed till now at the end of EGB will disappear and, consequently, the inequality of opportunities for continuation of studies and its negative impact on vocational training. For access to vocational studies at higher level it will be necessary to hold the title of *Bachiller*. The design and planning of the training cycles will include a phase of practical training in centres of work, and the participation of employers will be encouraged.

The law has encompassed, for the first time in a context of educational reform, extensive regulation of music and dance teaching, of dramatic art, of sculpture and of design, responding to the growing public interest in these themes, demonstrated in particular by a notable increase in demand. Several considerations advise that these areas should be incorporated into the general structure of the system and that, at the same time, they should be organized with the necessary flexibility and specificity appropriate to their particular needs and in order to provide for distinct professional grades up to qualifications equivalent to university level which, in the case of music and theatrical arts comprising dance and dramatic art, should be at the level of *licenciatura*.

To guarantee the quality of teaching is one of the fundamental challenges for education in the future. Achieving it is a priority of the first order for every reform process and a foundation stone for the capacity of the reform to put into practice substantial, decisive and educationally practical innovations. The modernization of schools to incorporate the advances that have been achieved in the social environment, public awareness of the importance of the teaching function, the value and attention accorded to its well-being, the active participation of all members of the educational community, the productive relationship of schools with their natural and social environments are, among other things, elements which will contribute to the improvement of that quality.

But above all there is a number of strictly educational factors where improvement will bring about a qualitatively better education. The law identifies and regulates these in its fourth section and dwells especially on teacher qualifications and training (the teacher training curriculum), educational resources, the function of management, educational innovation and research, educational and professional preparation, educational inspection and evaluation of the educational system.

The law considers in-service teacher training both as a right and an obligation for teachers, as well as a responsibility of the educational authorities. That perspective highlights the importance, assuming the necessary means, of the continuing adaptation of teachers to the process of renewal which is required by the versatile, diverse and complex education of the future. Equally valued is the pedagogic autonomy of schools which will allow them to develop and round off the curriculum within the framework of their own curriculum planning, while at the same time facilitating the shaping and implementation of curriculum management.

It is the responsibility of the educational authorities to promote research and innovation in the curricular, methodological, technological, didactic and organizational fields. This includes tuition and counselling as part of the teaching function and establishes the right of the student to receive such help in the areas of educational psychology and vocational guidance. The public authorities will exercise the function of inspection with a view to advising the educational community, collaborating in the renovation of the educational system and participating in its evaluation, thus assuring the fulfilment of the regulations in force.

The law attributes a singular importance to the general evaluation of the educational system, creating for that purpose the National Institute of Quality and Evaluation. Evaluation activity is fundamental for the analysis of the extent to which the different elements of the educational system are contributing to the attainment of previously established goals. For that reason, it has to be extended to educational activity at all levels, affecting all sectors participating in it. With a decentralized structure in which different territorial bodies enjoy a significant degree of autonomy it is even more important to be able to count on a device which serves to reconstitute a global vision and to provide to each and every part of the system relevant information and the necessary support for the improved exercise of their functions. In keeping with these considerations the National Institute of Quality and Evaluation will rely on the participation of the autonomous communities.

The extension of the right to education and the exercise of that right by an increasing number of Spaniards in conditions of developing homogeneity of quality are in themselves the best tools for the struggle against inequality. But besides containing throughout its various sections provisions equally relevant to that goal, the law also dedicates its fifth section to compensating for inequalities in education. By means of actions and measures of a compensatory character – sufficient offer of school places in post-compulsory education, policies for grants and study aid to ensure that access is only a matter of capacity and educational achievement – the educational system will contribute to a reduction of unjust social inequality. But additionally, the development of a policy for adults, connected with the principle of continuing education, and the integrated treatment of special education will be relevant contributions overcoming discrimination.

These are the fundamental aspects of the law which includes, in addition, numerous provisions related to the equivalencies and adaptations of existing qualifications, the modification of some clauses of LODE referring to schools, to the adaptations of current schools, to the attribution to teaching bodies of responsibility for the delivery of general and special training, as well as the basic conditions for access to these bodies, and teacher mobility, to the competencies and co-operation of the municipalities and other provisions which determine the transitional regimes of schools and of teachers.

The law, which directs the educational system with respect to each and every one of the rights and freedoms established by our Constitution and to the full development of the personality of the student, establishes among its provisions that the teaching of religion will be guaranteed with respect to the Agreements signed between the Spanish State and the Holy See, as also with other religious confessions.

Among its provisions the law brings together the foundations of the statutory regime for state teachers, establishing the framework for the organization by the autonomous communities of their state teaching function, and guaranteeing the rights of civil servants independently of their employment with particular autonomous communities.

With respect to the implementation of the goal towards which we aspire, we shall proceed towards it in a steady fashion, step by step, allowing time and opportunity for the integration of the changes into our current situation so as to transform it. The law sets out a calendar of ten years for the total implementation of the reform: a realistic and prudent period which will allow, in addition, progressive evaluation of the effects of such implementation.

Introduction of the reform over a prolonged period highlights the appropriateness of securing a broad commitment which will ensure that there are the sufficient and necessary means for its effective implementation – a political and social commitment which must be constructed on the basis of the plan contained in the economic appendix which accompanies the legal text and which has to be reconfirmed in successive legislated budgets.

The law is an unavoidable and decisive instrument for reform without which the essential elements of the reform would not be possible. But it is not the beginning nor the end of the reform. The changes introduced in recent years which have been directed by the underlying rationale of the reform not only have contributed to preparation for it but already form part of it. Frequently we have succumbed to the temptation of thinking of legal norms as paradigmatic acts which would bring about corresponding transformations of practice. The law contains sufficient flexibility that we can hope it will serve as a framework for Spanish education for a long time to come, being capable of assimilating within its structures the reorientations which future changes to our situation may advise.

For the same reason, reform will have to be a continuous process, a permanent putting into practice of the innovations and the means which will allow education to achieve the goals which society has entrusted to it. For that reason we have before us a law with a sufficient degree of malleability to guarantee a firm framework and appropriate direction, but also to allow for possible adaptations and later developments: a law which therefore has avoided the danger of excessive prescription.

The very decentralized structure of the State favours such malleability. Its full development requires not only the simultaneous exercise, so habitually shared, of respective competencies [between State and autonomous communities (ed.)], but their permanent co-operation. As regards the autonomous communities, even more, and most immediately those which have assumed full competencies, there derives from this perspective the need to play an absolutely decisive role in the task of completing and guaranteeing the effective implementation of reform. From that point of view and following on from a more decentralized conception of education, one that is closely related to its most proximate environment, the local administrations take on greater relevance.

The law refers to the general ordering of the educational system and, in the provision of education as a public service, integrates public education, private education and direct-grant education. The reform requires and guarantees participation in the necessary planning of teaching.

No consistent reform, especially an educational reform, can take root without active social participation. The reform will require and guarantee participation in the necessary planning of teaching. Particularly relevant for the attainment of its objectives is the participation of the different sectors of the educational community, above all the parents, teachers and students. Such participation, underwritten and guaranteed by the Constitution, guaranteed and regulated by our judicial arrangements, is promoted by this reform, which will bring together the different sections and levels of the educational system. Equally, all these sectors must lend their support to it for the benefit of the whole community.

With this determined effort and support we will succeed in raising the Spanish educational system to the level of quality that is demanded and deserved by our society, by a forward-looking outlook on to the twenty-first century and by the developing framework of Europe.

REFERENCES

Ministerio de Educación y Ciencia (1980) *Ley Orgánica del Estatuto de Centros Escolares* (LOECE). Madrid: Centro de Publicaciones, MEC.
Ministerio de Educación y Ciencia (1983) *Ley Orgánica de Reforma Universitaria* (LRU). Madrid: Centro de Publicaciones, MEC.
Ministerio de Educación y Ciencia (1985) *Ley Orgánica del Derecho a la Educación* (LODE). Madrid: Centro de Publicaciones, MEC.
Ministerio de Educación y Ciencia (1987) *Proyecto para la Reforma de la Enseñanza: Propuesta para Debate*. Madrid: Centro de Publicaciones, MEC.
Ministerio de Educación y Ciencia (1988) *Formación Profesional: Proyecto para la Reforma de la Educación Técnico Profesional*. Madrid: Centro de Publicaciones, MEC.
Ministerio de Educación y Ciencia (1989) *Libro Blanco para la Reforma del Sistema Educativo*. Madrid: Centro de Publicaciones, MEC.
Ministerio de Educación y Ciencia (1990) *Ley Orgánica de Ordenación General del Sistema Educativo*. Madrid: Centro de Publicaciones, MEC.

6 Educational reform in Spain and in the UK: a comparative perspective

Oliver Boyd-Barrett

Originally prepared for a conference on educational evaluation in Madrid (Boyd-Barrett, 1993) on the eve of a new era of educational evaluation in Spain marked by the establishment of the Instituto Nacional de Calidad y Evaluación *and of general recognition of the necessity for evaluation of the implementation of LOGSE, this chapter draws on the contrasting experiences of Spain and the UK to argue the importance of an international dimension to evaluation, with particular reference to the themes of democratization; decentralization; comprehensivization; curriculum standardization; vocationalization; multi-culturalism; and professionalization.*

My purpose in this chapter is to focus on a number of key themes which emerge from consideration of reform in Spain and which also figure prominently in discussions about educational reform in the UK – and to ask why it is that two countries within the European Community sometimes seem to be moving in quite different directions and propelled by quite distinct discourses. The question is the more intriguing because the reform debate in Spain has drawn inspiration from UK theoreticians of the 1970s and 1980s in such areas as action research, the role of teachers' centres and constructivist theories of learning. Yet evaluation of Spanish reform rarely takes explicit account of what is actually happening in UK education. In neither country is policy development related systematically to analysis of relevant international practice. This then raises the question: what place should comparative analysis play in the evaluation of educational reform, and what questions can most usefully be addressed by any such analysis? I cannot answer such questions directly or exhaustively in this chapter, but I hope to show that they deserve higher priority than they at present receive.

The chapter offers brief discussion of the following key dimensions: democratization; decentralization; comprehensivization; curriculum standardization; vocationalization; multi-culturalism; and professionalization. I choose these because they seem to me to be essential axes of the discourse of reform in the two countries and because they are structurally fundamental to the conceptualization and implementation of reform.

Simply to take them for granted and to adapt evaluation and assessment to whatever structural parameters prevail is seriously to undermine the role and potential of the task of educational evaluation. Of course, merely to list such structural concepts is to invite discussion about issues of definition and signification and these are challenges far beyond the scope of this chapter. Broadly speaking, I would argue that in Spain there has been positive movement along each of these dimensions (multi-faceted as they are), with the exception of curriculum standardization, which now exhibits a mixed picture of curriculum specificity and homogenization, with improved opportunity for local adaptation, and optionalization. In the UK, on the other hand, there has been a negative movement towards a diminution in at least some facets of many of these dimensions, with the important exceptions of vocationalization, and curriculum standardization.

DEMOCRATIZATION

Education in Spain has been transformed in the space of twenty years, and not least with respect to the opportunities for consultation and participation. The role of education in the Moncloa Pact, later enshrined in the Spanish Constitution of 1978 with its provisions for the protection of the educational rights and duties of citizens, is perhaps so fundamental an achievement that it is sometimes taken for granted. On this constitutional bedrock LODE was constructed, with its provisions for the involvement of parents, students and teachers in the government of schools – including even those private schools in receipt of state finance – and for the establishment of widely representative consultative bodies at state and community levels. Central Government has adopted a much more open approach to policy development, best represented by the systematic, carefully timetabled plan of consultation in the development of LOGSE.

It is in the nature of democratic procedures to frustrate and disappoint as often as they enable. A UK observer of Spanish school governing bodies (*consejos escolares*) after LODE might well have predicted on the basis of UK experience that they would be excluded or marginalized in relation to the key decisions of teaching and learning at the heart of school life, and that the participation and organization of parents and students (school children are not represented in the UK) would be lukewarm, uninformed but, occasionally, disruptive and seen by teachers to be undermining. The rhetoric of consultation prior to LOGSE lacked total conviction: participants were generally not well informed about the pilot reform experiments (which in themselves raised complex methodological issues, even if the important thing was that they happened). The debate was largely driven by two groups: progressive educationists on the one hand, and their ideologically sympathetic but more pragmatic colleagues in the Ministry, on the other. Arguably, the discourse was framed in a manner that effectively excluded more traditional and conservative interests. The reports of the national *Consejo Escolar de Estado* are a welcome addition to a widening but still modest range of sources of evidence and evaluation. Whether this national consultative machinery (the closest institutional parallels during post-war UK education have not survived) can be sufficiently unified, critical or innovative to become a major force for influence in the system has yet to be demonstrated. At the level of the autonomous communities, the consultative bodies enjoy little visibility and perhaps less influence. But pessimism with respect to the school governing bodies (*consejos escolares*) would certainly be premature, especially if Spain moves towards greater managerial autonomy for schools. UK experience suggests a positive relationship between autonomy and the power of governing bodies. Greater managerial autonomy for schools in Spain, if it comes, will certainly intensify demand for more effective internal school management, and here there awaits a painful balance to be established between criteria of democracy (which maintain continuing commitment to election of school heads, for example, despite severe shortages of candidates and consequent recourse to nomination by the administration) and managerial effectiveness. The extent to which this matters is dependent on the range of parameters over which schools can exercise real choice and real control, at present still very limited. The teacher unions have, in my view, made a strong contribution to educational debate and policy development in Spain, although this is in some measure contingent on the respect upon which they can count within mainstream government, a respect which may not be apparent until one looks at the UK, where it has been almost entirely absent. This raises the question of whether the exercise of democracy actually requires a commitment to consensus politics. The UK experience suggests that the rejection of a consensus model (in this case justified by an ideology of the 'freedom of market forces' which puts the concept of consumer above that of citizen) is a serious threat to democratic institutions and processes within the education service, even if the Government considers that it has acquired a popular mandate in national elections. This, then, may become an increasing dilemma for a Socialist Government that is increasingly seduced by market ideologies prevalent in the broader sphere of Europe.

DECENTRALIZATION

Estimations of centralization or decentralization are complex, for centralization in one sphere can be offset by decentralization in another, and so on. In the context of Spain it can safely be said that in most important respects there has been significant decentralization over the past twenty years, albeit starting from a point of such extreme centralization that the degree of subsequent decentralization may still seem modest. The establishment of autonomous communities with educational competencies, a process to be extended across the peninsula, is both a measure of decentralization but also highlights the retention of very important powers at the centre and these pose the question of how far processes of decentralization are actually accompanied by real differences of provision between communities across key areas of decision-making. If we compare Spain with a federal system such as that of Switzerland, we can conclude that in the most important parameters (structure of institutional provision, ages of compulsory schooling, hours of schooling, etc.) Spain remains more centralized than decentralized. The curriculum is still essentially a national curriculum, albeit with significant new spaces for local autonomy, not least with respect to provision for the teaching of and teaching through the languages of Spain other than *castellano*. (I do not wish to underestimate the complexities that arise from local administration of national provisions as we have seen in such areas as the creation of places for new categories of teaching staff in secondary education, or in the controversies that surround the 'continuous day'.) But there is also an important distinction to be made between what is legislated and what actually happens, and information about the latter is still relatively scarce and unsystematic (although this is an area where significant and rapid improvement can be expected). While Spain has had and will continue to have a strongly defined national curriculum, for instance, the curriculum as it is delivered and assessed appears to be remarkably free of external moderation and review.

If we can describe Spain essentially as moving from high centralization to moderate decentralization of educational provision, what can we say of Britain (or, at least, of England and Wales – the histories of provision in Scotland and Northern Ireland are somewhat different), which appears at one and the same time to be moving towards high centralization (with national curriculum and assessment, and the undermining of local education authorities (LEAs) – until now the bodies with major statutory responsibility for provision), and high decentralization (through LMS – local management of schools – and the encouragement to schools to opt out of LEA control in the form of grant-maintained schools)? There are indeed complex paradoxes here, which in this case relate to the right-wing political ideology of the market place. This ideology has focused attention on questions of parental choice of school as the one factor that can most appropriately drive quality – through competition between schools for parents and the managerial autonomy of schools to respond to competitive forces, increasing the pressure for selection of children at entry, and thus for a subtle dismantling of the comprehensive system. The Conservative Government believes that comprehensivization has failed (despite, ironically, an improvement in the numbers of children taking and passing terminal examinations at ages 16 and 18), but finds it difficult openly to advocate a return to the old tripartite (more commonly bipolar) structure, whose manifest inequalities and injustices constitute an important memory within the national psyche. Instead, change has to be accomplished within a framework of commitment to the 'protection of standards' (allegedly eroded by the comprehensive schools), hence the need for a national curriculum, and a need for national testing to ensure that parents have the 'objective' information which they require in order to make informed judgements about their choice of schools. The necessity for a national curriculum and national testing, together with the brutal centralist intervention which is required to undermine the LEAs and to promote the opting out of schools from LEA control, has created an overriding and paradoxical impression of a Central Government anxious to destroy any mediating influence between itself and thousands of individual, insecure and fearful institutions, dependent directly on Central Government for their finance and survival. This appears to be the understanding of the schools themselves, given the relatively slow rate of take-up of GMS status (despite tempting but temporary financial bribes), which may yet provoke the Government to coercion in place of persuasion.

COMPREHENSIVIZATION

Through LOGSE Spain has set itself to accomplish, in a climate of general support and self-congratulation, the ending of a post-14 curriculum divided between BUP and FP, replacing it with a single national system of compulsory education up to age 16 (although the economic recession has caused delays in the implementation of reform so that provision of compulsory secondary education to 16 will not actually be in place until the year 2000). It is remarkable that in the build-up towards comprehensive schooling in Spain so little publicity has been given to the crisis of comprehensives in the UK, where the middle classes generally bewail the collapse of standards and discipline, especially in inner-city areas. It is also arguable whether the working classes have benefited in terms of educational achievement, or access to the more prestigious institutions of higher education. For them the old selective grammar schools may have been a more secure ladder of upward mobility, albeit one that depended on an injust (because premature and nationally uneven) system of selection on the basis of national standardized tests at the age of 11. A popular Conservative view is that comprehensivization has populated all state secondary schools with significant minorities of un-educatable children – the product of anti-educational social sub-cultures in British society, who create serious disruption and unrest, consume and exhaust teacher time and energy, reduce teaching strategies to the safe and the unimaginative, and create tense, unpleasant environments not at all conducive for the effective education of 'mainstream' children. As yet, no proposal that would involve the systematic and direct removal of such disruptive minorities from the mainstream has been contemplated. For complex ideological reasons, however, the perceived problems of UK (and especially English) education are typically dealt with evasively and dishonestly. Almost from the beginning, the principle of comprehensiviz-ation had been corrupted by various strategies for streaming and other methods for the separate education of children of different abilities and aptitudes. Fernández Enguita (1990) has predicted precisely the same range of evasions for Spain. While these may protect the more able children, it is still debatable whether they offer as effective a route for the able and the bright children as would separate institutions empowered to sustain an institutional and professional ethos that is unambiguously and unashamedly committed to high academic standards. At the same time streaming can lock the less able, or less motivated, into low-achieving and self-reinforcing sub-cultures. The existence of a strong direct-grant (*concierto*) 'private' system of church schools in Spain could in itself provide an alternative to the mainstream, simply by becoming a preferred choice of middle-class parents or by substituting academic for religious criteria for their continuing separateness. Right-wing critiques perceive in comprehensive education the prevalence, rooted through institutional practice, of an ideology of professional practice geared to, or driven by fear of, the interests of a non-achieving and anti-educational sub-culture (whose strength and influence were exacerbated by the raising of the school-leaving age from 15 to 16 in 1973), that has made many teachers feel incapable of or disenfranchised from a commitment to academic values. New legislation taking effect from 1993 is intended to induce a rapid increase in grant-maintained ('opt-out') schools, free of LEA con-trol, and the provisions of that legislation may lead to a situation where, increasingly, 'difficult' students are referred to the special care of LEAs.

VOCATIONALISM

At the same time, there have been significant attempts to increase non-academic, pro-vocational routes through the curriculum from age 14 onwards, driven in large measure by a concern for the 'non-academic' sub-cultures, but also by employer complaints about the competencies of school leavers. These have their parallel in the proposals of LOGSE for a foundation of vocational training in the final two years of compulsory secondary schooling (a feature of LOGSE, incidentally, that has attracted little subsequent attention). In the UK the theoretical objective is the replacement of academic criteria and norm-referenced testing by criteria of 'capability' and criterion-referenced testing, as represented, *par excel-lence*, by a new framework of national vocational awards (NVQs). Within the school sector, however, there is still a long way to go before the dominance of the 16+ GCSE examinations (themselves an amalgamation of what was once a dual system of GCEs for the more able and CSEs for the less able) or of the 18+ GCE 'A' levels are seriously weakened by vocational substitutes. Implementation of the 1993 Dearing Report (SEAC, 1993) may have the effect of propelling at greater speed the introduction of more vocationally relevant and less academic lines of study and qualifications into the 14–16 curriculum. Such a measure is seen by the report as the key to raising pupil motivation and achievement at this level of education, and the proposals are inspired by particular reference to European experience.

It is in the sphere of vocationalism that there exists the greatest commonality of ideology between the two countries, supported by their common membership of the European Community, one of whose principal educational preoccupations has been the harmonization of vocational qualifications. In both countries there have been moves towards better integration of education-based and work-based training, identification of 'families' of vocational skills and transferability of skills. Spain has also had to focus on the rapid modernization of its range of qualifications, but there is a broad consensus as to the need for reform, with attention mainly on post-16 provision. In the UK much of the original energy for reform came from outside the Ministry (DES), and was located instead in the Manpower Services Commission (MSC, now TEED (Training Education and Enterprise Division – of the Department of Employment)), within the Department of Trade and Industry. There was a struggle between ministries to seize the initiative in vocational Education and Training, and the Education Ministry lost this battle. At a more preparatory level, a succession of major innovations under the Conservative Government have sought to revolutionize the traditional academic curriculum at school level in favour of newer criteria of competence. The introduction of City Technology Colleges (within secondary education) in some of the inner cities powerfully symbolizes this ambition. Designed to bring together government and business finance, the CTCs have depended in practice mainly on government finance. They are considerably better resourced than other schools and cannot therefore easily offer a general model of provision. For other schools there have been substantial grants available for the introduction of new lines of study that respond to the ideology of enterprise and initiative hailed by government, and there has been a move to extend vocational award-bearing courses from colleges of further education into schools. The underlying ideology is one of the market place, to supply the skills which are supposedly in greatest demand. Sadly, the recession has proved that demand is dictated by much more than a supply of the 'right' skills. The introduction of the NVQ – national vocational qualification – provides a means of accrediting a vast array of different skills according to a standard gradient of levels, which can be mapped on to traditional school, college and university qualifications, and which are criterion-referenced, work-based and focus on skill rather than knowledge. It is a movement with powerful backers, whose ambitions are to strike at the heart of academic culture, even at degree and post-degree levels. There is certainly concern about the reductionism inherent in these attempts to substitute 'competency' for 'academic' criteria which leave scant space for the development of critical skills and independent thinking. For Spain many of these issues do not yet exist. But extension of compulsory education to 16 will radically increase the heterogeneity of the ESO population from ages 14 to 16, which in turn may introduce similar pressures for change.

CURRICULUM STANDARDIZATION

The concept of a national curriculum is, of course, very well established in Spain, and follows the French Napoleonic tradition. LOGSE introduces both a more detailed and yet more flexible curriculum, appropriate to a modern, democratic, pluralist society. Some of its content was foreshadowed by parts of the 1970 *Ley General de Educación* (e.g. in the matter of continuous assessment): unqualified application of the term 'technocratic' to describe that law has recently and rightly been criticized by Manuel de Puelles (1992). LOGSE is strongly underwritten by a constructivist ideology which did not exist in 1970. Given the relatively short life-cycle of academic theories, such a strong theoretical underpinning may prove unfortunate, as the same content could probably have been underwritten by a variety of theories or by none at all. But at least it can be said that Spain, unlike the UK, is a country where academic (as opposed to nakedly political) theory is still seen to influence official educational policy.

It used to be said that there were two main approaches to curriculum control in Europe: some countries prescribed a curriculum, other countries prescribed assessment, but few did both. Spain has a national curriculum but it has, as yet, no system of *national* external assessment of individual students: guidelines, yes, but the actual practice of assessment is left to the schools. The nearest thing to external assessment is the network of university entrance examinations, each one catering mainly for students in its respective geographical area, and who actually intend to study at university level. Long-standing concerns about their validity and reliability, and about their usefulness as predictors of university success, are creating pressure for more standardization. In the UK (or rather, in England and Wales, given the contrasting histories of Scotland and Northern Ireland) by contrast with Spain, there was until 1988 no national curriculum. Increasing concern about school standards, voiced particularly by right-wing pressure groups in the 1960s and 1970s, induced worries about variations of curriculum between schools, among many other complaints. Such variation was said to create significant problems in a country with high population mobility, and was intensified by the fashion for modularity in the upper levels of secondary schooling during the 1970s. But it is very doubtful whether there was anything other than a fairly traditional preoccupation for English and Maths at primary level, where these two basic subjects accounted for roughly 50 per cent of the curriculum. The main source of effective curriculum control at secondary level came from the examination boards, setting examinations at 16+ and 18+. There were many different exam boards and variations between them in syllabuses and, possibly, in standards of assessment. Less able children were entered for a different examination at 16+, the CSE, which could be taken in any of three modes, one of which took the form of moderated school-based assessment of school-designed curricula. Overseeing the role of the examination boards was a national body, the Schools Council, which, until its abolition by The Conservative Government in the early 1980s, had broad responsibility for advising the Minister on matters of curriculum and examinations. Too much under the control of teachers for the Government's liking, the Schools Council was principally engaged in the development of innovative curriculum materials. Up to that time the general philosophy of Central Government was that the curriculum was a kind of 'secret garden' into which politicians should not stray. The 1988 Education Act, which introduced the National Curriculum Council (shortly to become the School Curriculum and Assessment Authority, SCAA) hammered the final nail into the coffin of that philosophy, and introduced, without challenging the continuing role of the examination boards or the principle of school inspections, both a very detailed national curriculum and also compulsory testing at the ages of 7, 11, 14 and 16. The introduction of standardized testing has occasioned anxiety among many teachers and parents for whom the idea of national testing is associated with the iniquitous system of selection of children on the basis of standardized tests at 11+, which prevailed before the introduction of comprehensive schools and on the basis of which children were sent either to grammar schools, whose provision of places was very uneven across the country, or to the supposedly non-academic secondary modern or technical schools. The new National Curriculum resulted in an extraordinarily over-determined, top-heavy bureaucracy of curriculum prescription and curriculum assessment. Ironically, the situation has been made worse by pressure from the teaching profession for maximum validity of tests. The search for the 'holy grail' of validity led to the construction of a testing machinery hopelessly over-complicated and demanding, so much so that it seriously intervened in the day-to-day education of children and has quickly proved unworkable. Teacher demands for a reduction of the work load for which they themselves are partly responsible had been resisted by Secretaries of State, but following a period of acrimonious struggle, and the publication in 1993 of the Dearing Report, which was commissioned by the Ministry to try and find common ground between the combatants, the trend now is towards a very substantial reduction in the amount of testing and record-keeping required, reducing these in all subjects other than English, Maths and Science. This in turn, however, has excited fresh fears that the curriculum of primary education will be too narrowly focused: only on those parts that will be subjected to testing. Given that the place of English and Maths in the primary curriculum actually fell from 50 per cent to 40 per cent after the introduction of the National Curriculum, it could be said that despite the contrary demands of Conservative politicians in the 1980s for a 'return to the basics' the National Curriculum did actually establish a broader curriculum at primary level than had previously existed, but one that proved to be unsustainable. The testing fiasco of the past few years has partly been justified on the basis of 'parental right to know', since the intention was that test results should form the basis of public 'league tables' of schools. At secondary level, arguably, this need has been fulfilled more cheaply, quickly and effectively by publication (enforced by earlier legislation) of league tables of schools in terms of their GCSE and GCE examination passes. The ideology of 'parental right to know' developed from the experience of many parents in the 1960s–80s who considered that schools released insufficient information about the performance of individual children or about the schools' own institutional performance. Parents vary, of course, in the freedom they enjoy to make rational decisions about schools on the basis of relative academic performance: other factors such as geographical proximity can be much more influential for the less wealthy. Teachers try to insist on the importance of contextualizing 'raw' examination and test scores with reference to the standards of children on entry to particular schools – the 'value-added' concept.

As Spain moves towards establishing a more effective machinery for the evaluation of education (CIDE (*Centro de Investigación, Documentación y Evaluación*), INCE (*Instituto Nacional de Calidad y Evaluación*), etc.), a process that in itself is greatly to be welcomed, it will choose whether to adopt rigorous national testing for all children, with all that this entails with respect to the associated controversies of validity and reliability, concerns about the use and limitations of such tests as tools for diagnosis, and the problems of curriculum 'backwash' (the extent to which teachers 'teach to the tests' and thus narrow the curriculum), or whether it wishes to focus solely on broad, systematic evaluations, which will not embarrass particular schools or groups of children. In determining in which direction to go (and the 3–year agenda established for INCE in 1994 suggested that it would be the latter), it would in my view be very regrettable if careful consideration was not given to the experience of countries such as the UK. The Dearing Report is moving education towards a view of testing where standardized national tests are regarded as 'summative' and teachers' assessments are regarded as 'diagnostic'; the proposal that these two modes of assessment should be equally weighted is welcomed by most teachers, but there is controversy as to whether the two forms of assessment can or should be aggregated to provide overall scores. The Dearing Report recommends that the National Curriculum be reduced to 80 per cent of school time up to the age of 14, then reducing to only 60 per cent for 14–16-year-olds, moving in a direction of increasing flexibility very similar to that already established by LOGSE in Spain.

One tool of curriculum standardization, overlooked because not understood in the UK, and unpopular among progressive educationists in Spain, is the textbook. In the UK there are no political controls over textbook publication and schools are expected to provide all curriculum material. There is an acute shortage of funds to buy books, hence children too often do not have any or, if they do, the books have to be shared or are seriously out of date, and parents rarely see them. In Spain, on the other hand, textbooks are subject to procedures of ministry approval. Parents buy them, children have them, they are generally up-to-date and the standards of production are increasingly impressive. Progressive educationists continue to fear that textbooks undermine the development of a more flexible curriculum, responsive to the needs of particular teachers, students and regions. These fears are understandable, based on distant memories of a system where the entire curriculum rested on a single, ideologically infused, textbook. But they fail to take account of instances in other European countries where textbooks have been used as major tools of curriculum reform. They undervalue the considerable ingenuity and the resources that are today invested in the design of texts to support rather than to lead teachers, and they underestimate the additional work that teachers must undertake in the absence of support texts. A curriculum without textbooks requires an investment of teacher time and energy that is frequently undeliverable without diminution of quality. This is an issue that I do not believe has ever been formally investigated in the UK. Textbooks bring the curriculum into the home, with the children, and at best they can provide a bridge for the actual involvement of parents in the processes of teaching and learning.

MULTI-CULTURALISM

Commitment to multi-culturalism in Spain is most convincingly represented by the evolution of policy towards the teaching of and teaching through the various national languages of Spain, that is to say, principally, *euskera, catalán, gallego* and their respective variants where these are sufficiently standardized, as is the case of *valenciano*, for instance. This has brought about an interesting and healthy proliferation of models for bilingual education. There is tension between the enthusiasts who argue that it is those children whose mother tongue is the 'dominant' language (*castellano*) who most of all require immersion in the alternative national language in order to acquire competency in it, and others who feel that the actual scope for choice of language education in particular geographic areas is threatened. None the less, this tension has been surprisingly low-key. That is to say, policies of bilingualism have been developed and are continuing to be implemented with a commendable degree of tolerance on all sides. Perhaps the networks of private or direct-grant (*concierto*) schools provide alternatives to the locally prevailing models of language provision. In general one can say that provision for bilingual education is most advanced in those areas with the strongest histories of demand for political autonomy, the strongest traditions of literary culture in national languages other than *castellano*, and where the 'standard' variant is both well defined and commands consensus. There are problems with respect to variants other than those which have been officially standardized, or which do not map neatly on to political borders (such as Portuguese in Galicia). Minority cultures such as those of the gypsies, or of North African immigrants, are clearly much more problematic although they are sympathetically dealt with at the level of national policy-making and in the national press (a sympathy that is sometimes much less in evidence at informal neighbourhood level), to a degree which I would say, sadly, is no longer common in parallel contexts in the UK. In general, therefore, one can say that Spain shows strong movement towards greater pluralism, and LOGSE is very emphatic on the necessity for adaptation of national curriculum guidelines to local and individual needs. In the UK there is a less certain forward movement. Security of provision for teaching through the medium of Welsh, for example, is threatened by the undermining of Welsh LEAs (mainly socialist) by Conservative Central Government. There is little mother-tongue teaching for immigrants in UK schools. The place in the curriculum of 'language awareness' in relation to non-English or non-Standard English variants has been called into question by recent attempts inspired by the Ministry to rewrite the English curriculum with a view to requiring Standard English as the normal language of schooling from the earliest ages, and by the partial eradication of 'Section 11' monies which had hitherto funded the employment of mother-tongue instructors mainly to assist children of immigrant parents for whom English was not a first language. Although the Christian churches, most notably the Church of England and the Catholic Church, have enjoyed well-established networks of schools in receipt of government subsidy for many generations now, grave impediments are still encountered by other religious groups such as Muslems when they try to establish schools of similar status. Religious education, a requirement in all schools, emphasizes Christianity and Christian values.

PROFESSIONALIZATION

In both Spain and the UK there was a feeling prevalent in the 1980s that teachers were badly paid and poorly respected, least of all by their respective governments. In Spain there have been considerable improvements in pay and conditions in more recent years, albeit starting from a low base. Negotiation between government and teacher unions is marked by respect, critical yet on the whole positive. But considerable hurdles must be jumped by individuals who wish to secure permanent employment in the teaching profession. The rules governing participation in management have made teachers more accountable to a wider variety of interests than before, including parental interests, but the *claustro* (the body of teachers within any school) has its own defined role in such matters as the curriculum, and is well represented on the governing body (*consejo escolar*). Structural reform has shaken up traditional divisions between teaching bodies, and there are undoubtedly injustices which can and do arise in the process of reintegration of teachers into the new structure. The extension of compulsory education may yet become the major issue, but it has at least occurred in parallel with curriculum reform (in significant contrast with UK experience).

In the UK, teachers have lived through an extraordinary decade, one that began with a demoralizing succession of unsuccessful strikes in the 1980s, but which may have ended by 1993 on a more victorious note with respect to the issue of the scale of work required for assessment and record-keeping. Throughout most of this period, teachers, alongside other public service workers, have been subjected to a continuing, pompous, political harangue from central government which has treated them with open contempt, all the more extraordinary in the case of teachers, the majority of whom have traditionally supported the Conservative party in national elections. Pay policies have been massaged to increase the gap between senior school managers and ordinary classroom teachers, but in contrast with some other professional groups (e.g. university academics) teachers have improved their relative position. Intensified hierarchization of pay, together with LMS (Local Management of Schools) and 'opting-out' have enhanced the climate of managerialism and undermined collegiality. Teacher training is being pushed away from higher education into the schools and the accomplishment of an all-graduate profession achieved in the 1980s is increasingly undermined by the proliferation of non-graduate routes. In Spain, on the contrary, while there has been greater reliance on teachers' centres for in-service education, there are moves to strengthen the role of higher education in teaching training with the development of faculties of education, which may eventually unify the functions of teacher training, initial and continuing, and research, now divided between the less prestigious university schools and the university institutes of education sciences.

CONCLUSION

If, as is sometimes argued, educational systems of developed countries are responding to broadly similar pressures regardless of national boundaries, how is it that two countries within the European Community exhibit such marked differences of direction? Is it that they are moving towards a similar point on a continuum but from different ends or starting points? Is it reasonable to assume that the directions which have been initiated will be sustained and, if not, why not? Should we conclude that cultural particularities are every bit as important in the analysis of educational reform as the more global socio-economic pressures experienced by the developed countries? While I leave these questions 'on the table', I offer at least one firmer conclusion: that comparative analysis has an important role in national evaluation, being an important source of critical insight into the ideological underpinnings of national theory and practice, whether or not these are explicitly recognized for what they are within their respective national systems.

REFERENCES

Boyd-Barrett, O. (1993) La Reforma Educativa en España y en el Reino Unido (R.U.): Una Perspectiva Comparativa, paper presented to *Seminario Sobre Las Reformas Educativas Actuales en España. Su Evaluación: Metodología y Resultados*, 26–28 October, Madrid.

Fernández Enguita, M. (1990) *Juntos pero no revueltos*. Madrid: Visor, pp. 29–50.

Puelles, M. de (1992) Tecnocracia y politica en la reforma educativa de 1970, in *La Ley General de Educación veinte años después*. Número Extraordinario de la Revista de Educación, pp. 13–29.

Schools Examinations and Assessment Council (SEAC) (1993) *The National Curriculum and its Assessment* ('The Dearing Report'). London: SEAC.

7 Problems of implementation in Spanish educational reform*

Javier Doz Orrit

The author outlines three major problems that may hinder the implementation of the process of Spanish reform which was formalized with the approval of LOGSE in 1990. These are: the parallel necessity for quantitative and qualitative improvements; the necessity for integration of education with the labour needs of a changing economy; and the difficulty of inspiring an appropriate level of teacher motivation. Each of these has budgetary implications as substantial as they are unwelcome in a period of economic recession, although relieved in small measure by falling school rolls.

There can be no doubt that it is, above all, in the field of education that the PSOE Government has demonstrated its reformist credentials. One could almost say that it is one of the few fields where policy has been actualized. In the majority of other spheres it has either not known how or has not had the will to do other than yield to the most extreme pragmatism.

It began with university reform in 1983, and after various attempts at reform of basic and secondary education it introduced a global reform whose proposals were concretized in 1989 with the *Libro Blanco de la Reforma Educativa* (White Paper on Educational Reform) and in 1991 with the approval of a law, LOGSE, which embraces everything from infant education (from 0 to 6 years of age) up to non-university post-secondary studies in vocational education.

Without wanting even to attempt a summary of the most significant aspects of the reform, I will mention those which seem to me to be the most essential:

1 The reform introduces an important change to the structure of education, leading from a basic education (EGB) of eight years (from 6 to the age of 14), and two subsequent alternative routes, BUP and FP (1 and 2), each of four years' duration (from 14 to 18 years of age) to a structure more like those of the educational systems of the developed countries: primary education (ages 6 to 12) and secondary education,

* This chapter translated by Oliver Boyd-Barrett

divided into an obligatory stage (the ESO, 12–16 years) and a *Bachillerato* of two years' duration (from ages 16 to 18), together with a more flexible system of FP of two years' duration. This involves a major restructuring of schools and teachers.

2 The inclusion of infant education (0 to 6 years) as an educational stage.

3 A profound change of vocational preparation, from two inflexible periods of study, with two courses each of two years' duration, to a more flexible system of modules whose duration varies from one to two years, studied after ESO – vocational preparation of medium level – or after *Bachillerato* – vocational preparation of higher level – with awards as demanding as those which are gained by students who choose more academic routes (access does exist without an award, based on professional experience rather than examination).

4 An expansive curriculum reform based on the principles of a more open curriculum, a comprehensive approach to compulsory education and – inspired, albeit with a certain eclecticism, by those principles of educational psychology known by some as constructivist – a focus on processes of learning and on individualized attention to students, principles which are notable for their practical implications and which constitute one of the principal problems for the application of reform.

In general terms the project of educational reform is progressive in orientation. While maintaining established commitments with respect to financing of provision of obligatory education in private schools, this is extended neither to infant education nor to the *Bachillerato*. Amplification of the supply of public places for infant education could support a strengthening of the public sector of education in the later stages. One has to take into account that the relative share of public provision in the current EGB has remained around 65 per cent of all students since PSOE came into power in 1982.

One of the principal reasons for the negative opposition vote to LOGSE in Parliament from the Spanish Conservative party – Partido Popular – was precisely to do with the fact that the law did not contemplate the financing of private schools at the non-compulsory levels of provision. LOGSE obtained the favourable vote of *Izquierda Unida* (a party to the left of the PSOE) and of the nationalist Basque and Catalan parties.

THE EDUCATION AND POLITICAL SITUATION OF SPAIN

In order to understand the circumstances of Spanish society in which the development of educational reform has been initiated through application of LOGSE and the new curricula, I believe that one must take into account the following considerations:

1 The indices of schooling in Spain have reached levels equivalent to

those which exist in other developed countries at the secondary and university levels. The strong decline in the birth rate, which has fallen from 3 per cent to 1.1 per cent in two decades, has brought about the disappearance of a common phenomenon of the 1970s and the beginning of the 1980s – social conflicts over the struggle to secure schooling, under adequate conditions, for children and young people. The educational conflicts of the period 1986–9 in great measure originated from the demand, on the part of students, for non-selective entry to university, and the demand by teachers for an improvement in their conditions of work.

These days, population pressures (the largest cohorts of students) are experienced most strongly at upper secondary and university levels. One should also note the proportion, unusual in Europe, of those who study the *Bachillerato* as against those who undertake vocational preparation (FP).

In reaction to the cultural and ideological changes suffered by the Spanish population there exists great regard for the importance of achieving the highest possible level of studies and qualifications in order to progress socially, that is to say, a strongly individualist desire for social mobility. In sum, one can say that the esteem in which the educational system is held by part of the population, and the level of confidence which it inspires, has increased spectacularly in the last decade. Nevertheless, the massive increase in the number of students has established, at those levels which have not yet been affected by the fall in the birth-rate, problems of scarce resource and overcrowding.

2 The political configuration of the Spanish State has not been consolidated. The distribution of powers between the Central Administration and the autonomous communities is still in the process of resolution, with important economic, political and administrative implications.

   The current model, in the so-called *Estado de las Autonomías*, is a quasi-federal model, with strong differences between the autonomous communities in the powers that they have; that is to say, between the historical communities of Cataluña, País Vasco and Galicia, those others which, for diverse political reasons, have sought equal status with them, and the other communities.

   Currently, the Ministry of Education and Science administers educational provision in 10 of the 17 autonomous communities which make up the Spanish state. In the other seven, education is the responsibility of the regional government. It is envisaged that the management of the educational system will be transferred to all the autonomous communities in the next few years.

   The parallel timing of the application of educational reform throughout the 1990s and the change in the location of administrative responsibility will introduce, without doubt, additional problems.

3 The Spanish economy entered into recession in the last third of 1992. The growth envisaged for 1993 is negative: −1 per cent. At the end of the current year (1993), the rate of unemployment will stand at around 24 per cent of the active population, and the percentage of persons of working age is, in turn, significantly lower than that of the most developed countries, due to the lower incorporation of adult women in the labour market. In our model of economic development, employment does not begin to grow until the rate of economic growth exceeds 2.5 per cent.

Given these brief statistics, among many other possible statistics, it is no exaggeration to declare that we are living in a crisis situation.

Superimposed on the collective crisis in Spain, and in common with the other developed economies, is a structural crisis with characteristic features which, if it could be summed up in a few words, is as much a crisis of industrial competitiveness as of the under-utilization of human resources.

The important economic growth of the period 1986–90 has been in good measure speculative. Financial capital has predominated over productive capital, with foreign capital acting as a motor of growth. The important public investment in infrastructures was not accompanied by an industrial policy which could make them pay. The monetary inspiration of the economic policy of the Government of Felipe Gonzalez, which has maintained the world's highest rates of real interest, has been an insuperable handicap for Spanish industry.

The expansive budgetary policy which did not control the growth in current expenditure of the three administrations – local, regional and central (still to be rationalized in the distribution of their functions and services) – was paralysed in 1993. By the end of this year (1993), the accumulated public debt was around 52 per cent of gross national product, and the budgetary debt for this exercise was 7 per cent of gross national product. These are not alarming figures, especially the first, in the context of Europe, but they are worrying. They demand austerity and spending efficiency and, on the other hand, they begin to serve as justification for those who demand cuts in social expenditure.

Spending on public education has grown in the decade 1982–92, from 3 per cent of gross national product up to 4.15 per cent. Nevertheless this growth has been insufficient to fit educational infrastructure, staffing and in-service training to the necessities of a quality educational system, at a time of strong expansion in the rates of schooling in the non-compulsory levels.

Spain has started from a very low historical level of public input into education, from a significant accumulated deficit, and has not yet reached the average rate of public expenditure as a proportion of national wealth (6 per cent) which pertains in the developed countries (EC and OECD).

Yet in the year 1993, which sees the beginning of the general application of educational reform to the first two years of primary education, the budget of the Ministry of Education had risen 3.1 per cent, two points below the rate of inflation for 1992.

THE MAJOR PROBLEMS OF EDUCATIONAL REFORM

The principal problem which has to be confronted in the process of educational reform in Spain is how to carry out the intention of simultaneously extending the period of schooling, at specific educational levels, and improving the quality of teaching, mainly by means of a profound curricular reform, in a context of economic crisis which has been translated by the direction of government policy into severe budgetary restrictions.

A second major problem is how to integrate the educational system, and in particular the subsystems of vocational education and the development of science and technology in the universities, with the Spanish system of production, in a context of a restructuring of the international economy, the outcome of a technological revolution with many economic, social and labour implications, which undermines the current international division of labour and for which there is no strategic economic policy.

A third group of problems centres on the teachers, the motivations and capacities with which they respond to the proposals for curriculum reform, related to their working conditions, teaching strategies and the training with which they fulfil their function, in a context of growing crisis of professionalism, in the sense of a rupture from the traditional paradigms of self-esteem of the teaching force.

None of these major problems, or groups of problems, are exclusive to the Spanish educational system. In different measures they are experienced in all the principal developed countries. They present particular characteristics which derive from the situation and history of our educational system. They remain outstanding even at the very point of putting into motion a global educational reform – whether structural or procedural, curricular or professional. Some voices, normally conservative, recognizing the difficulty of achieving a global reform of the Spanish educational system after twenty years of experience of the model inherited from the *Ley General de Educación* (1970), and of the economic, social, cultural and political changes that have occurred in this time, and of the persistent educational deficits, believe that a global reform is necessary. But if it is done badly, and without sufficient means, even its virtues can become defects.

It cannot be denied that ominous clouds loom over the educational reform which now begins to take shape.

From each one of the three major problems which I have just outlined can be developed an ample list of more concrete problems, together with the factors which have given rise them to them and the possible solutions which have been proposed to deal with them. The length of this chapter only allows me to offer a general account of these.

WILL THE BUDGET STRANGLE THE REFORM?

The educational reform now in force is ambitious and expensive. I trust I will not be accused of being 'economistic' if I assert that at the moment the principal source of problems is the scarcity of budgetary resources with which it has been launched. Although the economic appendix to the *Libro Blanco de la Reforma* already seemed insufficient to many analysts adequately to address the multiplicity of objectives and proposals contained therein, the investment chapters of the last three budgetary exercises (1991–3) have made provision for only between 40 per cent (1991) and 51 per cent (1993) of the initial estimate.

Certainly the Government had to find resources for significant increases in expenditure occasioned by salary improvements and by the incentive to voluntary retirement for teachers aged 60 and over – consequences, in turn, of the singular strike experienced in the public sector of education which took place over a period of five months in the year 1988. In any case, the improvement in salaries and in conditions of work for teachers was almost a necessary prerequisite for the reform, although it was not planned for in the economic appendix.

Up until now the major subsystems most affected by the budgetary reductions are those of infant and adult education. Here, the withdrawal of support of the Central Administration affects educational supply in its entirety. In infant education, the Ministries of Education and Social Affairs have blocked their collaborative efforts with regional and local administrations to support public and private provision, mainly affecting children aged 3 to 6 years (but not exclusively, as many schools also provide for the complete age range up to 6 years). There has only been an increase in the supply of places for 3-year-olds, in state EGB schools, sometimes without providing the appropriate material adaptations and with a relatively high (1:25) teacher–child ratio. One has to take into account that the level of demand for such provision – viewed as educational in the legislation of LOGSE, which is among the most advanced in the developed world – continues to grow despite the fall in the birthrate, due to the incorporation of young women into the work force (not so much into actual work, in the current circumstances of recession).

The demand that is not satisfied by either the public network or the grant-maintained private sector, nor by the very expensive high-quality private sector, turns to private nurseries, which are not subject to any kind of educational inspection, which in many cases do not meet minimum architectural or hygienic standards, and in which children are looked after by personnel lacking any teaching qualifications.

The rate of schooling for children of 3 years of age exceeds 85 per cent, and that of 4- and five-year-olds, 95 per cent. Provision is mainly in the pre-school sections of EGB schools.

Heavily indebted local and regional administrations have not increased existing state supply of infant education. There are exceptions, as in the community of Madrid (where PSOE governs with the parliamentary support of *Izquierda Unida*), which is developing a second plan for the construction of state infant schooling, in collaboration with the town halls which are committed to co-financing the maintenance of the schools.

But in general that promise of LOGSE remains unfulfilled, which obliges the public administrations (without specifying, of course, the respective degrees of responsibility between the different administrations) to ensure that there are enough places made available to supply all the demand for this stage of education. The establishment of reform at this first level offers a clear example of shock encounter between very ambitious objectives and a much more restrictive reality.

Adult education is another educational sector in which the translation into practice of an attractive 'philosophical legislation' is still to be realized. This very important subsystem in Spain – as much in order to remedy the cultural backwardness of the generations who were schooled before the 1960s, as to put into reality the principle of equal opportunities and 'education-through-life' – depends on the three administrations, local, regional and state, which very often fail to show convincing co-ordination. While expecting a potentially very high level of demand for the different types of programme, the Ministry has rejected up to now any proposal which would significantly increase the supply.

The politicians responsible for education have established that for the time being priority should go to strengthening efforts at the compulsory levels of education. Nevertheless, here, too, serious problems are manifest. Indeed, the delay of a year in the calendar for progressive application of the reform is due to the impossibility of completing the programme for the construction and adaptation of centres of secondary education.

The concept of compulsory secondary education as a common teaching core in accordance with a comprehensive curricular model is without doubt the most expensive of the possible options. This is apparent above all when one takes into account the educational infrastructure available – network of schools, internal and external school support services, the commitments undertaken for compensatory measures at particular points in students' educational careers and the curricular model chosen – to which I refer in the last section of this chapter.

It is clear, in my judgement, that the decision to go with this model, rather than others with different and earlier levels of segregation, marks one of the clearest differences between progressive and conservative

policies. If put into practice without sufficient means and with a demorali-
zed teaching force – and both things have much in common – it can lead
to a real deterioration in the levels of quality which will affect, in the
first place, the state network. The experience of the public comprehensive
school in Great Britain and the United States in the 1980s can tell us a
great deal in this respect. In fact it was an argument brandished by the
conservatives during the period of legislative debate, but they have
the audacity not to relate that situation to the political and economic
policies of Reagan and Thatcher that they themselves were then
defending.

The continuity of the restrictive budgetary policy can gravely affect the
conditions in which the new compulsory secondary education is introduced and in so doing can discredit the principal nucleus of the educational reform.

If the amplification of the network of secondary schools is not
accomplished in time, unavoidable as it is in the rural zones, and with a
combined policy of opening new schools and readapting existing ones in
the urban zones, we will find in many cases that teaching in compulsory
secondary education, derived from a curricular project which rightly aims
to be both global and open – in the sense of allowing for the possibility
of different outcomes in line with the particularities of the socio-cultural
environment and the learning needs of individuals – will be provided in
different institutions: the first cycle of compulsory secondary education,
from ages 12 to 14, may be provided in primary schools, and the second
cycle, from ages 14 to 16 years, in the secondary schools, by teachers who
have been trained differently, who have different pedagogic traditions
and who have not had previous relevant experience at co-ordinating the
two cycles.

The requirements that, as educational reform spreads, schools and
teachers should have at their disposal sufficient advisory and educational
psychology services, that the provision of in-service training for the new
curricula should be extended to all teachers, that curricular adaptations
and the support programmes for children and young people with learning
difficulties and for those who despite all else cannot reach the minimum
level required to obtain the qualification of ESO, should become a reality
leads forcibly to a significant increase in educational expenditure.

If this is not forthcoming, the simultaneous outcome of the objectives
of amplification of the offer of education and the improvement in the
quality of education will not come about, and given that this is what
the reform demands, it will have failed.

ECONOMY AND EDUCATION: CAN THEY BE RECONCILED?

I start from a non-mechanistic conception of the necessities and possibilities of adapting the educational system to the systems of the production

of goods and services of an economy currently characterized by full participation in the world capitalist economy and, therefore, subject to the current cyclical and structural crisis, and by the vertiginous speed of the introduction of new technologies – especially those related to information and communication – with the consequences of every kind which these bring about in the work-place, in the quantity and quality of work, and in demands for initial and continuous training. Any educational system, although it may struggle to introduce measures for adapting to the labour market, will always lag behind it, and now more than ever.

On the other hand, we are not exactly living in a time of great clarity with respect to the future of world society and its consequences for the fields of work and education, and the relationship between these. The collapse of the centrally planned economies antagonistic to capitalism has perplexed thinkers, economists and politicians alike, and not only on the left.

Some general considerations can be offered with a certain measure of certainty:

1 The current model of growth of the capitalist economic system is not sustainable indefinitely from the ecological point of view (including in this concept the physical and the human environment).
2 Within this or some alternative model, and if scientific and technological capacity (both actual and potential) were put to use, the labour time necessary in order to produce goods and services, both those that are necessary and those that are superfluously induced by the consumer society, would tend to diminish. Reduction in the working day, or work-sharing or alternating patterns of employment–unemployment, are different ways of dealing with this situation.
3 Technological changes, especially those related to information and tele-communications, will lead to an economic system which will polarize the training needs of workers, with a highly qualified minority of scientists, engineers, managers, etc. and a majority of semi-qualified operators and subordinates.

   At the same time there will be an increase in the demand for labour in the large traditional public services or in the new service industries, with a varied range of requirements either in line with the traditional professions or requiring little in the way of qualifications.
4 Compulsory education which affects all citizens must be founded on a broadly based scientific and humanistic base, in touch with social reality, which will allow for later, specialized training experiences. Even initial professional training must develop an important degree of polyvalency, complementing more specialized training, with periods of work-based practice or training.
5 The investment of human resources and endeavour in scientific research

and technological development is an essential component of any model of economic and social development.

I do not share the positions of those on the left who strike an attitude of resistance to the problem of the possible and manageable adaptation of the educational system to the demands of the production system. Sometimes the sum total of humanist, academic and anti-capitalist thinking results in a leftist academicism which is of little use for social change. Of course it is necessary to defend the humanist components of the curriculum, education for community, democratic values and the development of critical capacity, but not at the expense of separating the educational system from irreversible social and economic processes.

In every case one must educate to develop a capacity for redirection, by means of political and social change, and for putting self at the service of a model of a more just and more fraternal society.

Given the benefit of substantial funding from the European Community in recent years, the principal problem of professional education in Spain has not been economic, at least not so far as it concerns occupational training. The same cannot be said in the case of funds for research and development designed for research training. During the triennium 1989–91, Spanish expenditure on research and development reached an average of 0.7 per cent of gross national product. Today it is around 0.8 per cent, with a slight regression in 1993. In 1982 it was only 0.35 per cent. These figures place Spain among the industrial countries which have invested least in research and development, far behind the rate of 3 per cent of the most advanced countries in this respect.

Returning to professional training, the principal problems which must be confronted by the model proposed in LOGSE are:

1 The traditional lack of inclusion of Spanish entrepreneurs in vocational training programmes.
2 The continuing separation between initial or regulated professional training and occupational and continuous training, with distinctive conceptualization and separation of structure, media, programmes, etc.
3 The absence of a unified administration for vocational training, aggravated by insufficient co-ordination among those who today have responsibility for the different kinds of programmes: the State – shared between the Ministry of Education and the Ministry of Work – the region and, on occasion, the localities.
4 The delay in defining new curricula for vocational training, and the uncertainty as to whether these will integrate (while respecting their differences) the provision of training in the educational institutions and training in the work-place. The recent approval, with the agreement of employers and unions, of the National Programme of Vocational Education suggests integration, but the practical obstacles are numerous.
5 The adaptations of secondary schools and of teachers to the new curri-

cula assume a very significant augmentation in supply of equipment and teacher re-training, the likelihood of which is seriously affected by insufficient budgetary provision. Modes of provision for the incorporation of specialists and in-service workers into education have not yet been clarified. Similarly, the development of provision for practical work experience is precarious and suffers from the absence of a relevant tradition, to which I have alluded.

6 The requirement for certification that is demanded for vocational training at middle and higher status, namely at ESO and *Bachillerato*, respectively, can amount to a serious handicap: on the one hand for that sector of the adult population which has a low level of education, without certification, and on the other hand for the percentage of young people who do not graduate successfully from ESO. For these last there are provisions, within the so-called programmes of social guarantee, or short modules of vocational training which can facilitate work placement.

So that these two groups do not get stuck in some kind of low prestige training, it is necessary to develop and to put into practice special programmes to help them pass the corresponding examinations which they are required to take in order to enter the general system of vocational education without the requisite qualifications. Positive action of this kind would allow us to tackle these problems with a certain confidence of success. And if the result were an increase in the social prestige of vocational education, it would relieve the pressure for entrance into the universities which otherwise will increase with the implementation of ESO.

The fact that implementation of the new FP will not be complete, according to the reform calendar, before the end of the century, suggests a serious setback for this approach. The new FP should be fully generalized before the end of the decade. The obsolescence of the current system permits no delay. Nevertheless it is not at all clear that delay will be avoided.

THE TEACHERS: CRISIS OF PROFESSIONAL IDENTITY AND THE NEW CURRICULUM

My starting point is that teachers are the fundamental agents of any educational reform, the ultimate and principal mediators of the curriculum. It is they who define, in interaction with the students and with the educational and social environment, the curriculum-in-practice, the essential component of the curriculum, by means of which are realized the intentions and proposals of other agencies.

Legal requirements, regulations and circulars can prescribe, with varying levels of specificity, that which the teacher must do, but what he or she finally does is conditioned by a great number of factors, processes and complex practices, some of which are not explicit, but which evolve from the context of society, the school and the classroom, and which decisively condition all teaching practice and all learning processes.

Before the launch of the educational reform, and before the new curricula were formulated, the teaching profession of Spain was showing some signs of a crisis of professional identity, also in evidence in many other developed countries. The abundance of university graduates in search of employment has meant that there is not the scarcity of teaching candidates for certain subjects in secondary education which had been experienced in many developed countries during the second half of the 1980s. But in the common rooms all the signs are there of demoralization, and of wanting to get out of the profession, accompanied by an increase in absenteeism and psychological illnesses. The principal factors which have brought about this situation and which have been analysed by studies of this issue are:

1 Contradiction between the growing demands that society, through its political and educational spokespersons, makes of the educational system and of teachers and the means and capacities that these have in order to meet them; new contents, new methods, new roles, more administration, more facets of work (e.g. educational psychology) which before had formed no part of the life of the teacher in his or her career and which were not included in either academic or professional training; technological, social and cultural changes; advances in research into educational psychology and the possibilities which these offer for improvement of the processes of student learning; the legitimate aspirations of broad sectors of society, convinced of the role of education in social mobility, and of the educational authorities in improving the quality of teaching and in reducing the rates of 'educational failure' (without taking heed of the means which society and its political representatives are inclined to put at the disposal of schools to achieve this). All these factors are translated into demands that bring with them, to a greater or lesser extent, more work for the teachers to do and more responsibility.

2 At the same time, there is a decline in the social esteem of teachers in mass educational systems. Although it does not result in a reduction of their pay, and may improve on it, it does not keep pace with the additional burden of work, nor with the new specialized qualifications which it is assumed the teacher should possess. Whether their work is or is not effective depends on the efficiency of systems of control (authorities, inspection, etc.). In any case, the teaching profession loses hold of any semblance that it may have conserved of being a liberal profession which, in the manner of false conscience, had previously provided partial consolation to its practitioners.

In these conditions, taking refuge in classroom authority, not in itself free of all sorts of problems, acquires defensive characteristics.

In analysing the fall in professional self-esteem one should not leave out of the account the growth in the remuneration of other professions and other activities undertaken by graduates.

3 The extension of compulsory education will retain within the educational system many students who are poorly motivated – often on account of the kind of teaching which they receive, academicist and alien to the cultural codes of their own domestic environment, and in the face of which the teacher does not know how to develop strategies for satisfactory learning. Scholastic failure, very high in the least favoured social environments, with its consequences for classroom indiscipline, also demotivates the teachers.

4 The teacher is aware of the declining influence of the school and of its capacity to help young people acquire knowledge, values and guidance, in the face of the influence of the audio-visual media. Moreover the challenge posed by the media to the work of teachers is growing. Teaching activity and curriculum practice are far removed from media-derived culture and incapable of critically integrating the media into processes of school learning.

If these phenomena – common in my judgement to what has happened throughout the developed world, albeit with different levels of intensity – were present in the Spanish educational system in the 1980s, then the basic approaches of the new curricula of educational reform can only sharpen them, provoking a critical situation which could be very positive – if it leads to individual and collective reflection about how to realize these approaches in practice, if the means for doing so are available and if the teachers are motivated to apply these new approaches. Otherwise, the most positive aspects of the curricular reform will be cancelled out, and could even produce a counter-reaction from a broad sector of the teaching force.

The applicability of these considerations will vary according to educational level and type of school in relation to social environment. I will look in greater detail at the most problematic stage, that of compulsory secondary education, and at the teachers who will be responsible for it, whose backgrounds are in teaching the *Bachillerato* (BUP) and vocational education (FP). In the first cycle of ESO, the teachers will be *maestros* with subject specialisms until such time as they are joined by teachers coming from new systems of initial training with a higher education qualification which will include educational psychology.

The curriculum change proposed by the educational reform is based on the following principles among others:

1 An open curriculum which must be tailored to the level of the school, subject area and classroom as an expression of environmental charac-

teristics and special learning needs, whether individual or collective. Within the regulations established by the minimum educational specifications the arrangement of content remains in the hands of the curriculum plan (*proyecto curricular*) of each school, and teachers' curriculum planning, including the requirements of children with special educational needs.

2 Individual adaptations of the school's curriculum project and teachers' curriculum planning must accord with the different rhythms of learning, including the requirements of students with special educational needs.
3 Content will be organized by area of knowledge, although in the final years the organization will be arranged more traditionally, by subject or subject area.
4 The principal focus of pedagogic action must change from the transmission of knowledge to the processes of learning. Active teaching and individualized attention to learning problems should develop naturally from this approach.
5 The new curricula demand a change in teaching practice away from the individual and towards team teaching: at the level of school, area of knowledge, classroom, tutorial relations, relationships to counselling and educational psychology services, etc.
6 Tutorial activity is considered central to teaching practice.

By contrast, the prevailing reality in educational practice in current institutes as regards *Bachillerato* or vocational education (theoretical studies) is:

1 Initial teacher training is sufficiently broad in the scientific–academic mode but offers little on educational psychology. Programmes of in-service training have not yet covered this gap.
2 Through its contents, and its curricular formats, teaching is strongly academicist. No strong tradition exists of inter-disciplinary work, and as there is a lack of correspondence between the curriculum and areas of knowledge this can lead to a fierce rejection of the new method of organizing curriculum content.
3 Teaching practice is traditionally individualistic, not very responsive to external demands and little inclined to group work and the different kinds of co-ordination which this entails.
4 The approaches of educational psychology to the new curricula and the role of the tutorial require appropriate training which a significant proportion of current teachers do not have, as well as a change of outlook, which they resist.
5 At the end of the day, the curriculum is generally delivered through textbooks.

The shock encounter between proposals for change and this current reality is well illustrated in compulsory secondary education. Motivating teachers to undertake new curricular practices must become a priority task for the process of educational reform, centring on:

1 Emphasizing the positive values of a new kind of teacher autonomy, which it is proposed should be integrated with the concept of a teaching team.
2 Stimulating a generalized reflective process in schools on ways of introducing the new curriculum.
3 Supplying high quality continuous training, in line with school needs, for implementation of new curricula.
4 Having available in each centre, as soon as the reform is introduced, appropriate counselling and educational psychology support.
5 Promoting an improvement in working conditions, not just in terms of current salary, but also in terms of teaching materials. The reduction in the number of students per classroom will become one of the fundamental ingredients in the progress of reform.

I have serious doubts that all these things can be achieved with due speed and intensity. The lack of means, due to budget economies, and the weak motivation of many teachers may yet hinder an ambitious and necessary educational reform.

8 Finding the evidence*

Mark Blaug, Francisco Bosch and Javier Díaz

This chapter comprises two sections from the book La Educación en España *(Bosch and Díaz, 1988): the prologue to the book, by Mark Blaug, and a section by its principal authors on the difficulties of estimating educational costs. The principal purpose of including these sections in this volume has to do with the historical significance of the inadequacies of available data to which the authors refer (the book appeared too early for extensive reference to or comment on the results of pilot reforms inaugurated by the government in the early to mid-1980s). In the years following publication of the book, there have been significant measures improving upon the collection and dissemination of data about the educational system. These include: annual publications of educational statistics by the Ministry of Education and Science; research studies published by the* Centro de Investigación, Documentación y Evaluación *(CIDE), which was established in 1983; the setting up in 1994 of the* Instituto Nacional de Calidad y Evaluación *(INCE) (and of similar bodies to promote and assess quality in the autonomous communities, such as the* Instituto para el Desarrollo Curricular y la Formación del Profesorado *in Eúskadi, established in 1992); annual reports since 1987 on the state of education by the* Consejo Escolar del Estado *(a national consultative council) and its equivalents in the autonomous communities, together with the annual reports of the participative governing council (at the levels of the State and of the autonomous communities) for the universities'* Consejo de Universidades *established in 1983 and, since 1993, for vocational training, the* Consejo de Formación Profesional, *together with the results of extended consultations by government in the period leading up to reform legislation, and the often well-informed critical appraisals of government initiatives by the trade unions. Legislative requirements on school governing bodies to develop annual reports, annual programme and curriculum plans,* proyectos educativos *and* proyectos curriculares, *together with action research initiatives and evaluation work carried out under the auspices of the university-based* Institutos de Ciencias de la Educación *(ICEs) or the recently established*

* This chapter translated by Pamela O'Malley

networks of teachers' centres (CEPs), may also be adding significantly to the development of grass-roots data that can address questions of process as well as outcomes. The re-shaped schools inspectorate is also beginning to focus on more empirically based evaluative investigations (for example, the Plan EVA *in progress at the time of writing in 1994 has involved evaluative investigation of 350 primary and secondary schools). The fruit of many of these initiatives, however, has still to be harvested, and there can be no doubt that there is a great deal still to be desired. The processes of devolution of educational responsibility to the autonomous communities, while these may improve data collection in particular communities, also greatly heighten the potential for lack of co-ordination and standardization between them. In particular it is doubtful whether studies of the sophistication proposed by Blaug, Bosch and Díaz are much in evidence, but the growing maturity and confidence of the educational administration and of the academic establishment in the field of education suggest that there may be significant improvement in this area. The reality of the historical dearth of reliable data, however, will continue to hinder longitudinal comparative study.*

PROLOGUE TO *LA EDUCACIÓN EN ESPAÑA*

Mark Blaug

The authors (Bosch and Díaz) of this book (*La Educación en España*) wished to confine their work to a description of the economic aspects of the Spanish education system drawing on existing data. As a general rule they have avoided recommendations for reform, given their view that in the present circumstances it is much more urgent to evaluate the results currently obtained in the light of the information available than to add new reform proposals to the many already in existence. This seems to me to be the best approach. Spanish education authorities are currently proposing to put into practice, in a period of five to seven years, a large number of reforms across various areas of the education system. While one may have serious reservations as to the possibility of implementing all these reforms in such a short period of time, there is little reason to suppose that even if the reforms are implemented there is going to be a significant improvement in the whole of the system. Indeed, so little is known about the effectiveness of Spanish education that there is scarcely sufficient basis to embark on projects of reform. On the basis of existing data it is difficult to know with certainty which reforms might work and which might not. It is no wonder, therefore, that the authors of *La Educación en España* have prioritized the examination of existing studies of the economics of Spanish education in an endeavour to present the current state of knowledge on this subject. They have achieved their objective. Of the studies published on this matter, I do not know of any other which provides such a precise panorama of what is known about the economic aspects of Spanish education.

The current state of Spanish education is characterized by a series of specific features which set it apart from its European neighbours: an exceptionally rapid rate of growth in the provision of compulsory education for the 6 to 14 age group, achieved over a comparatively brief period, and which has effectively brought about the universalization of primary education; an even faster rate of growth of higher education during an equally short period, almost eliminating the differences in higher education that previously existed between Spain and the rest of Western Europe [NB – participation in higher education by the 18 to 25 age group in Spain is now (1994) higher than in all other developed economies, with the exception of the United States and Japan (eds)]; a high-profile private sector – 50 per cent of all infant schools, 30 per cent of primary schools and 50 per cent at secondary level are privately owned – 80 per cent of whose running costs are financed from public funds; and the coexistence of four different languages spoken in different parts of the country, an issue recently accentuated by a strong decentralizing tendency away from the Central Administration towards the autonomous regions. As a result, the Spanish education system shows all the characteristics of a hurried and uncontrolled expansion which has exceeded its capacity for self-administration.

Over and over again the book, *La Educación en España*, emphasizes the problem of the lack of data, an insufficiency which makes it difficult to ascertain what has really happened in the different areas and even more difficult to assess the results of what may have happened. Spain faces the urgent task of significantly increasing its research effort in the field of education, without which, I fear, a large part of the present educational reform movement will come to nothing. With a view to contributing to the generation of such an effort, I would like to develop through these pages a proposal for possible educational research for Spain.

We might begin with educational demand, a subject which is dealt with in Chapter 4 of the book. The question of estimating demand for infant education in relation to the estimated birth rate is a familiar challenge for educators the world over. Less well known are the problems with regard to estimations of the demand for post compulsory education, since this depends not only on the diverse individual variables of each family – such as examination results, gender, place of residence, family income, parental level of education, etc. – but also on the offer of places. The education authorities may to a certain extent stimulate or curb the demand for post compulsory education by means of their more or less expressed disposition to satisfy such a demand. Therefore, if we wish to predict the effect on demand which, for example, an increase in the available places in secondary schools would have, we must maintain as constant those individual and specific variables of each family which will also have repercussions on the total demand for school places at the post compulsory level.

But this is impossible if one does not have available data on these variables covering a number of years, and such information does not exist for any Spanish region. Consequently, from the point of view of educational research, a top priority would be the design of a sample of young people of 14 years of age, collecting information on their personal characteristics, and carrying out a follow-up on their educational route during the following three or five years. By annual repetition of this type of study for each new group or cohort of young people of 14 years of age, a broad picture would be established of the young people who complete their compulsory studies, after which it would be possible (using a multi-variable statistical analysis) to forecast the effect on the demand for post compulsory education of a modification of one of the variables which influence it, maintaining as constant the rest of the pertinent variables.

Another outstanding question concerns the private and social costs of education, which are in turn intimately related to aspects such as efficiency and financing. In Spain, as in other countries, it is relatively easy to ascertain the current costs of education, but practically impossible to determine what different schools really cost in terms of a hypothetical alternative use ('opportunity cost') of the resources assigned to them. The accountancy figures which are so readily available confuse capital costs and running costs and do not usually include indirect costs. In order to establish educational costs with greater precision specific studies of individual schools are needed, which could be carried out based on samples from different geographical regions and at different levels of the education system. Without such studies, it is idle to argue about the efficiency or inefficiency of any given school, or to discuss how to distribute the burden of finance for educational activity among parents and taxpayers in general.

But in order to be able to speak about educational efficiency it is necessary, besides an analysis of the costs, to analyse the results of the education process. When all is said and done, efficiency implies a relationship between such results and the cost per pupil. This does not mean that the result of educational activity merely consists of the acquisition of certain knowledge of a factual and conceptual nature, but it is true that these constitute one of its principal elements, especially in the lower levels of the education system. In other words, at some point in the assessment of primary education and of the first cycle of secondary education, such simple questions as what level has been reached by the average pupil in reading, writing and numeracy after four, five or six years of schooling must be answered.

In spite of the fact that the study of school results is commonplace in such countries as the United States, many European countries (among them Spain) have scarcely progressed at all in developing educational assessment at different ages, in spite of the fact that the International Association for the Assessment of Educational Results (IEA), whose headquarters are in Stockholm, Sweden, is the institution which has most distinguished itself by promoting throughout the world the scientific analysis of linguistic and mathematical competencies acquired by young people of 13 and 16 years of age. It is clear that Spain needs to become one of the countries of the IEA in which pilot studies are carried out on this matter, which would immediately enable Spain to share in the considerable experience of this organization in research on educational assessment. Without carrying out analysis of this type, it is quite absurd to speak of possible improvements in the Spanish education system.

And now we arrive at the third and last question: the transition from school to work. One of the best chapters of the book (*La Educación en España*) is the last (Chapter 9, on Education and the work-place), in which, with great wisdom, the authors avoid engaging in the many evasions which often characterize discussions on qualified unemployment or the transition between the education system and the labour market. In effect, if there is unemployment among the young people who finish compulsory schooling, it is usual to blame it on the education system: the schools must be teaching what they should not be teaching, and promoting academic rather than vocational study, thus reducing the employability of young people, etc. The solution, therefore, would be to vocationalize secondary education, introduce more vocational schools at second and third level and, in general, suppress academic studies. This approach is fallacious, since it presupposes that school curricula have only one objective: to stimulate the acquisition of concepts and information of a cognitive nature. It forgets that schools are equally interested in promoting the acquisition of psycho-mobility – how to do things – and, even more, in developing certain characteristics or ways of behaviour – the values and attitudes of punctuality, obedience, order and responsibility – which are what in Chapter 7 of *La Educación en España* are called generically 'socialization'. Indeed, even if the schools were not interested in developing such characteristics, the reality of school life would make it difficult for them not to do so, as part of the hidden curriculum.

It is not simply the fact that schools inculcate defined behavioural characteristics (as well as knowledge and mental and physical skills), but rather that these are perhaps precisely what employers most value in schooling. Employers are prepared to pay more to young people with a higher level of schooling not so much because of what they know or are capable of doing, but because of the way they behave. In other words, a majority of jobs are learnt by practice and not through any formal training that can be given in schools.

It is worth while emphasizing this point, on the one hand because it has still not been assimilated by the world of education and much less by journalists or by the general public, and on the other, because it suggests how to avoid some of the gravest errors committed in the past by education reformers. Once we have understood that the economic value of education has more to do with the hidden curriculum than with the explicit one, we will not feel tempted, in view of qualified unemployment, to hasten into a vocationalizing of study plans or to rush into building more vocational schools. There may be very good *educational* reasons for introducing vocational elements at secondary level – thus offering an opportunity for pupils who lack the ability or the will to go on to higher studies – but this does not allow us to hope that it will bring an end to qualified unemployment or that it will serve as a way of achieving a perfect correspondence between the training acquired at school and its use in employment. There will always be certain maladjustments between what is learnt in the education system and what is required in the world of work, but to a certain extent this is something natural, which cannot easily be eliminated.

I have not said anything which is not repeated in Chapter 9, but I feel it is worth while underlining. The reform of higher secondary education with a view to making it more practical and relevant may be in principle praiseworthy, but it runs the risk of failure if it is implemented by people who trust in what has come to be called the vocational school fraud; that is to say, the belief that education consists of acquiring the cognitive ingredient and nothing more. Those who for a long time have believed that in order to resolve the world's problems it is only necessary to reform the education system by making it more vocational should read Chapter 9 of *La Educación en España*, not once, but twice!

Much of the information on which the conclusions reached in that chapter are based, however, derives from studies carried out in the United States or Great Britain and not in Spain. This is not surprising, because the area of relations between education and employment is one of the most complex. The majority of employers, and even of those in charge of company personnel management, do not have very clear ideas about why they prefer, all else being equal, to recruit their new employees from among those who have higher levels of formal education. The young qualified people themselves are often surprised that the education level they have reached has enabled them to receive a higher salary, even when they do not see much relation between what they have learnt and the task which they now have to carry out in their job. In order to study these questions we need controlled 'tracer studies' of groups of young people from the moment they end their compulsory studies over a period of various years of employment, observing how they are contracted, what they do in their work, how they achieve promotion, etc. Such studies should form part of a wider programme of information about the labour market for school leavers and university graduates, specifying the sector in which they are employed by age, gender, level and type of education; the remuneration they receive by age, gender, level and type of education; the annual flow of those who are joining the work force, classified according to the different sectors in which they work, the total stock of individuals employed in the different sectors, by level, type of education, etc. This information would not only contribute to the improvement of individual options with reference to their career choice (as suggested in Chapter 9 of *La Educación en España*) but would also serve as a support for the tracer studies mentioned above.

ESTIMATING THE COSTS

Francisco Bosch and Javier Díaz

The public expenditure figures contained in the budgets are an inevitable starting point in attempting to establish the cost of educational activity in Spain. These budgets contain information concerning running costs and capital expenditure, and while a different weight is given to the different titles which form one or other type of expenditure, according to each Spanish autonomous community, there is no doubt but that the running costs – among which personnel costs occupy a prominent place – make up, in a general way, the immense majority of all public expenditure on education.

The total sum of public expenditure on education will represent, therefore, our first approximation to the cost of educational activity, although in the case of Spain, and due to various circumstances (which include inadequate accountancy and the irregular periodicity of certain items), not even this total expenditure figure can be calculated very exactly. In any case, in order to reach the total cost it is necessary to add to the total of public expenditure in education the considerable expenditure on private education, as well as indirect costs, including opportunity cost, which greatly exceed monetary payment.

Estimations of the average cost per pupil at the different levels of the education system have an undeniable, practical importance, which at present is accentuated by their relevance to certain provisions of LODE. However, this does not allow us to overlook their limitations. On the one hand, such estimations of average cost are unsatisfactory for establishing an economic model per school unit, given the difficulties posed by calculations based on existing budgetary figures (a calculation which, besides, does not take into account to what extent the ratios and expenditure are optimal in the state schools which are used as reference). On the other hand, the estimations in question are useless for evaluating and comparing the efficiency of various schools (for example, private with regard to public), an objective which demands a previous specification of the intended educational outcomes, establishing an order of priority within them and studying the effect of different school variables in relation to outcomes.

Improving educational results by means of a more appropriate assignation of the available resources involves, in effect, the identification of all the traditional elements of resources distribution in any given sector of production. In the field of education, in addition to the aforementioned specification and prioritization of educational outcomes, other aspects have to be taken into account – such as educational performance – or the cost per unit of the factors employed in the production process, about which there is almost no information available today in Spain.

Nevertheless, it must be observed that in the sphere of education, and owing to the fact that the schools simultaneously generate diverse products (knowledge of various subjects, preparation for civic life, socialization . . .), the evaluation of the results cannot be confined to mere cost-efficiency analysis with reference to a determined outcome, but rather demands the establishing of explicit preferences with regard to the relative importance of different outcomes, which in turn would realize corresponding value judgements.

REFERENCE

Bosch, F. and Díaz, J. (1988) *La Educación en España: Una Perspectiva Económica*. Barcelona: Editorial Ariel, SA.

9 Education in the State of Autonomous Communities*

Joan Carlos Gallego Herrerz

The distribution of political power in Spain demonstrates many features of a federal system, with a complex and as yet variegated distribution of power (which is charted in this chapter with specific reference to education) between the central government and its administration, on the one hand, and the governments and administrations of the autonomous communities on the other. There are seventeen autonomous communities, only seven of which had assumed 'full competency' in the provision of education by the early 1990s, but a 1992 pact between the governing party, PSOE, and the leading party of the opposition, PP (Partido Popular), approved plans for the extension of educational responsibility to all the other communities by 1996–7 (and responsibility for universities as early as 1994–5). By 1997 the Central Government will control only 51 per cent of public expenditure. In those communities with full powers in education, the education department of the local government is the principal source of power, subject to central laws governing the basic parameters of the system, and the educational rights and duties of all citizens. In the other communities, education continues to be provided by the Ministry for Education and Science, either directly or through its provincial offices. The author also considers the municipalities whose role in education, although weaker than in most other European countries and limited to such matters as the provision of sites, maintenance, and janitors (thus creating a problematic duality of administration in potential conflict with the bureaucracy of the Educational Administration), has shown signs of development and in some areas, such as Barcelona, there is a tradition of more active municipal involvement in mainstream educational provision. Municipalities can help define training needs, provide nursery education and continuing adult education, language and music education, and participate in schools' educational planning.

* This chapter translated by Pamela O'Malley

POLITICAL AND ADMINISTRATIVE STRUCTURE OF THE SPANISH STATE

The Spanish State is structured on three political and administrative levels: the State as such, autonomous communities and municipalities. Certain political and administrative responsibilities correspond to each level. The autonomous communities and the municipalities enjoy varying degrees of autonomy which are established by law and by the Spanish Constitution of 1978. As we shall see later, different responsibilities may be exercised exclusively, in full or in part, at any one of the three levels of the state structure.

ORIGINS OF THE STATE OF AUTONOMOUS COMMUNITIES

During the years of Franco's dictatorship and especially in its final years, the demand for recognition of the autonomy which had been enjoyed by certain constituent nationalities of Spain during the years of the Second Republic was added to the general demand for democracy. The claims for autonomy, political freedom and amnesty were forcefully expressed from the very earliest moments of the political transition and, as a consequence, had considerable influence on the process of drawing up the constitutional texts in 1978. Justifications for the claims to self-government of Cataluña, País Vasco and Galicia had their roots in a more or less distant past, in their own political institutions which had been restored during the Second Republic and which had enjoyed a brief but fruitful existence, and in certain elements of cultural and geographical identity. Among these elements the existence of their own language contributed to intense identification with nationalistic claims among the citizens.

Section VIII of the Spanish Constitution of 1978 started with a recognition of the State of Autonomous Communities in the political and administrative structure of the State which it established. This recognition seemed then to be a satisfactory response to the demands of the historical nationalities – the País Vasco, Cataluña and Galicia – that they should take responsibility for their own mechanisms of self-government and for a wide range of responsibilities which they could regulate and administer directly. At the same time, the Constitution established a framework for the political structure of the State which enabled those other communities or regions which were unable to press equivalent historical claims to advance by means of constitutional procedures towards the development of their own political structures, within which they could administer such responsibilities as the Central State transferred to them. In this way, with the passing of the 1978 Constitution, the process of shaping the State of Autonomous Communities commenced.

The Constitution itself established two different approaches to the creation of autonomous communities, that of article 143 and that of article

151. The latter introduced the possibility of recognizing the cultural, historical and national identity of certain Spanish regions, thus enabling them to accede by the 'fast lane' to the drafting of their own Autonomous Statute, whereas the former established a different route which would make possible the generalization of the development of the State of Autonomous Communities to all the other regions.

Establishment of the State of Autonomies meant that the structure of political and administrative responsibilities of the State would be shared between the Central State and the autonomous communities. Each would exercise the responsibilities laid down by law, either by the community's own statutes, or by state Acts regulating the transfer of responsibilities, or designating responsibilities that belong exclusively to the Central State or which are shared between the State and the communities.

In addition to these two political and administrative levels of the Spanish State – the State and autonomous communities – local government (municipalities, counties, provinces) occupy a third level which completes the administrative structure. This level also enjoys autonomy in the management of its interests and carries out those responsibilities which the law confers on it.

DEVELOPMENT OF THE STATE OF AUTONOMOUS COMMUNITIES

The first historic nationality to accede to the State of Autonomy was País Vasco in the year 1979 which, following the route established by the Spanish Constitution, drafted its own Statutes of Autonomy which were then endorsed by the Basque people by referendum. Cataluña followed in 1979 and Galicia in 1981. The three historic nationalities which during the Franco period had maintained their demands for autonomy thus recovered, by means of constitutional mechanisms, the political institutions of self-government which had been eliminated by the breaking out of civil war in 1936 and the subsequent imposition of General Franco's dictatorship.

The rest of the communities later joined in the process of setting up autonomies: Andalucia (1981), Valencia (1982), Islas Canarias (1982), Extremadura (1983), Murcia (1982), Rioja (1982), Islas Baleares (1983), Cantabria (1981), Asturias (1981), Aragón (1982), Madrid (1983), Castilla la Mancha (1982), Castilla-León (1983). Thus, the process of development of the State of Autonomies is in practice concluded. It remains to be decided what specific status should be given to Ceuta and Melilla, Spanish cities which are situated in Morocco and which have already been conceded a special political, administrative and geographic status in the Spanish Constitution of 1978. These cities require specific autonomous statutes which take account of their special characteristics and conditions.

Once the different autonomous communities were constituted and their statutes passed, there began the process of transferring responsibilities, functions, services and resources from the State to the autonomous communities. This is still an unfinished process; out of the seventeen communities in existence, ten have not yet had responsibilities transferred to them. Only in seven communities has there commenced the process of transfer of services and resources across the particular domains in which they are competent to assume responsibility – in País Vasco, Cataluña, Galicia, Valencia, Andalucia, Islas Canarias and Navarra – and in some cases this process has now been completed. In those autonomous communities to which there has been no transfer of responsibilities, the corresponding institutions of state continue to exercise administrative responsibility.

THE PROCESS OF TRANSFER

The process of transferring responsibilities to the autonomous communities introduces the problem of dividing the responsibilities, determining which belong exclusively to the State or to the Autonomous Community and which are shared. This is a highly complex judicial and political process. The Spanish Constitution lays down which are the exclusive responsibilities which belong to the State, regulated in article 149, 1.1: 'Regulation of the basic conditions which guarantee the equality of all Spanish persons in the exercise of their constitutional rights and in the fulfilling of their constitutional duties . . .', and in article 149, 1.30: 'Regulation of the conditions for obtaining, granting and recognizing academic degrees and basic professional norms for the carrying out of article 27 of the Spanish Constitution, so as to guarantee that the obligations of the public power in these matters are fulfilled'.

In article 148.17, the Constitution lists the responsibilities which the autonomous communities may assume: the fostering of culture and, where appropriate, of the teaching of the language of the autonomous community. Mechanisms for the extension of the responsibilities of autonomous communities are foreseen in article 149. 3: such matters as are not attributed to the State by this Constitution may correspond to the autonomous community, by virtue of their respective statutes. The responsibility in matters which have not been assumed by the Autonomous Statute corresponds to the State, whose norms shall prevail, in the case of conflict, over those of the autonomous community in all matters which have not been attributed to its exclusive responsibility. State rights shall in all cases be supplementary to the rights of the autonomous community. And in article 150.1: 'The Parliament, in questions of state responsibility, may concede to one or all of the autonomous communities the faculty of drawing up, for themselves, legislative norms contained within the framework of the principles, bases and directives established by State Act'; and in article 150.2: 'The State may transfer to or delegate to the autonomous communities, by state Act, faculties which correspond to matters of state responsibility but which by their very nature are susceptible to being transferred or delegated. The Act will provide, in each case, for the corresponding transfer of financial means, as well as of the means of control which the State will reserve for itself'.

Autonomy statutes once passed, and the implementation of the State of Autonomous Communities begun, the process of autonomous development has involved the creation of a system of autonomous law common to each autonomous community. Acts have been passed within a general framework intended to promote the harmonizing of the autonomous process, among which we may quote the Finance Act of the Autonomous Communities of 1980, which set up the mechanisms which regulate the transfer of economic resources to the different communities, an Act which has undergone different adaptations and modifications and which has involved negotiations between the autonomous communities and Central Government in order to revise the financial funds. Also there is the Autonomous Process Act whose aim is to complete the autonomous process. This Act cedes state revenue to the autonomous communities, conforming to the Finance Act so as to guarantee for the autonomous communities a greater capacity for self-financing, but excludes income tax and VAT which continue to be administrated by the State. These taxes are, however, now being claimed by the autonomous communities who wish to participate in their administration so as to guarantee for themselves more rapid access to the sources of state funds. The Interterritorial Compensation Fund Act of 1984 is intended to set up mechanisms of solidarity (or homogenization) among the different autonomous communities according to whatever social and territorial imbalances may exist. The reform measures for the Civil Service Act establish a framework which lays down the basic characteristics of the Civil Service with regard to access, mobility, code of conduct, ascription to different bodies, etc. The autonomous communities are obliged to respect this Act in the development of their systems and consequently in the specific regulation of their civil servants.

Conflicts have arisen throughout this process between the autonomous communities and Central Government, deriving from both the economic assessment of the services transferred and from the exercise of levels of responsibility which may have impinged on the responsibilities pertaining to Central Government. The settling of disputes over the economic assessments is carried out by the Mixed Transfer Commission which determines the value of the services transferred, quantifying the credits and relating them to the institutions, means, personnel and budgets necessary for the exercise of the responsibility concerned, in order to reach a solution by means of negotiation and agreement between the different parties. The resolution of problems which arise concerning the determination of responsibilities is achieved through political negotiation between the autonomous communities and Central Government, or through the law courts using the right of appeal to the Constitutional Tribunal, which will determine who should exercise a given contested responsibility.

RESPONSIBILITY IN EDUCATION

Article 27 of the Spanish Constitution establishes the right to a free education as one of the fundamental rights of every Spanish person. The exclusive responsibilities of the State are established in article 149 of the Constitution, and the first paragraph of this article establishes that the State is responsible for regulation of the basic conditions which guarantee equality for all Spaniards in the exercise of their rights and in the fulfilment of those duties established by the Constitution. Article 149 also attributes as an exclusive responsibility to the State in the field of education the regulation of the conditions for obtaining, issuing and validating degrees and certificates, as well as the basic norms of article 27 of the Constitution, covering:

- the general organization of the education system and the establishment of compulsory schooling;
- the regulation of the conditions for obtaining, issuing and validating academic and professional degrees and certificates throughout all Spanish territory; and
- the Central Inspectorate.

All other responsibilities may be carried out by the autonomous communities, either through an Act which transfers such competencies to the autonomous community or according to the provisions of the corresponding Statute of Autonomy.

Educational administration in Spain is consequently an administrative instrument of the State or of the autonomous communities, according to the distribution of responsibilities which exists in each case. The political and administrative system of the Spanish State must guarantee the unity of the education system, which may be provided and administered in each autonomous community with different educational programmes, priorities and objectives, provided that these observe the minimum requirements established in state legislation governing the validation of degrees and certificates and the essential unity of the system.

Article 28 of LODE established the setting up of a Conference of Education Counsellors (constituted in 1986) made up of representatives of the autonomous communities and of the central Ministry of Education, to ensure the co-ordination of educational policies and the exchange of information. This is the highest–ranking body of educational planning of the Spanish State. It is competent in all matters which are shared by the autonomous communities and Central Government.

The State Administration is equipped with an administrative instrument, the Central Inspectorate, which guarantees and monitors the exercise of the exclusive competencies of the State: minimum requirements in education, general organization of the system, academic certificates, pupils' documentation and records, the exercise of the right to education in accordance with the principle of equality, information and statistics.

The functions ascribed to educational administration, both of management and regulation, are shared by different administrations – central and autonomous. Central Government is responsible for the establishment of norms in relation to the basic aspects of the working of the education system, as well as the drawing up of state legislation governing the right to education (LODE, 1/1985) and the organization of the education system (LOGSE 1/1990) or of university autonomy (LRU, 8/1983). The autonomous communities with competencies in education are responsible for drawing up the norms which adapt central legislation to their historical, cultural and territorial conditions, guaranteeing respect for centrally defined basics. The management and administration of educational resources will be exercised by whichever administration is competent in each specific territory.

The different autonomous communities with responsibilities have also exercised their legislative capacity in the field of education, drawing up basic legislation for their territories. Thus we find autonomous communities which have drawn up a specific Civil Service Act, Cataluña (Act 17/ 85) and Andalucia (Act 6/85), extending the basic state norms, which in the case of Cataluña will in future allow it to regulate teaching in a specific manner within the framework of qualifications and requirements governing access dictated by LOGSE and by the State Civil Service Act. The autonomous communities have also promulgated Acts which regulate the use of their own language, in Cataluña (7/83), País Vasco (10/82), Galicia (3/83), Valencia (4/83), and which also affect the field of education in that they establish the status that is to be accorded to community languages in schools. They have also legislated for channels of participation for the education community within the autonomous community, in Cataluña (25/85), applying the basic state requirements of LODE and adding to them the creation of Municipal Schools Councils as a specific forum of participation. They have also drawn up a series of norms and decrees concerning the application of grant-aid agreements with private schools, the enrolment of pupils, registration procedures, regulations governing extra curriculum and complementary activities within the schools, regulations relating to parents' associations and other aspects, in which the different autonomous communities have used their legislative powers to elaborate on existing basic state-defined minima for education norms. Today, with the passage of LOGSE, the autonomous communities have begun the work of developing the Act in all the areas which refer to the adaptation of the minimum requirements – for the contents of the curriculum, the school calendar, the setting up of in-service training programmes for teachers, etc.

LOGSE AND EDUCATIONAL DECENTRALIZATION

The distribution of responsibilities according to LOGSE are as follows:

State Government (Ministry of Education)	*Autonomous communities*
Regulates minimum content of curriculum, up to 55% for community with own language and up to 65% of curriculum for the rest	Regulate rest of minimum content of curriculum (45 or 35%)
Establishes modules or special norms relating to the contents of each subject or area	Propose modules and the educational specialisms; vocational training
Establishes qualifications and validation	
Conditions and requirements for school buildings, basic norms for grants to private schools	
Statutory basis for civil servant teachers. Rights and duties. General framework. General open competition for mobility between posts. Teachers' qualifications	Organization of Civil Service Teachers
Sets up the National Institute of Evaluation	Participation in evaluation system
Establishes compensatory programmes	Establishes agreements for implementing compensatory programmes
Carries out the calendar for introducing new system	Apply and adapt new calendar
Establishes norms for repetition by students of school cycles	

In the areas which are shared (between State and community) or where there is co-operation, LOGSE establishes the manner in which the autonomous community will participate in the shared responsibilities, as well as laying down the mechanisms of prior consultation, prior information, agreements, etc.

MUNICIPAL ADMINISTRATION AND EDUCATIONAL RESPONSIBILITIES

The capability for establishing norms and regulations and the administration of education corresponds to the State and the autonomous communities whose responsibilities are recognized in their respective autonomous statutes or in the corresponding state Act by which responsibilities were transferred.

The municipalities form the basic unit of the territorial organization of the State, and their responsibilities are established by state Acts or by autonomous Acts in those communities which possess such responsibility (Act 7/1985 (LRBRL) (Ley Reguladora de Las Bases de Régimen Local), regulating the basis of local administration (articles 2 and 25)).

Neither the basic legislation for local administration nor educational legislation authorize the municipalities to be education administrators, as they assign to them neither competencies nor normative nor management functions in the field of education.

The law establishes the obligation for local corporations to co-operate with the educational administrations in the creation, building and maintenance of state schools, as well as in monitoring the carrying out of compulsory schooling (second additional disposition, LODE). Also the LRBRL indicates that the municipality is competent to participate in curriculum planning and to co-operate with the educational administrations in the creation, building and maintenance of state schools, to intervene in the governing councils of state schools and to participate in overseeing the exercise of compulsory schooling (article 25, LRBRL). LOGSE, in the additional disposition no. 17, reiterates the same responsibilities for municipalities, adapting them to the new education stages – second cycle of infant schools, primary and special education – allowing for the possibility of agreements between the educational administrations and the municipalities for provision of education of a special nature, ordering the educational administrations to establish criteria for the use of state schools by the Municipalities outside the period of the school timetable, and for adaptation of the system of obligation which article 88.3 of the Act of Regulation of Territories and Town Planning establishes in relation to the ceding of sites for basic education, which now covers both primary and compulsory secondary education.

In summary, the obligations for local administrations are:

- Monitoring compulsory schooling;
- Prevention of school absenteeism;
- Supplying sites and town planning;
- Conserving, maintaining and protecting state school buildings (second-cycle infant schools, primary and special education);
- Supplying cleaning personnel and janitors for school buildings at the levels of compulsory education; and
- Participating in school governing bodies (school councils) in the state schools.

Many municipalities, in addition to observing the obligations laid upon them by law, have intervened in educational matters by voluntarily taking on other obligations. This takes a variety of forms in different municipalities, depending on the political programme which happens to govern the municipality, the weight of local tradition of involvement in education and the intensity of concern exercised by its citizens.

Municipal intervention has been exercised by the assumption of functions that complement those of the educational administration, and has even reached the stage of assuming supplementary functions. Among the responsibilities assumed in recent years are:

- The creation and management of schools (especially in infant schools and artistic teaching, although also in EGB and secondary education);
- Supplying resources and equipment to schools (especially computers in recent years, also musical, physical education and library equipment, etc.);
- Pedagogic encouragement and aid for teachers (by means of creating municipal institutes of education, teachers' centres, educational psychology advisory teams, etc.);
- Supplying support and specialist teachers;
- Organizing school dining rooms and transport;
- Organizing and carrying out complementary activities;
- Encouraging associations (parents' associations, students' associations, etc.);
- Developing adult education (creating centres, contracting teachers, etc.); and
- Services which help to relate the school to the world of work, orientated towards the transition to employment, helping to organize work-experience, putting the school in contact with sources of professional and occupational training).

While this is not an exhaustive list, it is intended to give an idea of the wide range of ways in which local authorities have been intervening, sometimes to complement the involvement of the educational administration in improving the quality of educational service which the citizens receive, and sometimes to compensate for education deficits and so to attempt to relieve deficiencies in local educational provision.

In LOGSE there are no real changes in relation to municipal power, although it does introduce a stronger role for local administration in the field of education. The preamble to the Act proposes a perspective of greater decentralization and a closer relationship with the immediate environment, over which local administrations have the greatest influence. All through LOGSE there are many references to the public authorities and the public administration, and these permit one to assume that there will be greater consideration for the role of local administrations in certain areas, no longer limiting them exclusively to the field of educational administration, whether state or regional.

Thus we see that an important role is given to the public and local administrations in infant education and in the provision of school places to guarantee an adequate supply (articles 7, 2 and 7, 3). The law also opens up the possibility of establishing agreements between the educational administration and the local corporation (article 11, 2).

Article 54, 3 opens up the possibility of agreements between the educational administration and local corporations in the context of the development of adult education.

Section IV of LOGSE, concerning the quality of education, delegates to the public powers the provision of priority attention to the factors that favour quality and improvement in education. In article 57.5 it specifies that local administrations may collaborate with schools in order to encourage extra-curricular activities and promote a relationship between the curriculum planning of the school and the social and economic conditions of its environment. Article 60.2 lays down that the educational administrations should guarantee that there be a relationship between the academic activities and services of educational psychology and professional orientation that are carried out with the pupils and those that are carried out by the local administrations.

Article 65 establishes that the public powers will guarantee a free school place to all pupils in their own municipality, and close to their residence in the case of small municipalities.

Through this rapid review of LOGSE in relation to the local authorities we can see that there are clear references to the role which the municipalities should play, but a specific field of municipal action is not established in the area of education. We continue to move within the field of voluntary responsibilities and that of co-operation and participation.

10 The process of pedagogic reform*

José Jimeno Sacristán

A characteristic of the approach to educational reform espoused by the Socialist Government from 1982, in sharp contrast with previous approaches to reform in Spain, has been its enthusiasm to integrate philosophy with processes of piloting and experimentation. This empirical approach has not had the benefit of an established national tradition of critical evaluation and inquiry (echoing a point that is made by other contributors to this volume), and is possibly hindered by a substantial dependence on internal modes of student assessment (none the less yielding high rates of scholastic 'failure') although significant measures have now been undertaken to develop a culture of evaluation. The author reviews the history of educational innovation under the Socialist Government, and detects a significant shift between its first and second terms of office (i.e. 1982–86, 1986–90) from a grass-roots trial-and-error approach which concentrated on classroom practice but was poorly resourced and co-ordinated, to a more global, all-encompassing process of reform which threatens to swamp desired changes in classroom practice with a discourse of system and curriculum regulation which is, ironically, also committed to principles of school autonomy and curricular flexibility.

> Hurricane winds sweep across the sea tossing up twenty foot waves, a fathom below the surface turbulent waters swirl, while on the ocean floor there is unruffled calm.
>
> (Cuban, 1984, p. 2)

Before embarking on a chapter dedicated to the pedagogic implications of educational reform, I need to draw attention to certain limitations. One is of general validity, applicable to all educational systems, and the other is of specific relevance to Spain.

It is a difficult and perhaps impossible task to identify, precisely, the origins of the main features and processes of the educational system or to assess a brief historical period in terms of the educational practices which define it. The culture of teaching pedagogy that is expressed in

---

* This chapter translated by Oliver Boyd-Barrett

educational practice and in curriculum development does not have a sudden take-off point, nor is it transmitted overnight as a consequence of particular policy changes. One can establish a date for the proposal of certain ideas or of principles in the official curriculum but it is quite another thing to translate these into the practice of teachers and the operation of schools. We know that programmes of qualitative reform within educational systems have contradictory effects, which make it difficult to attribute to a particular political programme the absolute credit, or blame, for having brought about certain changes within the system. Educational practices depend on established traditions and beliefs, they are a response to the organizational conditions of classrooms, they are related to the quality of the teaching force, to the style of teacher professionalism, and are connected to the available means for curriculum development.

The difficulty of analysing the quality of teaching is all the more evident in a situation where, as is the case with Spanish educational policy, there are no (1994) regular or reliable global assessments available of the quality of education, the implementation of the curriculum-in-practice, methodologies, approaches to student assessment, or the utilization of curriculum resources. There is not even a tradition within the system of Spanish education of the study of change, monitored in the light of the objectives of the policy-makers, as a routine practice of the educational administration, apart from the normal study of statistical data or participation in international programmes for the study of scholastic achievement. None the less, over the past ten years evaluation programmes have been initiated, financed by the Administration, examining certain very concrete factors or innovation projects, although the dissemination of results among teachers or through public opinion has remained very limited. The reform inherent in the development of LOGSE foresees the creation of a National Institute for Quality Assessment in education [INCE began operations in 1994 (eds)] which can begin to establish such a tradition of qualitative systematic assessment.

The Spanish educational system has experienced an important process of administrative decentralization, wherein responsibility for the management of affairs pertaining to quality is shared between the Central Administration and the autonomous communities, governed in some cases by different political parties, with different programmes, different attitudes and values towards education. Decentralization across different political approaches to qualitative systematic reform makes it more difficult to develop and to offer an overall picture of the school system on the basis of assessment and analysis.

For these reasons, therefore, when we discuss the effects of reform on the pedagogic quality of education we can rely on very few objective data on which to form a judgement of the general situation. Accounts and evaluations are usually limited to very particular points and above all to the analysis of proposals and initiatives disseminated by the Administration, rather than focusing on contrasts of situation before, during and after the application of programmes of innovation. Such absence of evaluation of the effects of implemented proposals detracts from the capacity for critical judgement and lends legitimacy to proposals, assuming them to be accurate and efficacious by the simple fact of their being made public and developed. The discourse about the qualitative functioning of the educational system is circumscribed and basically determined by the Educational Administration, with few opportunities to test assertions against reality or to supply alternative diagnoses. It has to be said that such a discourse is generally full of good intentions and of progressive pedagogic ideas.

DISSATISFACTION WITH THE QUALITY OF EDUCATION

The quality of education has been a significant concern in recent years. The four major objectives for education in the period of socialist government have been: *democratization* of the functioning of the educational system, regulating the participation of the different social sectors of the educational community; guaranteeing the *right to education*; the *redress of inequalities*; and improvement in the *quality* of education. The two latter aspects are perceived as interconnected: 'It is about a policy whose aim is equality of results more than equality of opportunities' (Maravall, 1984, p. 89), rather than simply the extension of schooling merely to provide 'more of the same'. Both public opinion and the rhetoric of the Administration are in agreement that the quality of the current educational system is not acceptable.

These political preoccupations have been accentuated by a concern to defend the quality of education against an impression cultivated and propagated by certain influential social, religious and political interests that private education is superior to state education – a superficial impression which does not take account of the socio-cultural and economic differences between students attending one or other form of education.

In Spain, discussion about educational quality basically turns on two fundamental indices or criteria: the student-teacher ratio, and the rate of scholastic failure in each of the different elements of the system.

With respect to the ratio, the authorities are committed by legislation to reduce the levels to twenty-five students a class for primary education and thirty for compulsory secondary education. The more outstanding problem is that of scholastic failure. The OECD Report (1986, p. 38) on Spanish educational policy echoed this problem in recognizing that if scholastic failure is an index of quality then evidently the percentages of students required to retake examinations, or who abandon their studies, or are required to repeat years or who do not achieve any qualifications at the end of their period of study, are too high. In this sense, the reality today is practically as bad as it was at the beginning of the reform era which we are considering and it remains to be seen how these rates will move in the future, given that the lengthening and universalization of compulsory education up to 16 years will certainly increase these rates if other measures are not introduced.

The data which best represent this diagnosis of a 'quality deficit' include the following. According to the reports *Les desigualdades en la educación in España* (Educational inequalities in Spain) (CIDE, 1992) and *Informe sobre el estado y situación del sistema educativo, 1990–1* (Report on the state of the educational system, 1990–1) (*Consejo Escolar del Estado*, 1992), 19.7 per cent of EGB students (aged 6 to 14 years) are behind in their studies (i.e. are not at the level that corresponds with their age), which is almost a fifth of the school population in this phase. At the end of this phase, 23.2 per cent of EGB students 'fail' in that they do not obtain the qualification of *Graduado Escolar*. If we accept the validity of such indices of educational quality, then the period 1980–88 has seen an improvement on this last percentage, as students who obtained the *Graduado Escolar* have risen from 65.46 per cent to 79.8 per cent. The situation at the secondary level of the *Bachillerato* (BUP), on the contrary, has deteriorated in this period. In *Formación Profesional* (FP), which starts at the age of 14 (albeit for students from a lower social background and with fewer possibilities of academic success than those who study for the *Bachillerato*), only 42.8 per cent pass all their subjects.

Studies in recent years are indicating that failure rates are concentrated primarily in the areas of Mathematics and language.

It is important to consider the academic results of the *Bachillerato*, given that with LOGSE a part of these studies will form an element of compulsory secondary education (ESO). In the current *Bachillerato* system (ages 15 to 18 years), 14.7 per cent of students repeat their first year, 16.7 per cent repeat the second and 15.1 per cent repeat the third. Only 55 per cent of students pass all subjects at the end of the course and 31.9 per cent of all students abandon the *Bachillerato* at some point. Failure rates have climbed during the period 1980–88, as we have said. A combined assessment of the various indices (accumulated failure at the end of EGB, together with those who abandon BUP in the first or second year) bitterly reminds us that currently 47.8 per cent of students do not achieve success in education at the levels which will become compulsory secondary education with the implementation of LOGSE.

This problem is a long way from being tackled decisively by concrete programmes of action. Rather, it is taken for granted that the discourse and the measures adopted for establishing new curricula will of themselves reduce the problem of scholastic failure. What is certain is that in the reform period which we are examining, policy discourse has moved away from emphasizing these structural and deeply rooted deficiencies, introducing other themes of a pedagogic and more technical character.

Naturally, scholastic failure or success cannot be explained exclusively or fundamentally by the inadequacy of the curriculum or of methodology, by the shortage of good teachers, lack of didactic materials or poor school management. It is evident that behind school failure lie other hidden factors: cultural deficits originating in domestic life tip the balance, as well as high student-teacher ratios in some schools, lack of family involvement, and poor co-ordination between the different levels of teaching. But it is obvious that the deficiencies identified in the pedagogic realm have some effect on the teaching–learning process, on the content offered and on the outputs of the system. In any case, any project which aims to reduce failure and student drop-out must find alternative approaches to content, improvements of resource and changes in pedagogic methods, if it wishes to transform education. We should not forget that the failure or success of a student in Spain is determined by means of an assessment carried out by the educational system itself, which depends on internal assessments, in accordance with norms and demands established by teachers, and in line with the levels marked out by the compulsory curriculum, by prevailing academic goals and by textbooks. In Spain there is no external assessment of students, only the entrance examination for entry to university.

TEACHING REFORMS: DIFFERENT TACTICS AND CONTENTS FOR INNOVATION

The reform of teaching practice inspired by the Administration has passed through two different stages in the period 1983–92, directing messages to the teachers that have not always been consistent, which have comprised two strategies for the change of prevalent practice in teaching.

1   A first stage of encouragement and loosely defined curriculum experimentation at every level of the educational system except university amounted to little more than publicity and exhortation to observe certain general principles and suggestions for curriculum development in the various areas of the curriculum, in a limited number of schools. The teaching teams had to specify and concretize such exhortations and suggestions through activities and contents for their students. These programmes were complemented by others, directed at stimulating the use of computers and audio-visual media, and assisting in the realization of extra-scholastic activities. This phase extended from 1983 to 1987.

2   Another stage of generalized innovation derived from a global project, better defined and more centralized, but without involving the teachers or schools directly in activities for the transformation of practice. This

phase had as its point of departure the *Proyecto para la reforma de la enseñanza* (MEC, 1987), a debate which gave place later to the *Libro blanco para la reforma del sistema educativo* (MEC, 1989) and the approval, finally, of LOGSE in 1990. From this point there has existed a national curriculum with objectives, contents, evaluation criteria and directions which mark out a philosophy of innovation for the whole system.

First stage: trial and experimentation

In 1983, at the start of the first Socialist Government, the Minister for Education and Science decided to bring to a halt the introduction of the new curriculum for EGB which had been started by the previous Government of the *Union de Centro Democrático* party.

The model of innovation bequeathed by Francoism involved the Administration in deciding certain homogeneous and defined curricula for the whole country accompanied by directions for teachers, in pursuance of a policy of in-service teaching led by a central body (CENIDE and INCE) and undertaken by means of the *Institutos de Ciencias de la Educación*, tied to the universities. The teachers played no part in the establishment and development of these programmes. The contents of such in-service training generally had little to do with the needs of teachers. A policy for textbooks which standardized the products allowed on to the market completed a model of centralized innovation, defined bureaucratically in the form of vertical control.

The socialist tactic in 1983, taking its cue from the most progressive sectors of the teaching force, was to adopt an alternative philosophy to curriculum development and pedagogic innovation, whose starting point was that real change in the quality of education requires the adoption and putting into practice of processes of experimentation and collaboration among teachers. New curricula, before being standardized for the entire system of education, must be piloted to demonstrate that they meet the needs of actual students and that their guiding principles are assimilated by the teachers who must implement them, paving the way for an innovatory pedagogy which recognizes the professional autonomy of teachers. In order to initiate that process the reforms had first to be tried out in a limited number of schools who voluntarily – this is important – wished to participate in them. The experimentation was not embarked upon throughout an entire school but by a voluntary group of teachers. The project was not school-based – an important condition which detracted from the usefulness of this model for change.

This strategy implied that the processes of innovation would be driven by teachers, adapting teaching to different contexts and piloted before innovations were adopted for the entire system, thus establishing a commitment to verification of their suitability, in acknowledgement of the high rates of scholastic failure already mentioned. The rhetoric which had sustained the most progressive teachers since their emergence after 1975, approximately, now acquired legitimacy in the discourse of the Educational Administration. Indeed, policy now was one of convergence and consultation between the Administration and these groups of teachers (*Movimientos de Renovación Pedagógica* (MRPs)).

This new approach also served another function from the political perspective. Experimentation demonstrated prudence and it gained time. The socialist party had obtained an electoral victory with a well-designed programme for government which included reference to structural transformations that would promote democratic control and participation in education (Gomez Llorente y Mayoral, 1981). But it could not logically claim any basis in research, nor had it developed models or programmes to transform the system internally, even less to acknowledge its lack of quality or to propose a reform of teacher training to raise its level and integrate it with the historic tradition of progressive renovation represented mainly by the MRPs and *Colegios de Licenciados* which advocated a democratic, high-quality state school responsive to the different languages and cultures of Spain.

The experimental innovations explicitly put their trust in a particular model of innovation, the 'oil stain' which would progressively spread to a growing number of schools and teachers, further amplifying the process of experimental reform. There was confidence in the wisdom of this strategy and confidence that teachers, anxious for reform, would adopt the new measures. It was soon realized that this strategy was illusory.

From the pedagogic point of view, the educational model which now won official blessing brought together the principles of progressive pedagogy from Europe and America, of activist pedagogy and, more specifically, the popular school of Freinet, the Italian co-operative movements; it borrowed Dewey's approach to learning, the anti-authoritarianism of 1968 French pedagogy, ingredients of Romantic pedagogy which favoured new humanist relations in teaching, of Piagetianism, aspiration to interdisciplinarity and complementarity in intellectual formation, and a certain militancy against hegemonic textbooks. It stressed the importance of incorporating popular culture, of artistic expression through diverse media, a formative model of student assessment, introduction of new technologies, excursions into the outside world to study social, geographical and cultural realities, and generally making use of the environment, establishing connections between intellectual and physical development, stimulating the participation of students, flexible groupings of students and the take-up of action research.

Within this early perspective there was no shortage of disparagement of curriculum content, under the pretext of a struggle against traditional academicism, explicable by a pendular movement that was now favouring pedagogic processes and skills transferable to any content – learning to learn – guided by the rhetoric of child-centred learning.

All these reformist principles were strengthened and disseminated from 1975 by the journal *Cuadernos de Pedagogía*, popular among the most reform-minded teachers, particularly at primary level. It was a proposal for change which adopted the pedagogic perspective of the so-called hidden curriculum of educational psychologists such as Basil Bernstein. This discussion was evaluated in the following documents: *Hacia La Reforma* (MEC, 1983), *Hacia la Reforma, 1* (MEC, 1985) and *Vida Escolar* (MEC, 1984, pp. 229–30), all of them publications of the Ministry.

The most important aspect of these pedagogic reforms was an attempt to bring an end to the dual structure of BUP and FP from the age of 14, establishing a common curriculum up to 16 which, in its content and methods, tried to synthesize intellectual and manual training. These ideas could not but facilitate the hoped-for loyalty of teachers and intellectuals but it alarmed BUP teachers who could not see where the reform was going, who regarded it as an extrapolation of the pedagogic principles accepted at primary level to the whole of education, and who were worried about the possible loss of quality and the marginalization of the value of classic subject areas and disciplines. The new pedagogy implied a profound change in the pedagogic role of the teachers.

These experimental reforms assumed a significant mobilization of teachers which would stimulate contact and grass-roots innovation, economic support from the Administration in supplying those schools which were piloting the reform programmes with additional resources and teaching posts, and with a promise of stability in their place of employment for a given period, and the assurance that the participation of those teachers involved would constitute a professional advantage for the future advancement of their careers.

The imprecision of the programmes went on for too long, and demanded of teachers an intense dedication in order to concretize the curriculum guidelines, to prepare alternative materials to textbooks, to meet with parents, to co-ordinate other teachers. The reforms intensified the burden of work, thus rendering them less attractive to other teachers while reducing the enthusiasm of those who were involved in them.

The 'pedagogic culture of the reform' was distinguished within a given school from 'normal' education, without involving the school as a whole, which reduced the opportunities for promoting the reform. One should recall that not even the school management teams were engaged in the experiment. The group of teachers who applied innovation within the school did not enjoy the promised stability of employment, which made it more difficult to establish a clear and stable line of study.

The promised pedagogic principles were easier to talk about than to put into practice in the day-to-day life of schools without an adequate pedagogic training for the teachers, which could not come of itself, and without a transformation of the working day in order to make viable the additional commitment required of teachers.

In 1984 the *Centros de Profesores* (CEPs) were established, under alternative titles in some of the autonomous communities, based on the model of the UK teachers' centres, underwritten by a philosophy that was favourable to teacher participation but which in itself could not secure the practice of participation in the on-going processes of reform, which continued to be co-ordinated by the Administration. What was missing was a system of specific training, simultaneously tied to the reform, as an instrument for its establishment and diffusion.

Apart from ideas that had already been announced, and some guides which were sent to teachers, the reform of the curriculum did not start from a clear plan that could act as a quality alternative to textbooks, nor were measures undertaken to make available new materials in the short time available. Curricular development was nourished by certain proposals drawn up by the Administration which in practice were insufficiently focused and which were converted into a direct substitution for textbooks. It was due to the creativity and working dedication of voluntarily committed teachers, as can now be seen, that those schools that did introduce the reforms developed styles of teaching distinguishable from those that did not.

In sum, the reform began as a project to stimulate experiment but was then extended without first creating the necessary conditions for the realization of the ideas which it propagated: in-service training of teachers, alternative curriculum materials, organizational flexibility in schools, resources and opportunities for the commitment of teachers. Under these conditions it was unthinkable that the model could be sustained into the medium term.

Contributing to this predictable wearing down of processes of innovation that were both limited but very much welcomed in general terms was a political attempt to establish a professional career structure designed to improve the quality of the teaching force, but which merely provoked a confrontation with teachers. A teachers' strike motivated by salary demands decisively undermined the climate of confidence within the most progressive sectors of the teaching force who were supporting innovation in government policy. The Administration began little by little to lose confidence in initiatives which required a decentralizing impetus, which demanded strong commitment on the part of the teachers and which gave them an awareness of their importance and of needs which the Administration could not satisfy. If the Administration could not satisfy teacher demands, then it could not ask so great a commitment from the teachers.

Innovation within a global project for reform of the structure of the educational system

A second period of office (for the Socialist Government from 1986) provided an opportunity of proposing a restructuring of the educational system in its entirety, establishing compulsory education up to the age of 16, and bringing together in one unitary project all the experimental reforms. In this manner, the discussion of pedagogic innovation would be established from now on within a project of radical transformation. While gaining coherence within a general framework of transformation, certain ideas languished – above all, the dynamic of innovation which had begun in 1983 and which with great intensity had involved teachers in the transformation of educational practice. Experimentation by trial and error could no longer continue. Although they were not negated, the previous pedagogic principles have been substituted in the debate by another discourse.

The new reform turned the organization of education upside down, and put forward proposals for change that were of more vital interest for the teaching force than those related to educational quality. What level of teaching were they going to deliver? In what kind of school would it be taught? Were there going to be non-specialized teachers or teachers specializing in one or more subjects? The problem of quality as indicated by the failure rate would now be attributed to the structural inadequacies of the educational system, regarding as inseparable the re-ordering of the system and the reform of contents and pedagogic methodology (*Libro Blanco*, MEC, 1989, p. 91), an extremely questionable presupposition that ties qualitative reforms to changes in structure.

From this point onwards the debate went beyond the schools which were experimenting with the reforms, moving to discussion of the general, prescribed compulsory curriculum for the overall school system – though not its actual implementation in classroom practice – something which went over the heads of many teachers given the complexity of its grand objective and the technical language in which it was presented. Rather than being a debate about contents or about methods, or about the transmission of culture, discussion was orientated towards problems of curricular organization and, fundamentally, about the model of design to be adopted, preoccupations which did not connect with the more immediate classroom worries of teachers. Pedagogic discourse, diffused in a vertical manner, upon the structure and internal rationality of the curriculum, started from a project initially drawn up in preparation for the first phase of the reforms in Cataluña, which was later accepted by the Ministry of Education (Coll, 1987).

The major pedagogic ideas in this phase were the following: Coll, 1986, 1987, 1989, 1991; *Diseño Curricular Base, Educación Primaria* (MEC,

1989b) and *Diseño Curricular Base, Educación Secundaria Obligatoria* (MEC, 1989c):

1 Constructivism, together with other principles of cognitive psychology, is the theory which lends the most coherence to the proposals of the official curriculum, also influencing the design of curriculum materials and orientating tutors and children towards the practical. In assuming a theory for the entire educational system, the Administration makes it 'official'.

This idea is easy enough to announce but more difficult to apply to concrete contents, to the selection of objectives and contents in the distinctive areas of the curriculum, to the materials or to the processes of teaching and learning. In general terms it can be said that the new proposals tend to be justified from above, supported by psychological concepts and analysis rather more than by social and/or pedagogic concepts. This curricular discourse has been extended and has triumphed. To this extent it is real, as Reid (1984) concurs. But it remains far distant from the common training of teachers and it has not been translated either into the elaboration of materials or into concrete pedagogic practice.

2 Categorization of the components of the curriculum, differentiating between (a) one line of vertical decisions which connects the following steps: general objectives for the cycle for each curricular area and the terminal curriculum objectives of the different curriculum areas, each of which has to specify the 'type and grade of learning which must be achieved' (Coll, 1987, p. 140); and (b), the qualitative dimension, distinguishing between objectives and components, relative to concepts, procedures and attitudes, across all the areas, classes or themes.

This structure, more appropriate to the models of the *diseño de instrucción* than to a proposal which would provide basic guidance for teachers, is imposed by the Ministry on the autonomous communities and the teaching profession, in order that it be followed through into the curriculum planning of schools and the individual curriculum plans of each teacher. In the regulations governing the conditions under which the use of curriculum materials can be approved, the publishers are required to distribute their products according to the system managed by the Ministry, concerning concepts, procedures and attitudes. A first indication of the unsuitability of these proposals is that the prescriptions that are being elaborated by the autonomous communities at the present time are already departing from this taxonomy of objectives and contents.

3 It is stressed that school teachers should draw up plans which concretize the curricular directives of the Administration, which it describes as 'flexible' despite what was said in point (2) about plans which must specify the what, how and when of teaching the components of the

curriculum in schools and classrooms. This acknowledged autonomy contrasts with the increase in technical regulations and the necessity for the approval of some very precise criteria for the evaluation of student learning.

Obviously, without adequate preparation of teachers, without a tradition of collegiate functioning in schools, without adequate training of school heads, without a reduction in the daily work of teachers to make time for planning and without a help network for all teachers, it is easy to predict that the assigned autonomy will have no reality for a large majority of schools, unable to escape beyond the directions established through textbooks. As a point of departure, a philosophy that recognizes pedagogic freedom is very acceptable to teachers, but it is also a source of a certain degree of anxiety and professional insecurity for fear that autonomy will be translated into further intensification of pressure of work.

4 Prescriptions of content that are described as flexible must facilitate the adaptation of curriculum design, undertaken by each school and each teacher, to the diversity of social and cultural contexts and of students within compulsory education.

In secondary education this pedagogic principle is reflected in the configuration of an optional part of the curriculum to bring about compatibility between mixed-ability students and the prolongation of schooling. As for its application in differentiated teaching strategies, attention to interests, consideration of the rhythm of learning of each student, etc., the viability of the idea remains at the mercy of teacher training, of the current, homogenizing rigidity of schooling, with a market of very homogenized curriculum materials and a manifest lack of provision in school libraries.

To diffuse these innovations through channels other than official and semi-official publications, the programmes of in-service training have been reorientated in a more centralized manner towards the themes which have been proposed by the rhetoric of the Administration.

REFERENCES

CIDE (1992) *Las desigualdades en la educación en España*. Madrid: Ministerio de Educación y Ciencia.

Coll, C. (1986) Hacia la elaboración de un modelo de diseño curricular, *Cuadernos de Pedagogía*, no. 138, pp. 8–10.

Coll, C. (1987) *Psicología y curriculum*. Barcelona: Paidos.

Coll, C. (1989) Diseño curricular base y proyectos curriculares, *Cuadernos de Pedagogía*, no. 168, pp. 8–14.

Coll, C. (1991) Concepción constructivista y planteamiento curricular, *Cuadernos de Pedagogía*, no. 188, pp. 8–11.

Consejo Escolar del Estado (1992) *Informe sobre el estado y situación del sistema educativo 1990–1991*. Madrid: Ministerio de Educación y Ciencia.

Cuban, L. (1984), *How teachers taught: constancy and change in American class-room, 1890–1980.* New York: Teachers College Press.

Gomez Llorente, L. and Mayoral, V. (1981) *La escuela pública comunitaria.* Barcelona: Laia.

Maravall, J. M. (1984) *La reforma de la enseñanza.* Barcelona: Laia-Cuadernos de Pedagogía.

Ministerio de Educación y Ciencia (1983) *Hacia La Reforma.* Madrid: Centro de Publicaciones del Ministerio de Educación.

Ministerio de Educación y Ciencia (1984) *Vida Escolar.* Madrid: Centro de Publicaciones del Ministerio de Educación.

Ministerio de Educación y Ciencia (1985) *Hacia la Reforma. 1.* Madrid: Centro de Publicaciones del Ministerio de Educación.

Ministerio de Educación y Ciencia (1987) *Proyecto para la reforma de la enseñanza.* Madrid: Centro de Publicaciones del Ministerio de Educación.

Ministerio de Educación y Ciencia (1989a) *Libro blanco para la reforma del sistema educativo.* Madrid: Ministerio de Educación.

Ministerio de Educación y Ciencia (1989b) *Diseño Curricular Base. Educación Primaria.* Madrid: Ministerio de Educación.

Ministerio de Educación y Ciencia (1989c) *Diseño Curricular Base. Educación Secundaria Obligatoria.* Madrid: Ministerio de Educación.

OECD (1986) *Examen de la politica educativa española por la OCDE.* Madrid: Ministerio de Educación y Ciencia.

ADDITIONAL SOURCES

CIDE (1988) *Evaluación externa de la reforma experimental de las enseñanzas I, II y III.* Madrid: Ministerio de Educación y Ciencia.

Gimeno, J. (ed.) (1992) *Proyecto de investigación para la evaluación de la reforma de las enseñanzas medias in la Comunidad Valenciana.* Valencia: Consejo Escolar Valenciano. Conselleria de Cultura Educación y Ciencia.

Gimeno, J. and Pérez, A. (1986 and 1987) *Evaluación de la reforma del ciclo superior de EGB. II: Los profesores de la reforma, III: Los centros de la reforma. V: Los padres ante la reforma.* (Informe de investigación). Madrid: CIDE.

Martinez Rodriguez, J. B. (1992) *El alumnado y la reconstrucción del curriculum en la reforma.* Granada: Universidad de Granada.

Perez, A. and Gimeno, J. (eds) (1991) *Evaluación de la Reforma del ciclo superior de EGB en Andalucia.* Sevilla: Consejeria de Educación.

Reid, W. (1984) Curriculum topics. Implications for theory, in Jodson, I. and Boll, S. (eds), *History of Social Science.* Brighton: Falmouth Press.

Revista de Educación (1988) *Número monográfico sobre 'La reforma de las enseñanzas media: evaluación externa',* no. 287.

11 The value of diversity and the diversity of value*

Mariano Fernández Enguita

The drive to unitary or comprehensive education to the age of 16, the single most significant measure introduced by LOGSE, was a logical move away from the perceived weaknesses and injustices of the previous division at age 14 between a prestige academic route, the Bachillerato, *and a low-prestige vocational route (none the less criticized for being over-academic),* Formación Profesional, *and it accorded with the practice of many other developed countries. Like LGE before it, LOGSE is arguably based on a 'deficit' model of Spanish education which is perceived as being in various ways 'backward' in comparison with its more 'modern' neighbours, and needing to be brought more into line with 'modern' practice – but at the risk of being insufficiently critical of the 'modern'. More positively, different models of comprehensive education were piloted over several years prior to legislation. But it is arguable whether the discussions leading up to reform were sufficiently informed by any evaluation of comparable international practice that took systematic account of and responded to evidence of disillusion with aspects of comprehensive education in countries such as England and Wales. Some of the most critical analysis proceeded from the relatively young discipline (in Spain) of educational sociology, and the work of one of that discipline's foremost exponents, Fernández Enguita, raises important issues reminiscent of the debates surrounding comprehensive education in Great Britain some thirty years previously. This chapter investigates the implications of the offer of options (different models of optionality were tested in different regions of Spain, namely Cataluña and País Vasco, and in the area administered directly by the Ministry) in relation to principles of comprehensivization and individualization of the curriculum. Secondary education in Cataluña is to be organized in terms of credits or termly modules (with optionality increasing from 27 per cent of the curriculum in the first cycle to 35 per cent in the second), each of 35 teaching hours, whereas in other areas of Spain the curriculum will be organized in terms of 'areas of knowledge'.*

* This chapter translated by Oliver Boyd-Barrett

The problem of options (optional subjects) – whether or not they are useful, the relative weight they should or should not have, the range of subjects they include, the point at which they should be introduced, the extent to which they should be limited, their relationship to tuition and guidance, their consequences in academic and professional terms, etc. – has been one of the most controversial issues in the debate on educational reform and in particular how this affects the new unified track envisaged in the present proposals (ages 14 to 16, the second half of compulsory secondary education).

COMPREHENSIVE SCHOOLING AND OPTIONALITY

Segregation of the educational system into branches and diverse special-isms, each selected differently and of distinctive academic and professional value, has as a natural effect the configuration of relatively homogeneous groups of students within each segregated unit. In the segregated school the problem of optionality is of little relevance given that when it is introduced the options are always between similar categories of subject: Latin or Greek, English or French, Metalwork or Woodwork.

The comprehensive reform, nevertheless, maximizes the significance of options. All students, whatever their capabilities, attitudes, preferences ambitions, are brought together in a basically communal education. In principle, the problem of the diversity of individuals is inescapable for an educational institution. There are no two persons whose needs are so similar as to allow us to reinforce that similarity by means of a totally identical curriculum. None the less, what has kept substantial numbers of all students in harmony with the educational institution is not their identification with the actual curriculum so much as their acceptance of the goals of the institution: goals which these students – drawn principally but not exclusively from among the more 'successful' – accept not in terms of a particular combination of Geography, Chemistry, Physical Education, etc., but in terms of the idea that school knowledge is valuable and is useful precisely because it has been chosen as such by the school.

Internal diversification of the curriculum starts precisely from the moment that the (secondary) school caters for sectors of the student body other than those which have been most associated with it traditionally. In other words, internal diversification does not stem from the recognition of individuality, but from evidence that the composition of the student body continuing within the institution is very different from that which the institution was designed to serve. Otherwise, why was it that there was so little room for choice in BUP and COU (where it was restricted to choice between elements of what was officially a single subject), and there was none at all in FP? Surely, we did not have to wait until now to realize that people are different? Or are we dealing with a counter-offensive to the offensive against segregation which is represented by comprehensive education?

To begin the discussion, it is necessary to bear in mind constantly that the diversity confronting the school is two-fold. On the one hand, there is individual diversity which makes of every individual a unique being resistant to being reduced to some interchangeable entity. On the other hand, there is social diversity, or rather the totality of divisions of class, power, gender and ethnicity which cut across the society of which the school is part. To ignore either one of these two dimensions can only lead to simplistic conclusions and (if we are talking among ourselves) to a dialogue of the deaf, not to say idiots. If we concentrate only on individual diversity the solution is clear: that everyone should see the menu and choose the dishes they most enjoy. If we look only at social divisions – unless, of course, we wish to ensure that the school maintains and reinforces them – then the conclusion is *menu del dia*, a set meal for all.

I believe that the majority of the experts and educators who have participated in the debate on options share, at least vaguely, two objectives: on the one hand, that the school should recognize, acknowledge and attend to individual diversity; on the other hand, to eliminate, limit or at least to prevent the school from contributing to reinforcement of the great social divisions. I have no doubt – indeed I am convinced – that there are many other persons who do not share these objectives or who believe that to try and achieve them would be a remedy worse than the disease. Doubtless, it would be worth while to discuss this issue expansively but I shall confine myself to emphasizing the question of optionality in the context of shared objectives.

A BRIEF RECAPITULATION

In 1986, I published a book: *Integrar a segregar: la enseñanza secundaria en los países industrializados* (Integration or segregation: secondary education in the industrialized countries) (Fernández Enguita, 1986) whose fourth chapter, *Diferenciación y división social en la escuela integrada* (Differentiation and social division in the comprehensive school), warned against three kinds of internal division in the comprehensive school: the offer of alternative curricula, grouping by levels of ability (setting) and options. In dealing with the third of these, I was supported by the evidence of two countries which had proceeded further down this route: the UK and the USA. In both countries the weight of optional subjects in the comprehensive secondary curriculum had attracted strong criticism in the previous decade, for two lots of reasons.

On the one hand, these options were criticized for permitting students – while not obliging them – to configure for themselves irrelevant curricula that would be of little value for their adult life, or which were formatively incoherent. One can debate what is relevant or coherent, but I will not do so here because it is not this critique that I am concerned about. Rather, it is the criticism of the right wing which takes its starting point from here and which then goes on to demand a return to the 'basics'; that is, a strengthening of the role of the traditional academic subjects, from which many pupils have escaped thanks to the balance between options and core curriculum.

On the other hand, critics have focused on the fact that, by means of options, many students compiled or were persuaded to compile pro- grammes of study which simply reproduced the old lines of segregation (from the social perspective) and the distinctiveness (from the individual perspective) of the 'academic' and the 'professional' branches. Besides, the choices of students were strongly influenced by their social context, by the internalization into their personal destinies of their unequal social opportunities, by the expectations of teachers, etc. In sum, the system of options allowed the school – without forcing it to do so – to reproduce social differences . . . and to reproduce them generationally, perpetuating class differences for successive generations of the same families, and differences of race and ethnicity for members of those corresponding groups.

A year later I published *Reforma educativa, desigualdad social y inercia institucional'* (Educational reform, social inequality and institutional inertia) (Fernández Enguita, 1990). This book was based on field research undertaken by several dozen schools which were adopting the reform programme on an experimental basis, at that time variously labelled *ciclo polivalente* (multi-dimensional cycle), *Bachillerato general* (general Bacalaureate), *ciclo de enseñanza secundaria* (cycle of secondary education) (in Cataluña) or simply 'REM' (*reforma de las enseñanzas medias* (reform of secondary education), that is, the new unified stage of two-year secondary education, ages 14 to 16. I set out to explore in the first three chapters what seemed to me to be the most relevant problems, advantages and risks of the three models of organization which were being tested out in the 'MEC territory' (those parts of Spain for which the Ministry of Education and Science has administrative responsibility), the País Vasco and Cataluña. Without any doubt it was my evaluation of the Catalonian model which occasioned the greatest debate, although it was not the most unfavourable of the three. Essentially, what I was saying was that although students were basically satisfied with the alterna- tives provided by options and that the teachers were divided but inclined to favour it, this system could reproduce within schools differences which were equal to or greater than those which used to exist between BUP and FP, only atomized to a symphony of individual cases rather than formally institutionalized into two scholastic branches. Without going into more detail at this point, I should say that I still think now as I thought then, and that I only regret not having insisted more on another dimen- sion of the problem, namely that with a system which allows ample autonomy to schools in the elaboration of optional schemes the differences which can be produced inside a school must be considered even greater than those which are manifest between different schools. I exposed personal curricula which were simply repetitions of those of BUP or of FP, but even more academic than BUP or more pragmatic than FP. Let us say, if I may be permitted the use of prefixes which correspond to prejudices, but to prejudices which have some rational foundation and significant social implications, that one could encounter a range from a very superior BUP to an excessively inferior FP.

Perhaps I did not emphasize this sufficiently because although it could happen and was happening, it did not happen *inevitably*. To have given it greater emphasis might have helped to fortify those teachers who were putting their best efforts into trying to ensure that students obtained, out of the multitude of possibilities which the optional system promises, something approaching an integrated education. I must also say, none the less, that to have emphasized this too much could have created the impression that I was complaining about a mere hazard, and hazards can be encountered in any system. On the contrary, what I thought and still do think is that if this situation could arise already, with teachers who have volunteered for reform and were identified with it, and with comprehensive education as their main priority, then it was all the more likely to occur among those who still believe that there are essentially two categories of students, those who have to go to university and those who have to proceed directly to employment.

Finally, I want to mention that in order to 'denationalize' the debate as far as possible, the book contained a critique – similar in vein, but stronger in tone – of the first experimental application of reform to the subject area of technology and art, within 'MEC territory' (i.e. within those parts of the country directly administered by the Ministry rather than by autonomous communities), where what had previously been the BUP institutes concentrated on information technology, photography, video, gardening and other 'hobbies' or other appealing subjects, while what had previously been FP colleges offered their pupils metalwork, woodwork, automobile repairs and technical drawing.

SOME REPLIES TO MY CRITICS

As examples of two principal kinds of criticism of my argument I am going to take instances which, together with one of my own contributions, were published in No. 157 of the journal *Cuadernos de Pedagogía* (March 1988), one written by Josep Alsinet and Emili Munoz, and the other by Joan Badia i Pujol. Both were rather general contributions on the single theme proposed by the journal, 'Responses to Diversity', but both referred directly or indirectly to *Reforma Educativa, desigualdad social y inercia institucional* (Fernández Enguita, 1988) and, more specifically, to its chapter on Catalonian reform.

The response of Alsinet and Munoz, directors of two of the schools which were then piloting the reform – or rather, of two schools which were set up, if I am not mistaken, precisely in order to pilot the reform – is simple and, at the same time, clear. If in *Reforma Educativa* I had put forward various examples of disparate and socially segregated curricula, they could put forward various examples 'selected so as to represent various types of student', with respect to which they can affirm, despite the personal inclination of the students,

> the infrequent over-specialization and the absence of class . . . hierarchization, look wherever one may. . . . We stress . . . in good faith that we have not altered the sociological . . . destination of these five students. But no less certain is . . . the fact that we have not sanctioned it. . . .

(Alsinet and Munoz, 1988)

I am not going to enter into discussion about either the interpretation of the content, nor the selection of the five examples, as the same could be done with the examples I presented in *Reforma Educativa*. I shall take their selection as representative and I shall allow their interpretation. Besides, seeing that in my book I used code names in strictest confidence to protect the anonymity of schools, I cannot check to see if the examples I chose corresponded with any of theirs; nor does it make any sense to try, since this is no place for discussion about any one school, and a basic respect for the ontology of social research stops me from pointing the finger. Consequently, we take as read that which neither of the two parties has put into question, namely, that the field work on which *Reforma Educativa* was based disclosed cases (not isolated cases) of reproduction of the old BUP/FP divisions – even amplified – by means of options, while the examples offered by these authors, on the contrary and as a result of researching their own schools – and without doubt, others – yield instances of balanced selection.

Thus Alsinet and Munoz, on the one hand, and I, on the other, are saying different but not contradictory things. They maintain that by means of an optional system which offers a range of benefits, it is possible for students to configure a balanced curriculum. They even explain how in their schools they actively encourage this: first, by forcing choice between groups of options in predetermined areas of learning; second, in principle permitting total freedom of choice, but correcting possible imbalances opportunistically by means of tutorial action. For my part, I maintain that by means of the optional system, whose other advantages I accept, an imbalanced selection by students does occur, and can be accentuated by the school, and even more by differences between schools. All in all, I believe there are two common premises: that options have the advantage of flexibility and of responsiveness to the individual interests of students, and that compulsory schooling must provide everyone with a balanced

education, of social value and of equal weight. They say that from these
premises there may be a positive outcome, I say there may be a negative
outcome. And here, precisely, lies the question. What is it we need? A
reform which allows us to do things well or a reform which does not
allow us to do them badly? I think that both things are possible – and
this was, and is, my criticism of the Catalán reforms – the same flexibility
allows both miracles and disasters. And I think it is also what Alsinet
and Munoz believe when they write:

> It has to be recognized that curricular flexibility . . . however remote
> the likelihood, can be applied in a divisive manner if the school opts
> for premature specialization and for reinforcing diversity of the student
> body in terms of social class and hierarchy, division between courses
> or students in theoretical or applied orientation, or between academic
> and professional adaptation at the point of leaving school. Some of
> this can be found in some schools of Cataluña.
>
> (Alsinet and Munoz, 1988)

This is confirmed beyond doubt when, to avoid these problems, the
authors affirm:

> All activity we undertake in secondary education must be located
> within a framework of general and holistic education which distances
> itself from premature specialization. In this sense we think it is oppor-
> tune that the academic administration establishes the basic criteria
> which might govern the offer of options. These will have to guarantee
> the presence in the optional curriculum of awards from each area of the
> curriculum. It is not sufficient to control only the supply of options;
> we have to be prepared to control possible idiosyncracies of particular
> demands. In order to avoid these it is necessary, here also, to introduce
> suitable tutorial counselling which will influence and if necessary
> compel students to take certain given options.
>
> (Alsinet and Munoz, 1988)

A very different kind of critique is offered by Badia i Pujol. Here I must
choose between that which refers to me explicitly – by name and surname
– or implicitly – by making it clear that he has read *Reforma Educativa*
(which is said, in this author's judgement, to be full of 'exaggerations',
'irrelevancies' or 'jokes') – and which one way or the other concerns the
fundamental debate; I believe I must choose the second.

I believe that the arguments of Badia i Pujol can be synthesized into
three. In the first place, he says that to judge the Catalán model of
secondary reform by concentrating on the variable options, which make
up 30 per cent of teaching time, while leaving to one side the common
core, and the time allowed for remedial work, examinations and tutorial
counselling, is to distort its real character and its objectives. Secondly, he

says that the common core does not signify 'curriculum standardization' but merely the 'common objectives that all citizens should achieve by the age of 16', which is not the same thing as saying that 'it does not attempt any levelling of knowledge, conscious that this is impossible'. This argument is better explained with a quotation from Girod:

> The real problem is not to operate on the general structure of inequality of outcomes, but, more traditionally, to ensure that every student, whoever he is, achieves as much progress as he is capable of in all the disciplines which will serve him later.
>
> (Girod, 1984)

In the third place, it is argued that diversity among students will exist whatever the social environment and it is not the function of the educational system to achieve something that is beyond its compass; again, with the help of Giroud:

> For those who yearn for an education that can equalize all learning situations, or the educational achievements of all pupils, they must bear in mind that it would be less utopian to try to equalize the income of all citizens and their share of participation in power, or even to abolish all labour hierarchies by means of a restructuring of work to ensure that each person takes on the same proportions of manual and non-manual work, creative or management responsibility, than it would be to achieve equality of educational outcome for all students.
>
> (Girod, 1984)

I will concern myself here with the first and third arguments, given that the second is essentially the nub of the whole debate. On the first, I must begin by saying that if one is interested in the general organization of the curriculum, the only features which are specifically peculiar to the Catalán model are the optional modules. The common core modules are not only common in Cataluña, but also form essentially the same common programme that is shared throughout the whole Spanish State (regardless of the fact that this should currently be the curriculum model peculiar to the 'MEC territory', but with which the autonomous communities are obliged to align, and which is delivered in various proportions, as happens in País Vasco) except of course for subject matter related to regional language and culture. Counselling services are also available throughout the country although naturally they vary according to whether they focus on the context of the common core or the optional curriculum. Nevertheless, what our survey showed is that there was not just one form of counselling available, but several, as many as there were schools. Also, Badia y Pujol (who was co-ordinator at that time for the piloting of the reform), in a debate actually concerning the reponse to diversity with reference to options, could permit himself to speak of the importance of counselling while leaving its implementation to each school or teacher group, while Alsinet and Munoz demanded basic criteria to control both the supply of and the response to the demand for optional modules.

As for optional time for remedial work or for assessment, the first seems fine to me, and is not new (EGB was full of 'recovery' time), and the second is impressive, and this I have said or written on more than one occasion (including the controversial chapter on the Catalán model in *Reforma Educativa*). In practice, not all such ideas are intrinsic to the model, although they represent innovations in the context of Catalán reform and I applaud them as such, but the reform could survive without them (although I would hope that this does not happen) and they could perfectly well be applied to some other model (and I wish they were). What we are left with, and which continues to be the most distinctive feature of the Catalán reform of compulsory secondary education, its corner-stone, and the card on which all the rest is gambled, is the principle of optional modules. We should mention that in *Reforma Educativa* it was also shown that the optional modules could easily extend from 30 to 50 per cent of school time, and even to almost two-thirds.

The third argument may seem like a broad generalization with which it is tempting to agree, but it is more than that and takes on special importance in the context of a discussion about a model for the offer of options. In truth, it is an old argument, much older than Giroud, and it comes from the disenchantment of some expert observers and prophets of educational reform, British social democrats and their 'liberal' North American counterparts. It was popularized in the world of education by Christopher Jencks and A. H. Halsey. These authors maintained that egalitarian reforms in education (e.g. comprehensive reorganization or measures against racial segregation and resource inequalities), which had been perceived in the 1950s and 1960s as panaceas for the great social inequalities, had not had the effects expected of them. They therefore concluded that if one desired to eradicate inequalities, or to reduce them (and they enumerated all those considered by Girod, as quoted by Badia i Pujol, and some more), then one should not seek an answer in oblique and ineffective areas such as the reform of education, but rather one had to commit oneself to a direct attack, by such means as wage struggle, against employment practices and patterns of ownership. What they did *not* conclude is that one should give up on an egalitarian education, even if they could no longer regard this as a magic wand with which to resolve all major problems. At the time, the statement that reforms do not produce 'equality of results' (from the Coleman Report of the early 1960s) was used by the extreme right-wing conservative thinkers to argue that expenditure on educational reform was not worth the effort.

For ourselves, we have the luck and the misfortune to embark upon our comprehensive reform two or three decades later. We can and we must go one step further, moderating our initial optimism in order to avoid our inevitable disappointment. If we well know that social inequalities do not depend exclusively nor principally on education, we also know that they depend in great measure on it. We could say that they depend on three factors: on ownership, which determines the opportunities of one person to exploit the work of others, to live independently of their own labour or of having to sell their power of labour to third parties and become part of a salaried work force; on power, which is distributed in a manner no less unequal and which, in a world governed by institutions (public and private, political and economic, companies among them), allows adults to bequeath their status by various means to their descendants (including nepotism among some professions and occupational groups – from notaries and property registrars to shipyards – the celebrated 'relations', 'contracts' and 'connections', etc.); finally, educational credentials which, other things being equal, determine to a large extent the opportunities of people in the labour market. School is not simply an institution which educates individuals, as conservatives think, nor is it a mechanism for the legitimation of inequality, as certain radical theorists would have it i.e. the mechanism for the legitimation of inequalities which originate and develop outside its sphere. It is all these and much more and it is itself a significant source of social inequalities.

Precisely because ownership is highly concentrated in contemporary society, reducing the majority of the population to employee status, while power is subjected to greater public control in order to restrict its arbitrariness (i.e. capitalism within democracy, or vice versa) education takes on importance as a determinant of social opportunities, as long as it does not challenge the rights of ownership or power. What has reduced the capacity of educational reforms to overcome social inequalities has not simply been the persistence of other sources of social inequality such as ownership or power. It also, and perhaps even more, has to do with the fact that all comprehensive reforms, and other egalitarian measures, presented with great song and dance for the benefit of public opinion, were accompanied or followed by small counter-reforms taken in discreet shadow, removed from political debate and justified in the technical, individualistic language of pedagogy and psychology. Among these counter-reforms was included the introduction of uncontrolled optionality.

The problem of optionality is not that students learn different things, more or less desirable, useful or prestigious, from one view or another, but that it leads, albeit within a structure of obligatory, comprehensive and common education, to education credentials of sharply varying values in the world of work, or which open very different doors within the educational system itself, or that it simply allows, as a fact of life, very early and irrevocable choices. From my particular point of view, there is no doubt that these matters should be subject to a political judgement about the organization of schooling and its place in the wider society – and, consequently, of how this should be. No organization of optionality in compulsory education is acceptable which prevents or impedes such judgement. That signifies, as a starting point, that no optionality without controls is acceptable, nor any system which allows each school to offer different options for each student or lets them choose their options however they like.

Those who would do nothing to limit student choice of options make three assumptions. The first is that school qualifications need have no effect on the job market or on the structure of employment. On paper, this could come about in two ways: by eliminating the differences between jobs (in the broad sense of reward, not just in terms of salaries) or detaching employment differences entirely from educational differences. The first is proposed, or at least identified as something which should concern us, by Badia i Pujol, quoting Giroud in his support; the second has been proposed, some time ago, by Illich, who suggested an amendment to the US constitution to the effect that it should not discriminate between people by reason of their educational qualifications, similar to that which prohibits discrimination by reason of people's beliefs or their skin-colour, or which feminist movements are trying to secure with respect to gender in approving the Equal Rights Amendment. I have to say, none the less, that both possibilities would never amount to more than idle speculation for the distraction of civil servants or, worse, a flight towards the impossible or the unlikely which would cut us off from a sense of the possible and the likely.

The second assumption consists of what we can call a 'de-subjectization' of educational knowledge, apparent in the conception of the common curriculum as a collection of competencies, attitudes, skills, etc., not tied to specific disciplines but present in and attainable across all of them. The student can then choose whatever he wishes, because all roads should lead to Rome or because, as Kavafis has written and Llach has sung, Ithaca will be the road unto itself, the name of its final destination having no importance. This is the view which has been proposed for some time by at least a part of Her Majesty's Inspectorate in Great Britain, one of the countries in which the regime of options has flowered most liberally. To me, the result is tempting and yet at the same time difficult, if not practically out of reach of a school system with our traditions, but perhaps this is due to an innate, unjustified lack of confidence or perhaps simply because I know hardly anything of didactics.

The third assumption springs from the view that such options have always led to knowledge and academic awards of equivalent value in social and cultural terms, whose consequences are not irrevocable, which do not close doors, either legally or in practice, nor do they open different doors for different groups of students. Reassurance of this could be achieved very simply, through the mere procedure of requiring students to choose between sets of options, each set balanced in terms of subjects or curriculum areas, in order to ensure a minimum number or quota of subjects or areas for each student.

Let us suppose, for example, that a school can be allowed to offer twenty-five different subject options from which the student chooses five, and let us suppose these are as follows:

Physics	English	Mechanics	Economics	Music
Chemistry	French	Electricity	Communication	Theatre
Biology	German	Plumbing	Law	Pottery
Geology	Italian	Woodwork	Psychology	Video
Botany	Russian	Health	Sociology	Drawing

This example is not a proposal, as I am aware that it lacks areas such as language, humanities, elements of work-related experience, etc., but I do not want to complicate things unnecessarily. On the other hand, I have deliberately stressed the generic and disciplinary labels: Mechanics in place of motor vehicles, Biology in place of the human body, English in the place of the contemporary English novel, etc., in order to be as clear as possible and because my experience suggests the majority of such specialist courses are but mere fragments of traditional subject courses. I do not wish to venture into whether schools should offer 10, 20 or 30 options: the students choose three, four or however many, and it is possible to choose a termly, quarterly, annual or even variable duration.

This is simply an example which could be found in any school and which allows us to see that there are various ways of organizing options. The individual groups of options which tend to be concentrated along the vertical lines would represent, from the perspective of the individual student, a premature specialization and, from the perspective of the institution, an internal segregation equal to or more extreme than that which is experienced between schools and which it is proposed should be eradicated. Any student can choose the first whole column and thus achieve a science *Bachillerato* without anyone turning a hair. If we exclude the possibility of a young polyglot, the same mechanism would be able to turn out in succession a student of FP1, a modern *Bachillerato* of letters, a young artist and a dilettante academic.

Alternatively, a student could always choose from the horizontal lines which are formed by the columns, ordered in this or in some other way; that is, she/he would have to put together a set choosing one option from each column, whatever the academic value or social advantage of the resulting combination. Of course, it is arguable whether physical education is more or less important than biology (it is well known that at university men tend to study the first, and women the second), whether English is more or less useful than French, whether electricity requires a level of technical competence greater or lesser than woodwork, whether economists earn more or less money than lawyers, or whether a fascination for music is more or less refined than a fascination for theatre, but any such differences are small beer compared to the differences between the *Bachillerato* and the *Formación Profesional*. Besides, it will have escaped nobody's attention that the choices based on the vertical columns amount to a very specialized education while those based on the horizontal axes are the only choices which would approximate to an understanding of integral and all-round training or to the full and multi-faceted development of the individual.

More than one reader will have wondered whether in the example chosen the labelling of options needs to be bound to a disciplinary or specialist conception, and whether it would not be possible on the contrary to construct options of a more inter-disciplinary kind. Thus, to provide some new examples, 'The sea' could encompass Geology, Biology, Geometry and Economics; a term dedicated to the reading in its original language of *The Piano Player* could encompass English, Technology and its social repercussions, etc. I do not doubt it would be possible, and I think that if everything were like that we would confront the second assumption that I described at the beginning of this section. But I also have to add that although I have seen some notable efforts of this kind, and with good results, they are the exception rather than the rule, and will become more so foreseeably, in the short to medium term at least, when the reform extends beyond the voluntary framework of experiment/piloting to affect all schools. In any case, I would urge all teachers within a regime of options that they should start to experiment with structures which, besides offering vertical blocks like those we have seen, also offer modules conceived as inter-disciplinary themes.

It is interesting to observe at this point that in principle any educational administration or any teacher is faced with three choices: to promote options of the vertical kind, which we might call specialization; to promote options of the horizontal kind, which we could call multilateral; or, of course, to abstain from promoting any structure at all – whether in response to regulatory constraint or out of conviction – and to allow students to choose whatever they feel like. Although this last sounds good, and very liberal, I believe that the traditions of schooling and the pressures of society work in favour of the first strategy, but that none the less, what every administration and school should try to achieve, even to impose, is the second.

The questions of the reversibility or irreversibility of student choices and of an options structure that will not forever shut off future possibilities are even more complex than they seem at first glance. For at first glance it is simply a matter of ensuring that there should not appear to be any legal constraints or requirements, which is to say that whatever curriculum a student has compiled during compulsory secondary education, he or she should have access to every specialism at higher secondary level, be it the *Bachillerato* or, of course, professional or technical education. None the less, if any specialism at these levels presupposes as a given fact that students should have achieved a level of learning in some areas that goes beyond anything corresponding to what has been learnt in compulsory education, a mistaken choice can become a difficult obstacle for anyone to negotiate.

A solution to this would be to reduce such differences of level, which would have as a consequence the lowering of standards on entry to post-compulsory education in some specialist subjects. Another solution would be an access system to higher secondary education which would cater for students who have taken options that do not fit very well with the specialism they finally choose, to help them climb to the same starting point as those whose choice has been more appropriate.

REFERENCES

Alsinet, J. and Munoz, E. (1988) Book review, *Cuadernos de Pedagogía*, no. 157, March.

Fernández Enguita, M. (1986) *Integrar a segregar: la enseñanza secundaria en los países industrializados.* Barcelona: Editorial Laia.

Fernández Enguita, M. (1988) *Reforma educativa, desigualdad social y inercia institucional. La enseñanza secundaria en España.* Barcelona: Editorial Laia.

Fernández Enguita, M. (1990) *Juntos pero no revueltos.* Madrid: Visor.

Girod, R. (1984) *Politica educativa. Lo ilusorio y lo posible.* Madrid: Editorial kapalnz.

12 The place of evaluation in educational reform*

Angel Chico Blas

The 1970 Ley General de Educación (LGE) promised a radically new approach to educational evaluation which it did not deliver: student assessment (and above all the summative examination) remained the principal mode of evaluation, and rates of 'failure' stayed high. This chapter examines the gathering interest in a broader range of approaches to evaluation, especially in the light of LOGSE; the author looks at implications for evaluation at the different levels of system, school, curriculum, teachers and students. Of particular interest is his discussion of the links between teacher in-service training and remuneration, and the provisions in LOGSE for student progress from year to year or from cycle to cycle. Equally significant for an assessment of the current situation in Spain are some of the omissions: no reference, for example, to teacher appraisal, to standardized testing of children at specific ages, to provision for systematic moderation of assessment between schools. The author outlines some of the reasons why the university entrance examinations should not be expected to correct for some of these omissions and his criticisms retain their force even in the wake of recent efforts to promote greater consistency of standards between entrance examinations. The editors' postscript provides details of the constitution of the newly established INCE, and some results of a report of the Inspectorate on the implementation of the reform programme.

In this chapter I shall try to articulate some personal reflections on the role that has been assigned to evaluation in a particular period of educational reform. This refers to the process that started in Spain since the promulgation on 3 October 1990 of the *Ley Orgánica de Ordenación General del Sistema Educativo*, which I will refer to by its acronym, LOGSE. Application of this law will follow a timetable that ensures the complete substitution, within a maximum period of ten years, of the academic structure established in 1970 by the *Ley General de Educación* (LGE). I expect and I hope that the substitution will be more than a merely formal process.

* This chapter translated by Oliver Boyd-Barrett

I believe that within the curriculum framework which governs or which should govern every educational development or intervention, the evaluation of the process or of the outcomes is an essential factor. And in saying 'every educational development or intervention' I mean everything from the most detailed (e.g. the work of a group of students, a particular day, a curriculum theme, the training and appraisal of a teacher) to developments that are more global or transcendental (on account of their scope or of the resources they involve, e.g. the launching of an in-service teacher training programme or the very process of implementing an educational reform).

A BRIEF HISTORY

The 1970 LGE had the merit of generalizing the deployment of a technical, pedagogic and didactic vocabulary, although I believe that behind the smoke-screen of new terms there was, in practice, a scarcity of real change.

The idea that everything that can be said in education has been said used to be current among many teachers and inspectors, who adopted a sceptical attitude towards processes of innovation. In the summer of 1970, a course was organized at the International University Menendez Pelayo, dedicated to the analysis of *Educación General Básica* (EGB) which the LGE had introduced. In one of the reports (UIMP, 1970) the text stated that 'evaluation was introduced into our field by economists . . . when they arrived, the economists discovered that we also spoke prose; in other words, we were already practising evaluation, only we were calling it something else'. References to evaluation in LGE were multi-faceted and included:

1 The student's educational achievement;
2 Effectiveness of curriculum programmes and methods of application;
3 Achievement of teachers, assessed by the Inspectorate in collaboration with the University Institutes of Educational Science (ICEs);
4 School outcomes, in the light of criteria specified in LGE;
5 Adaptation of plans and programmes of study to emerging new needs with respect to in-service training and up-dating; and
6 The results attributable to LGE itself.

This is a wide and ambitious range of objectives for evaluation. The reality, in practice, was that the only evaluation that actually functioned was category (1) above, and even that was subject to the inertia of methods of assessment which had been recycled for application to the new structure.

The evaluation of student achievement – which was to have been continuous, systematic, qualitative, utilizing diverse methods, exploring not only the acquisition of knowledge but also of attitudes – strayed little, in practice, from the traditional modes of numerical qualification based on examinations, oral questions or exercise books.

At the beginning of the 1980s the *Proyectos de Reforma Experimental* (Projects for Experimental Reform), which started with *Enseñanzas Medias* (secondary education) ages 14 to 18, and with the highest cycle of EGB education, ages 11 to 14, attempted to design, experimentally implement and evaluate a new curriculum for these age groups which would overcome the weaknesses that had been identified in the operation of LGE. The central idea, which was an integrated curriculum for compulsory education up to 16 years, also remodelled the role and operation of evaluation.

As set out in the document *Hacía la Reforma* (MEC, 1985), the didactic principles of experimental reform introduced in 1983 included a section that revised our understanding of evaluation as a learning tool. Reviewing the accumulated experience of evaluation during the years of LGE, it recalled that 'evaluation must harmonize with the principles which underlie the reform'. A traditional system of evaluation would run completely against the educational goals of reform; evaluation had to be formative, and its formative character converted evaluation into an instrument of support, not of judgement.

The document emphasized that the essential purpose of evaluation is to service the progress of each student. Indirectly, the evaluation plan facilitates an analysis of the appropriateness of the curriculum at the levels of both classroom and school. The design of the pilot reforms included an evaluation of the reform process itself undertaken by the *Centro de Investigación, Documentación y Evaluación*, (Centre for Educational Research and Documentation) (CIDE).

None other than the Minister for Education and Science, in presenting the 1989 *Libro Blanco para la Reforma Educativa* (White Paper on Educational Reform) (MEC, 1989), cited the results of that evaluation in support of some of the issues and recommendations which he put forward for debate, in particular the controversy over how to provide for a heterogeneous student body without resorting to a segregated curriculum (for further discussion on this point see Fernández Enguita, 1986).

EVALUATION IN LOGSE

Now that LOGSE is approved and the first packet of regulations for its implementation are in force, I shall proceed to analyse how the issue of evaluation is to be dealt with across its various dimensions, and to indicate those aspects which most of all merit development, contingency planning and preparatory training.

LOGSE dedicates a specific article to evaluation within its fourth chapter on the quality of teaching, and it is addressed holistically. The location is appropriate. The educational community appreciates, perhaps intuitively, that there is a clear correlation between the degree of rigour applied in evaluating an educational activity and the overall value that is attached to that activity.

The generic aim which is attributed to evaluation is not particularly original: 'The purpose of evaluation of the educational system is the continuing adaptation of the system to social demand and educational need, and will apply to all students, teachers, schools, educational processes and, above all, to the educational administration' (LOGSE, 1990).

For each of the different levels which require evaluation I will discuss existing projects, their legal foundation and the most significant difficulties that can be anticipated.

GENERAL EVALUATION OF THE SYSTEM

A new agency, the *Instituto Nacional de Calidad y Evaluación* (National Institute for Quality and Evaluation) (INCE), has been established to begin work from 1994, and this may signify a qualitative change in approach to evaluation. The agency will have to develop systems of evaluation for the different kinds of teaching and different kinds of schools, and will carry out research studies and evaluations of the educational system.

The ruling party has not accepted, in the context of parliamentary debate, that this new organization needs to be tied to the existing *Consejo Escolar del Estado* (the National Advisory Council for Education), which is the national, participatory forum for all relevant sectors involved in education: teachers, students, parents, school administrative and service personnel, unions and employer organizations, universities and the national educational administration.

This view, together with the delay in setting it up, leads me to harbour the suspicion that the Institute will retain an 'official' character, which will diminish its potential scope. During the stage of the implementation of reform, an evaluation of the system is indirectly an evaluation of the reform process itself, and this should be undertaken with ample room for independence from the Educational Administration.

EVALUATION OF SCHOOLS AND CURRICULA

A serious attempt has been made to systematize a procedure for the evaluation of schools (i.e. a pilot plan for the evaluation of forty schools implemented by the Ministry in 1991, and since extended). Evaluation of the school should be the responsibility of the school's own community, on the one hand, and ultimately that of the governing body as the site of the school's management and participation, synthesizing the perspectives of its various interests. It should self-evaluate its own functioning, infrastructures and work plans. External evaluation by the Inspectorate, on the other hand, provides an opportunity for the inclusion of different techniques, methodologies and perspectives. The two approaches should be complementary, and external evaluation should be understood, by all parties involved, as an objective assessment. School evaluation also contributes to a data base for evaluation of the global functioning of the system.

In Spain, and in Cataluña to be precise, there had already existed practical precedents for a systematic evaluation of schools and of educational goals (Darder, 1980). To apply this type of evaluation more widely implies first of all the need to define a provisional, working methodology, controlling it experimentally, adjusting it after experiment, planning approaches to consciousness-raising and training for the services and sectors which will have responsibility for evaluation. To undertake all that would require a careful plan with substantial provision of resources and with sufficient personnel: neither suitably qualified personnel nor economic resources are abundant, although such deficits are all too common in programmes of educational innovation.

As for the programmes which are devised by educational administrations (of the State and of the autonomous communities) and for the projects which emerge from schools or from groups of teacher innovators, for which recognition and support may be forthcoming if the innovations are adopted, the assimilation of a resolute 'evaluating culture' is an indispensable and basic component. Once again, we have two faces of the same coin: the requirement for self-evaluation on the part of whoever is applying the project, and external evaluation in the hands of technical experts.

External and internal evaluation, partial or global, has already begun for certain specific programmes, e.g. counselling in secondary schools, the introduction of information technology, professional development for teachers, etc. Directions have also been given for the evaluation of school or group projects, but these generally lack the necessary degree of system and method.

EVALUATION OF TEACHERS

This brings us to the analysis of the controversial theme of the teaching profession. In Spain, to be a teacher of state education is to be a civil servant, together with the advantages and the inconveniences of that status. That it is a post which is held for life guarantees a certain independence and organized professionalism as protection against the whims of politicians, but also has the disadvantage that it tends to have a conservative influence. If this can be unfortunate in almost any other sector of public administration, in teaching, with its particular historical, social and scientific evolution, it can be disastrous.

Clearly, a recognition of the necessity for modernization should be tied to a commitment to corresponding practice, but sometimes only the recognition exists, and at times even that is absent. A period of global reform of the educational system with profound implications for curriculum change necessitates a process of galvanization. But how to achieve this without adopting coercive methods which would simply consolidate anti-reformist sentiment? The Educational Administration seems to have wagered its bet on the use of economic incentives.

Coinciding with the promulgation of the first legislative developments of LOGSE, there has been an effective process of negotiation and agreement with the unions for a new system of remuneration which allows for new salary increments for every teacher for each six years of service, provided that in each six-year period the intended beneficiaries have undertaken at least one hundred hours of approved in-service education.

Under the previous system of remuneration, all members of a school's staff, save for such specific functions as director, or head of department, were paid the same salary, except for a small automatic increment for seniority, and this favoured passivity.

But the new system is in danger of reproducing the one that it replaced. It may convert itself into an automatic system in which any teacher progresses on the basis of steady attendance at in-service training sessions, however passive their attendance, and whether or not attendance has any subsequent impact on classroom behaviour. Symptoms such as these are already in evidence. (Around 90,000 teachers took part in in-service education activities in 1991–2 and again in 1992–3.)

In negotiating this new formula, two alternative negotiating positions could be identified within the teaching force, which in principle was largely favourable (see a variety of contributions to number 124 of *Trabajadores de la Ensénsanza* (Federación de Enseñanza de Comisiones Obreras, 1991). The first position emphasized the necessity for a supplementary payment to compensate for a real and sincere effort involved in training, innovation and implementation of change, relating that payment to a positive evaluation of teaching practice according to a plurality of criteria. It would not therefore have been 'automatic'.

The second position, while sharing the fears expressed above, considered that given the inequalities and scarce opportunities for training and retraining, and the unequal chances for teachers to gain access to them (e.g. rural teachers), evaluation should not be a discriminatory factor. On the other hand, to set up a system of teacher evaluation would demand technical means, resources and qualified personnel, and these were not available. Besides, it could subliminally suggest to society that if a general evaluation of teachers could take place before an evaluation of the Inspectorate, of schools, programmes, etc., then the exclusive or main responsibility for the dysfunctions of the Spanish educational system must be laid at the door of the teachers. This second position, while arguably more conservative, was possibly the more realistic, and was the one endorsed when the time came to make deals.

EVALUATION OF STUDENTS

To conclude this general account of evaluation we are going to look at the way that LOGSE, and the first regulations that followed in its wake, deal with evaluation and the year-to-year progression of students.

Primary education, the first stage of compulsory education, will comprise six years of schooling, divided into three cycles of two years each. LOGSE requires for evaluation at this stage that it should be 'continuous and holistic'. The progression from one educational cycle to the next should occur whenever the objectives of that cycle have been achieved. Where that is not the case, the student 'may remain in the cycle one year further subject to the conditions and limitations which ... the Government shall determine'. The decrees which have established the '*enseñanzas minimas*' (i.e. basic state requirements for education in all Spanish schools) and the primary curriculum develop and concretize the broad terms of LOGSE (*Reales Decretos* 1006/91 and 1344/91).

The criteria for evaluation require that it should 'establish the type and level of learning which it is expected that students should have attained at any given point in time'. Nevertheless, the same legal text warns that the level of attainment should be assessed flexibly, taking into account the circumstances and the potential of the student. The conditions and restrictions that govern progression from one cycle to another are formulated in the following terms: if a student has not attained the objectives of a cycle, the teacher-tutor, on the basis of reports from other teachers, and having considered that complementary or remedial teaching during the following cycle will not be sufficient, can decide that the student should remain one further year in the current cycle. Parental consultation is also required, and the decision to keep a student back can be taken only once during primary education.

The regulations attempt to activate remedial strategies from the moment it is realized that the objectives are not being achieved to the required degree and as an alternative to having recourse to repetition which, through lack of precision, often fails to identify and to supply those concepts, procedures or attitudes in which a student shows him or herself to be deficient.

Compared with the system established under LGE for *Enseñanza General Básica*, for the 6 to 14 age range, the essential differences are that there used to be no limitation to the number of repetitions at the end of each cycle. In the top cycle from ages 11 to 14, progression was from year to year. The only positive feature of LGE which LOGSE does not have, but which should be recoverable, is that a student who had spent an additional year in a given cycle could catch up on lost time in the following cycle. Although this facility was very rarely applied in practice, there are circumstances in which a girl or boy could suffer an academic set-back for non-academic reasons, and if their level of maturity and subsequent effort allow them to recover lost time, then the legislation should make this possible.

For secondary education, which will normally be followed between the ages of 12 and 16 across two cycles of two years each, LOGSE establishes three basic prescriptions in the context of student evaluation, one to do with method ('evaluation will be continuous and integral'), another to do with decisions on progression, and another to do with certification.

With respect to progression, 'the student who has not attained the objectives of the first cycle of this stage can remain one further year in it', just as there can be repetition in any of the years of the second cycle. The decrees which govern the minimum conditions for teaching and the basic curriculum at this stage (*Reales Decretos* 1007/91 and 1345/91) require that assessment, and any corresponding decisions about progression, should be operated on a collegiate basis by the teaching team responsible for a given group of students, with the advice of the school's advisory service.

The teaching team has the power to allow the progression of those secondary students from first to second cycle, or from third to fourth year within the second cycle, who, even if they have failed certain subjects, are deemed to have achieved the *overall* objectives of the cycle or year.

The decision not to progress a student can generally be taken only once during this stage; only exceptionally, under certain conditions and in consultation with the student and the parents, can there be a further repetition. Just as in primary education, the reforms are designed to stimulate strategies for the provision of additional or remedial help, or curricular adaptation, as alternatives to having recourse to repetition for those students who are lagging behind.

While I am in basic agreement with the philosophy underlying these reforms I must not gloss over two concerns: one is that the potential for remedial work or curricular adaptation will not be realized to its full. Where there are insufficient numbers of teachers, rigid timetables or administrators, high teacher–pupil ratios or defects in curriculum design, the potential for remedial work or curricular adaptation may not be realized. This is not idle speculation: currently in BUP and FP colleges there are remedial classes only when there are the teachers available.

The second concern is that while student progression may not be as rigidly managed as it once was (e.g. failure in any three subjects required that a year be repeated), which is good, it also becomes less objective, which is bad. A girl or boy who may be held back in one school in the light of the curricular philosophy of that school, and according to the judgements of its respective teaching teams, might very well, in another school or even with a different teaching team within the same school, be allowed to progress.

It would seem advisable that the curriculum plan of each school should carefully lay down the procedures and the circumstances for decisions not to progress students, and identify the mechanisms of remedial education and revision which should be at the disposal of those students affected. The Inspection Service must be especially sensitive in its vigilance over progression and its implementation. It would also be desirable if the procedures and circumstances were similar for all schools, so as to avoid any hint of favouritism or élitism which, in cases of repetition and 'recommended' change of school for those who have fallen behind, would otherwise be intensified, creating some schools known to be 'softer', possibly even related to their status as private or as state schools.

With respect to certification at the end of compulsory secondary education, there is an error in its formulation. Under LGE, at the end of compulsory schooling a boy or girl would receive either the *Graduado Escolar* or, if not, the *Certificado de Escolaridad*. With the *Graduado* they could register for either BUP or FP but with the *Certificado* only for FP. There did exist pathways from FP to BUP but in practice these were little used. The problem of this 'dual certification' was one of the anomalies which LOGSE has tried to resolve.

The manner of doing so has the character of a semantic pirouette. The certification is unitary, but not everybody achieves it. The percentage of students who will not achieve certification – a percentage which the Ministry has not dared to estimate in any public document – will have access neither to BUP nor to the professional modules of middle grade, but will be eligible to take special courses under a 'social guarantee' programme. It is not easy to overcome the dilemma of how, without introducing discrimination at the end of compulsory schooling, it is possible to guarantee the acquisition of minimum skills and knowledge before the beginning of post-compulsory studies. A possible solution could have been to concede the title of '*graduado*' to every student, but at the same time indicating where appropriate the need for a boy or girl to pass a course of adaptation or reinforcement prior to the start of post-compulsory studies where their teachers consider it necessary on the basis of objective criteria.

For post-compulsory studies there are few significant changes from the situation established in the 1970 legislation. Legislative implementation, as a consequence of the calendar for application of the reform, proceeds very slowly. In the White Paper on the *Bachillerato* (MEC, 1991) a mechanism is defined for progression from first to second year based on subject assessment and the possibility of progression on the basis of passes in all but two subjects. To achieve the title of *Bachiller* it is necessary to have passed each and every subject of the curriculum of the two academic years which it comprises, between 16 and 20 subject passes according to circumstances.

The title of *Bachiller* will be sufficient to be able to start professional studies at the higher level (level 3 in EC terms) but not sufficient to gain access, directly, to university studies. 'In the latter case it will be necessary to pass an entry examination which, together with marks obtained in the *Bachillerato*, will objectively assess the academic knowledge of the students and the knowledge they have acquired.' This is textually a version of one of the most polemic and socially contested articles of LOGSE. Currently, the access examination is indispensable for the start of university studies at higher level (five-year course: the *licentiatura*) but not for medium level (three-year course: the *diplomatura*), although access to medium level is easier for those who have passed that examination.

The *Libro Blanco para la Reforma del Sistema Educativo* (MEC, 1989) justified the continuation of the entry examination on three grounds:

1 To ensure an adequate level of preparation for university study;
2 As a mechanism for correcting discrepancies in standards of assessment among schools; and
3 As a means of evaluating the educational system as a whole, and not just the students themselves.

None of these reasons, in my judgement, carries sufficient weight.

The preparation required for undertaking university (or professional) study – we do not understand why professional studies should be excluded – should come about as a consequence of the correct development and implementation of the curriculum, which should rely on its own appropriate mechanisms for evaluation, including student assessment, and which should not have to be validated by means of a written test which features several worrying and interrelated factors: unfamiliar location, restricted time, unknown examiner, the factor of luck, nervousness about the heavy administrative requirements, etc. Besides, the current test, which is passed by more than 80 per cent of students, does not guarantee any level of preparation for university, given the high rate of failure and drop-out from university study (CIDE, 1991).

Differences in standards of evaluation should be examined and corrected by an analysis of the curriculum theory and practice of each school. The Inspectorate should plan for this with the development of suitable survey methodology. The current examination has only been of consequence for the subjects which it comprises and it has not constituted a source of data to explain differences in standards of assessment among schools and their implications for the obtaining of university places.

Evaluation of the overall educational system should not concentrate exclusively on one part of the educational process, the end of the *Bachillerato*, and only one part of the educational community, namely, those who want to go on to university. Any educational expert could design a periodic evaluation of the system by means of synchronic and diachronic analysis of significant surveys of schools, pupils, geographical zones, specific groups, etc. which would yield a snap-shot of the system and of trends at a given point in time, valid for decision-making but clearly without direct implication for the pupils who are the sources of the data.

The real reason for the access examination is nothing other than to regulate and to channel the process of entry to a university system which is becoming more and more overcrowded. The problem of overcrowding is a separate problem, and to investigate it here would require analysis of what percentage of each cohort it is estimated should benefit from higher education, how long for, with what provision of different studies, taking into account the level of demand from the labour market for different professional/occupational profiles. Even with an optimistic expectation of matching global supply with the endeavours of careers advisory services in helping to balance career decisions with the jobs and skills actually required, we can still experience a surplus demand for certain studies. Various experimental researches have enabled us to design predictive models of success across a variety of university studies, giving heavy weight to the academic history of the student, which are correlated with results actually obtained, while some indices have been higher than those obtained when the correlation is with the results of the access examinations.

The development of these models, perhaps complemented by a process of interviewing, would allow us to adjust this phase of the assessment process – end of the *Bachillerato* and access to university – eliminating those aspects that are clearly at odds with the philosophy of LOGSE in favour of student assessment in the earlier stages of their educational careers.

EDITORS' POSTSCRIPT

Plan EVA (Plan de Evaluación de Centros Educativos)

The MEC-instigated *Plan EVA* (Assessment of Schools Plan) began in 1990–1, based on forty schools and broadening in 1993–4 to 154 primary and secondary schools within the reform programme. The first report on this programme by the Inspectorate was summarized in *Comunidad Escolar* (CE, 12 January 1994). The report deemed as satisfactory or good the material resources, utilization and variety of teaching resources, and economic and administrative management. It considered that curriculum planning had stimulated a notable increase in team work in primary schools, that there had been a notable improvement in pastoral care, and that students had acquired positive civic and social attitudes in their dealings with teachers, with evidence of tolerance for disagreement.

A number of areas were considered to be in need of improvement, including external sources of support. Team work was still relatively scarce overall, with evidence of the persistence of individualistic attitudes and behaviours among teachers. There was inadequate pedagogic debate in governing bodies and teachers' *claustros* (with reference to annual planning, identification of evaluation criteria, analysis of outcomes) which instead focused on organizational issues. Involvement of parents and pupils was very low. There were many shortcomings in the evaluation of students.

The inspectors recommended the following improvements:

1 Establishing criteria for evaluation of students by *claustros* and by departments, the determination of minimum demands on students in departmental curricula, clarification of criteria for promotion and strategies for evaluation of the teaching force;
2 Vitalization of participation in and activities of the governing bodies and the *claustros*;
3 Development of a process of reflection about current in-service training plans, with a view to relating them better to the actual needs of teachers; and
4 The work of inspectors should centre fundamentally on criteria of evaluation and student advancement, strategies for evaluation of teaching practice, assessment of the organization of team work and supervision of the processes of generating general annual planning and curriculum proposals.

INCE

The formal functions of the *Instituto Nacional de Calidad y Evaluación* (INCE) from 1994 are to evaluate the implementation of the minimum state curriculum requirements at all stages and levels of the system; evaluate the general reforms of the educational system, its structure, range and outcomes; develop a state-wide system of indices which will facilitate the evaluation of system efficacy and efficiency; co-ordinate participation in international studies of evaluation; issue reports on the functioning and outcomes of the educational system in the light of criteria agreed by the Conference of Education Counsellors (*Conferencia de Consejeros de Educación*) who preside over departments of education in the autonomous communities; supply and exchange information with the educational administrations to facilitate decision-making; collaborate with the administrations, and the schools, etc. in the design of methodologies of evaluation for the different kinds of learning provided for in LOGSE.

INCE is governed by a council presided over by the Secretary of State for Education, the heads of department of various departments of the Ministry, and representatives of each of the autonomous communities. Its plans are subject to the approval of, and the criteria and priorities established by, the *Conferencia de Consejeros de Educación* (CE, 21 April 1993).

The three main priorities of INCE for its first three years of operation from 1994–7 are to evaluate the results of the new system of primary education, and the functioning of schools which provide it; to evaluate changes in FP and of social demand for FP; and to establish a national system of indicators of quality in the educational system (e.g. relating to budgets, registered students, academic output, levels of participation, functioning of evaluation criteria, organization, hours dedicated to in-service training, teacher–pupil ratios). INCE will also attend to issues of equality of provision between the autonomous communities, and would monitor compliance with the requirements to provide for specified minimum levels of education (CE, 25 May 1994).

REFERENCES

CIDE (1991) *Las Jornadas sobre investigación educativa sobre la Universidad*, CIDE and ICE de la Universidad Politecnia de Madrid, May–June. Madrid: Centro de Publicaciones, Ministerio de Educación.
Darder, P. (1980) *Quesionari d'analisi del funcionament de l'escola*. Barcelona: QUAFE-80.
Federación de Enseñanza de Comisiones Obreras (1991) *Trabajadores de la Enseñanza*, no. 124, June, FECO.
Fernández Enguita, M. (1986) *Integrar a segregar: la enseñanza secundaria en los países industrializados*. Barcelona: Editorial Laia.
Ministerio de Educación y Ciencia (1985) *Hacía la Reforma. 1.* Madrid: Centro de Publicaciones del Ministerio de Educación.
Ministerio de Educación y Ciencia (1989) *Libro blanco para la reforma del sistema educativo*. Madrid: Ministerio de Educación.
Ministerio de Educación y Ciencia (1991) *Bachillerato: Estructura y contenidos*. Madrid: Ministerio de Educación.
Real Decretos, 1006/91, 1007/91 (1991) *Boletines Oficiales del Estado*. BOE, 26 June.
Real Decretos, 1344/91, 1345/91 (1991) *Boletines Oficiales del Estado*. BOE, 13 September.
UIMP (1970) Esquemas de Evaluación a nivel de centro y a nivel de alumnos, *La Educación General Básica*, Santander: Curso Universitario de Verano, UIMP.

13 The Spanish Inspectorate in search of a modern model of inspection*

Vicente Alvarez Areces and Arturo Pérez Collera

Reform of the Spanish Educational Inspectorate in advance of the implementation of LOGSE has been a particularly tortuous process. Inspection was once controlled by three different, powerful and autocratic bodies whose responsibilities had more to do with control than with advice and which ranged across a very wide range of matters. This situation has been transformed into one in which the inspectors form an integrated component of the established educational administrations, operating very much as teams, and whose responsibilities are focused on monitoring, advice, information and the assessment of teaching, learning and reform.

A MOSAIC IN CONSTANT MOVEMENT

Social and political evolution in Spain over the past fifteen years has been frenetic; other chapters have repeatedly alluded to this bubbling-over of innovation and change in Spanish education, now at last absorbed within the framework of LOGSE, the product of a broad social, political and territorial consensus which renders the educational system more durable and better adapted to the plurality of the State and to late twentieth-century society.

In most educational systems the Inspectorate represents a highly valuable instrument for information, analysis and technical assessment of educational practice, which gives it a key role in processes of change. It is not to be wondered at, therefore, that in this period it has been subjected to serious fluctuations, in some cases due to necessary state-wide and system-wide readjustments, in others due to the divergencies of interest and expectation that exist between a pluralist political power, a somewhat less pluralist body of teachers and education experts, and the much more diverse school communities.

Only thus can we understand how in such a short space of time decisions to restrict activities of the Inspectorate Corps dealing with essential tasks for the implementation of LOGSE have alternated with

---

* This chapter translated by Pamela O'Malley

decisions to greatly augment the size of the Inspectorate, while simultaneously reducing its sources of support, its sphere of influence and public esteem; how, likewise, trends towards maximum centralization have coexisted with centrifugal developments in the provinces; or how, under the same title of 'Technical Inspection', some education administrations have developed highly specialized models focusing on the supervision of teaching processes while others have developed extremely generic models for the assessment of school organization.

In the period 1989–92 there was growing contact and communication between those different autonomous communities which have responsibility for education, with greater intermixing of the different models of inspection. But one cannot yet speak of a consolidation of the essential features of the Spanish Inspectorate, even if the norms and regulations pertaining to them are no longer pending in the official gazettes, and even if the reservations and hostility towards the Inspectorate that were harboured within many professional and political circles have gradually disappeared.

In this process of the re-establishment and rediscovery of the importance of the Inspectorate, the concept of the school curriculum for which LOGSE sets the basic standard has been very significant. The degree of autonomy which is accorded to each educational establishment entails the compulsory reinforcement of supervisory mechanisms to ensure comparability of standards of students' learning, neither more nor less. This challenge and that of improving the quality of educational service by means of a systematic assessment of schools is what at present most preoccupies the Spanish Inspectorate. This will require readjustment and rapid change.

THREE MODELS OF INSPECTION IN EDUCATION

The 1970 Education Act distinguished two levels of inspection:

- *Technical inspection of services*, to inspect the administrative organization and functioning of all services, organizations and schools which depended on the Department, especially with regard to personnel, procedures, regime, installation and equipment.
- *Technical inspection of education*, which is the focus of this chapter and which was given the function of monitoring the implementation of laws pertaining to education, advising teachers on teaching methods, assessing the educational efficiency of schools and teachers, and collaborating with the planning service and with teachers' in-service training.

Reformulation some twenty years later in LOGSE still maintains this functional division:

1 an internal or service inspectorate, which supervises the organization of the administration; and
2 an external or management inspectorate, which monitors the educational administration and is closely linked to teaching and curricular processes.

In step with the territorial organization of the State established by the Constitution and the consequent distribution of responsibilities between the State and autonomous communities, a third variety of inspection emerges, namely *Higher State Inspection*, established, in the seven communities which have assumed responsibility for education, País Vasco, Cataluña, Galicia, Andalucia, Islas Canarias, Valencia and Navarra, whose functions are governed by the respective autonomous statutes and in accordance with the 1985 Royal Decree, which defines them as responsible for the supervision of the implementation of regulations within the educational administrations of the autonomous communities, covering areas such as study plans, textbooks, administrative documents, and in general having responsibility for ensuring that the basic conditions which guarantee the equality of all Spanish people in the exercise of their rights and duties with respect to education are fulfilled, including their linguistic rights and, especially, that of receiving an education in the official language of the State, in agreement with the relevant legal provisions.

The services of the Higher Inspectorate are integrated with the government delegations, which depend on the Secretary of State for Education by means of the General Directorate of Co-ordination of the Higher Inspectorate (Royal Decree, 20 July 1988), comprising merely a dozen civil servants who have been selected by open appointment called through public announcement in the official gazette.

The general inspections of services depend on the respective education administrations, and, within the area administrated by the Ministry of Education, on the Ministerial Secretariat. They represent a body of just over one hundred inspectors throughout the country, equally selected by open appointment from among inspectors or civil servants in possession of a university degree.

The technical inspections of education, finally, come under the education authorities of those autonomous communities which have taken responsibility for education or, in the case of the Ministry, come under the respective provincial directorates, and are co-ordinated by the General Sub-direction of the Inspectorate Service integrated within the General Directorate of Co-ordination and Higher Inspection dependent on the State Secretariat. Education inspectors represent a body, throughout Spain, of nearly two thousand (seven hundred of whom work within the areas governed directly by the Ministry of Education) and they are selected by means of open competition among teachers and education administrators with university degrees, based on a merit system as published in the official state gazettes of the corresponding administrations.

TERRITORIAL DISTRIBUTION

We have already referred to the process of transfer of educational responsibilities [from the centre to the autonomous communities (ed.)] which is dividing the Inspectorate Service, so that already powers have been devolved to Cataluña, País Vasco and others, in a process which commenced in 1983 and whose most recent application has been in Navarra in 1991: there are now seven substantial inspectorates. As the process continues, ten further inspectorates will be established – in Aragón, Asturias, Baleares, Cantabria, Castilla-León, Castilla-La Mancha, Extremadura, Madrid, Murcia and La Rioja. These autonomous communities are at present (1994) still administrated at provincial level within the common framework presided over by the Ministry of Education and Science, centred in Madrid.

The basic legislative framework for inspection is to be found in the Civil Service Reform Act 30/1984 and subsequent amendments in 1988 (Act 23/88) and in the definition of functions provided by article 61 of LOGSE which, while not obligatory, represents virtual consensus throughout the autonomous communities. However, each autonomous community has designed a model of technical inspection which it deems to be in accordance with its specific needs. Andalucia, for example, has opted for separation of the functions of control and assessment on the one hand, and functions of advice and consultancy on the other, with a separate team for each category. Cataluña and País Vasco have established generalist teams spanning the different levels, while maintaining specialized profiles for the different curriculum areas and specialisms. In Galicia, there is a clear separation between the levels of primary, secondary and vocational training; in Valencia there is an inter-level inspectorate which, unlike the others, co-ordinates and directs in-service training, etc. All this results in a rich diversity whose common characteristics can be broadly summarized as:

- Access by means of open competition from the ranks of teachers (minimum three to seven years' experience) which includes a rigorous, selective training course;
- Appraisal, and, if approved, extension of contract from three to six years;
- Preference for teamwork; and
- Preference for cross-phase teams led by a co-ordinating inspector reporting to a single Head of Service.

As one would expect, there is a greater degree of cohesion in the organization and functioning in the ten communities which do not yet have responsibility for education, in spite of any local emphases imposed by the provincial directorates of the Ministry. This atypical diversity may be understood with reference to pre-1980s history.

BEFORE THE DECADE OF REFORM

The Service of Technical Inspection was established by the *Ley General de Educación* (1970). This Act established for the first time a Service which combined the former cadres of primary inspectors and secondary inspectors. But realization of this intention to establish a single, integrated service was aborted in practice by a variety of factors. These included the different ways in which different responsibilities of primary and secondary inspectors were embedded in the structures of management and in lines of daily communication with schools; the hierarchical dependence they had established first with their respective general managements and then with the Secretariat; mutual jealousies during a period in which primary responsibilities had expanded while those of secondary education had contracted; the broad powers of the Educational Administration, and also the resentment caused by its preference for dependence on civil servants for effective control of the provincial delegations.

These corporate pressures were not only strong enough to block the implementation of article 143.5 of the 1970 Education Act and to limit it to a mere definition of functions in 1973, but they also brought about the creation of a third cadre of inspectors, for vocational training, first referred to in functional terms in 1975 and formally constituted in 1980.

In little more than a decade the cadres forming part of the embryonic Service of Technical Inspection of Education had won various battles:

- The maintenance of their own *esprit de corps* and respective organizational systems;
- They did not depend on the provincial delegations;
- They paralleled the highest level of the hierarchy, the sub-secretariat; and
- They resisted a more modern organizational regime, in preference for one that was more in accordance with their functions and with the levels in which their own system had been structured.

The relative independence attained by the inspectors had bitter consequences for academic authorities, who were frequently undermined by decisions of the Council of Primary Inspection in matters of administrative management, who lost the initiative in the development of the school map and in innovations in the *Bachillerato*, and who worried about what seemed to them excessive power, in which it was difficult to distinguish the professional from the political.

Teachers also shared a perception of enormous inspectorial influence in the case of secondary schools, of real command in the case of private and primary schools, and frequently of tight circumscription in the different zones or territories.

Laudable efforts to implement proposals in agreement with legislative plans were stalled – never proceeding beyond their initial stages of development or remaining as mere experiments – by the independence of the three services *vis-à-vis* the highest-level authority of the Delegation, by their detachment from ministerial hierarchies, their organization by zones or themes (programme direction) in the case of primary schools or by subjects in the case of secondary schools, and by their role as a parallel administration in the case of vocational training.

It is impossible, therefore, to speak of one homogeneous Inspection Service nor even of homogeneous practice by inspectors in their respective zones. Add to this the broad responsibility of their work as organizers and providers of in-service training, for implementation and application of the Education Act, and as standing intermediaries between the schools and the Ministry and we will have completed the diagnosis which explains subsequent political initiatives.

THE MANAGEMENT OF CHANGE: 1983

The Socialist electoral triumph in 1982 led to the formation of a government in the following year, with a popular mandate and a vision for the reform of education. Under the new minister, José María Maravall, projects were initiated which were going to have a decisive repercussion on the Educational Inspectorate: planning for reform of the whole education system, redefinition of the structures and governing bodies of schools, reformulation of relations between the Administration and direct-grant private schools, a reform of the Civil Service, a restructuring of the Ministry, modernization of educational management and an attempt to improve educational quality, to mention but a few. These were measures which had a very direct impact on the Service of Technical Inspection and on the cadres subsumed within this service. Its ponderous and acrimonious response, its vacillations, caution and tentativeness can only be explained by the tortuous dynamics of its internal relations prior to democracy and by the confusion created by the decentralization to the autonomous communities. Chronologically, the main legal steps towards the present Inspection Service may be summarized as follows.

First step: unification of cadres and provisional access to Inspectorate

In 1984 a bill of vital importance for the Inspectorate was passed in Parliament: Measures for the Reform of the Civil Service Act, a national Act for the whole of Spain, which includes in its fifteenth additional disposition two sections which radically modify the previous panorama:

- Inspection in education will be carried out by members of the teaching profession for periods of not less than three years nor, in any case, more than six years. At the end of this period the teachers may return to the locality to which they were previously designated as teachers.
- The three cadres of inspectors – primary, secondary and vocational training – will be integrated into one cadre, taking over from its predecessors the rights and obligations of inspection.

Both measures were particularly forceful, atypical and without precedent in any other recent educational regulation. They must be understood within the context of an extreme situation which had blocked implementation of a substantial part of the General Education Act of 1970 for almost a decade.

The integration of the cadres into one single cadre of inspectors at the service of the educational administration represented, finally, the implementation of the sixth additional disposition, point four, of the 1970 Act. Replacement of the previous cadres with teachers on short-term inspection contracts was an initiative aimed against the bureaucratization and stagnation which had characterized the former period, opening the door to professionals with a more recent and direct experience of teaching. The alleged instability and wasteful nature of this model (given that the selection and training of inspectors involve too substantial an investment of time and cost to justify dispensing with and replacing inspectors at the very point when they have just managed to master the requirements of the job) led to a legal amendment to the Act in 1988, permitting those inspectors whose work over a period of six years has been positively evaluated by the appropriate education administration to remain in post indefinitely. The amendment was incorporated among others in Act 23/1988.

Second step: provincial inspectorates

A Royal Decree of April 1985 modified the basic structure of the Ministry of Education, formally terminating the provincial units of primary, secondary and vocational training inspectorates and establishing a provincial service reporting to the Provincial Director of the Department. These provisions worked quickly to reinforce the structure of the provincial directorates, providing them with the ways and means of planning, management and extension of the educational programmes, which have relieved the Inspectorate of inappropriate tasks which they had been carrying from earlier times.

Of particular relevance was the clarification of hierarchical lines of responsibility, underlining the authority of the provincial directors, and eliminating the confusing division of lines of responsibility inherited from pre-democratic times.

Third step: creation and consolidation of educational programme units

The Ministerial Order of 15 January 1986 modernizes the structure of the provincial directorates on the basis of progressive decentralization of functions and of important tasks of educational reform in connection with the need for support, co-ordination and promotion of educational innovation. The creation of *ad hoc* curriculum units which immediately assumed areas of responsibility which had been previously assigned to the inspectorates (especially those connected with reports) deprived the inspectors of one of their most creative and influential roles.

While the inspectors immediately perceived that they now had competitors within their own field of expertise, it is perfectly legitimate to separate functions of management, animation, the generation of innovation and teacher training from those responsibilities most appropriate for the Inspectorate, namely control and assessment, which require that they maintain an element of distance from, or at least are not directly associated with, particular areas of provision.

Fourth step: LODE

One further central concern of the Socialist Government was to have major repercussions for the work of the Technical Inspection Service. The desire to democraticize school management, accomplished in 1985 through the passage of LODE, introduced certain complications. Attribution to governing bodies of oversight of the general working of schools introduced a degree of confusion between community control and bureaucratic control. Growing tension between the different collectivities which make up the school community made it necessary to establish areas of activity, methods of work and even a language that was different from the traditional register employed by the inspection services.

The autonomy of schools and the power of their governing bodies required a serious reconsideration of the relationships between inspectors and schools so as not to undermine the responsibilities of the governing bodies, while at the same time not hindering the exercise by government bodies of their responsibilities for control and assessment. If the first three of these above measures had introduced Copernican changes to their administration, functions and responsibilities, this Act led indirectly to a substantive and necessary change of attitude in professional approach.

Fifth step: action plans and team building

Having shelved the issue for three years, a circular was finally published in January 1986 by the newly appointed first Sub-Director General of the Inspectorate Service of the Ministry of Education. The circular explained the first Action Plan for the integrated service. At last the first requirement for the operation of an institution was in place: there was a plan.

From then on the activities of the Inspectorate were inscribed in successive annual plans for the entire service, drawn up in agreement with the needs identified by the Educational Administration itself and concretized with respect to the area of each provincial directorate by means of plans of activities for each provincial service.

This planned activity has been successfully sustained through all the inspection services of the country. In those parts of the country which are directly managed by the Ministry, the activities of the Inspectorate have acquired a special status, with public dissemination of information about its activities through the Ministry gazette, and an assessment by means of the Annual Inspection Report, which has been published since 1988.

Complementing the Activity Plan for the year 1985–6, organizational objectives were set that served as the main thrust of subsequent developments:

1 That the basic working unit of each inspection service be the *team*, its responsibility territorially defined by the demarcation of educational divisions for which it would have responsibility for control and assessment, and which would provide self-sufficiency of resources and a social and educational identity.

2 That these inspection teams encompass a *sufficient diversity* of specialists to allow them to carry out their functions in schools with appropriate professional authority and competency.

3 That the criteria employed by team members be suitably co-ordinated with the other teams by means of *periodic meetings* to guarantee uniformity of criteria in control and assessment. This would entail the existence of *co-ordinators*, who would be responsible for this task in each team.

4 That apart from the collective responsibility inherent in each team the *individual responsibility* of each member for his or her specific tasks should be preserved.

5 Complementing this territorially defined team structure there should exist another more provisional structure of *working parties*, which, subject to the same provisions for co-ordination, should attend to specific tasks of a thematic nature which do not coincide with territorial demarcation, e.g. programme assessment, control of resources, emergency actions, special studies, etc.

6 That the *Chief Inspector*, reporting both to the Provincial Director and to the General Director of Co-ordination of the Higher Inspectorate, should have main responsibility for the direction, organization and assessment of each provincial service, and should ensure the drawing up, development, accomplishment and assessment of the plans.

These basic organizational features were confirmed by Royal Decree 1524 in December 1989 and Ministerial Order on 27 September 1990, and rounded off with measures for the organization of inter-team rotation; a five-year limit on membership in any given team; development of planning mechanisms and of weekly monitoring of tasks; the identification of sources of external support; and specialization by curriculum expertise. Team-work structure creates a generalized networking within the communities and constitutes a prerequisite for any modern organization aspiring to basic standards of efficiency. Its composition provides a natural point of confluence for different specialisms and experiences, and guarantees a desirable level of co-ordination and coherence.

Sixth step: recruitment of new inspectors

In 1986 there took place the first merit-based competition for entry to the renovated Inspection Service. After a virtual five-year freeze, the competition was arranged to fill 120 vacancies, representing over a quarter of the full staffing complement, in accordance with an order agreed with the different autonomous communities and which combined technical merits with teaching and management experience in the first selective stage, together with the presentation of reports in which candidates demonstrated their technical mastery of a variety of set themes, followed by a second stage based on attendance at a selective combined course of theory and practice.

This process has been reinforced in subsequent years, to the extent that a large majority of contemporary inspectors have entered through this selection procedure, so that in addition to their youth and recent familiarity with teaching, many are distinguished personalities in educational innovation, doctors, technologists, managers and professionals of established repute, offering a wider and more diverse range of experience than those attracted by previous selection methods.

Seventh step: redefinition of functions

Various factors connected with the strengthening of educational administration have tended to eliminate from the Inspectorate many central and long-standing features of their profession, namely planning, distribution of materials, equipping schools, managing teaching staff, control of buildings, selection of teachers, special educational programmes, etc. – all examples of executive areas which have now been assigned to other departments of the administration.

This redistribution of tasks has been achieved without neglect of tasks reassigned to the Inspectorate such as information, needs analysis and follow-up across all areas. The Service has experienced a real measure of relief from management tasks while matters of control, advice, assessment and counselling are more appropriately highlighted as the main activity of a modern inspectorate.

The redefinition of functions contained in the Royal Decree 1592/1989, which identify the regulations for the Inspectorate Service of the Ministry of Education, take into account precisely these essential aspects, enumerated as follows:

1 Ensure that the laws, regulations and any other legal dispositions of the educational administration are fulfilled in schools and services which are referred to in article 1, as well as the implementation and development of educational programmes and activities which are approved or authorized by the Ministry of Education and Science.
2 Collaborate in educational reform, teacher in-service training, processes of pedagogic innovation and experimental programmes, and participate in their extension, follow-up and assessment.
3 Assess the educational outcomes of the system, by means of an analysis of the organization, functioning and outcomes of schools and services, and of the execution and development of programmes and activities of an educational character promoted and authorized by the Ministry of Education and Science.
4 Advise and inform the different sectors of the school community and both heads and collegiate managements in the exercise of their responsibilities and obligations concerning the norms and regulations legitimately relating to them.
5 Collaborate with planning units in the study of the educational needs of each province.
6 Report on all matters as are required by the competent authority or which have come to their knowledge through their professional activity. In both cases, the resulting proposals, if there are any, should be implemented through the recognized channels.

A new element that should be highlighted is the arrangements for educational evaluation because these are extended to encompass the whole of the education system. This concept of external, global accountability, including the Education Administration itself as forming part of the system, is not yet a customary practice of the Inspection Service, and there are doubts as to its viability. What is, however, undeniable is the firm and deep commitment on the part of the Ministry of Education during the past few years to strengthen the Inspectorate so that it is capable of carrying out rigorous assessment of schools: in its second stage of development, the Assessment of Schools Plan, begun in 1991, has already involved hundreds of teachers in an assessment model which boasts among other advantages that of combining with and reinforcing internal assessment procedures within the schools themselves.

On the other hand, the functions of control and advice at the heart of education have been greatly strengthened in the process of implementing curricular development in those schools and colleges already involved in the reform, and they represent the most decisive challenge for the consolidation of a professional, efficient Educational Inspectorate, esteemed by all those most closely involved in education.

Both the advisory supervision of the design of curricular projects and the Assessment of Schools Plan constitute the *priorities* of at least two recent action plans of the Inspection Service. This is the best proof of growing correspondence between the declaration of intentions published by the state official gazette and a real determination to make reality match such intentions, just as the articulation in the last three academic years of an In-service Plan for Inspectors has already involved all inspection staff. This is the promising panorama now offered by the Spanish Inspectorate.

EDITORS' POSTSCRIPT

The annual report of the Inspectorate for 1992–3 (*CE*, 9 February 1994) notes that on average each school was visited four times, a doubling in the number of visits over a six-year period, achieved with a modest 27 per cent growth in the number of inspectors. Fifty per cent of primary school management teams were reported to consider the Inspectorate as their only source of external support in the implementation of reform (MEC, 1994).

The report judges that team work has improved the distribution of responsibilities and the adoption of criteria on the basis of consensus. There was also reported to be good co-ordination between the Inspectorate and other units and services of the district offices (*Direcciones Provinciales*).

REFERENCE

Ministerio de Educacion y Ciencia (1994) *El Plan de Seguimiento de proceso de implantación de la LOGSE en el curso 92–93*. Madrid: Centro de Publicaciones del MEC.

14 Professionalism, unionism and educational reform*

Antonio Guerrero

Teachers in Spain have always been and continue to be a heterogeneous body representing diverse interests. They are not greatly differentiated in terms of salary, however, and salaries (for a profession which was once considered synonymous with poverty) have been rising while, as a result of falling rolls and the introduction of new teaching specialisms, the conditions of work may have improved, at least for primary teachers. There is a relatively high level of trade union participation and even if the attitudes of most teachers towards educational reform have been ambivalent, even ignorant, the unions have been active in negotiations related to the implications of reform, in particular in relation to the number of teacher guilds (the cuerpos, *corporatist bodies representing various groups of state employees, dating at least as far back as the dictatorship of Primo de Rivera, 1923–30, with significant powers and influence in the training and influence of new members) and the conditions of schooling. The author argues that the four most important implications of the reform for the teaching profession concern the number of guilds, the reorganization of schools, new bodies of students for each school, and new curricula.*

Processes of reform usually generate a mixed response of expectation and fear, a conjunction of anxiety in the face of the unknown and the fear of losing what was once secure. Whether it is fear or expectation which prevails within any given group depends on how well the group is positioned in the share and enjoyment of the means and resources that would allow it to capitalize on the new reforms. This explains the dynamics of competition between different groups, vying for relative advantage throughout the process of reform.

From the creation of a modern educational system in the middle of the nineteenth century, education in Spain has been subject to a permanent process of reform, its most outstanding milestones being the *Ley Moyeno* of 1857, the processes of educational institutionalization and regeneration at the turn of the century, the Second Republic and the *Ley General de*

* This chapter translated by Oliver Boyd-Barrett

Educación of 1970. Throughout this process the leading players, or the architects of the curriculum, have consistently been the Catholic Church and the State administration, representing – to a degree – the 'ancient humanist' universities and the 'state educators', but not the 'captains of industry', who traditionally have been more noted for their absence.

At the heart of the educational system there has been a fragmented and hierarchical teaching force, with university professors reigning supreme and primary school teachers playing the role of faithful infantry.

With the processes of industrialization and democratization of Spanish society, the professional aspirations of the most alienated sectors of the teaching force have entered a process of realization, through fierce struggle and mobilization, above all in 1978 and 1988, in which years the *magisterio* (*cuerpo* or guild of primary teachers) managed to reinforce its recently acquired semi-professional status. For strategic or other reasons, this status has been extended to other marginal sectors (including teachers on temporary contracts) and has been subject to revision in the reforms undertaken by the socialist party since its assumption of office.

The objective of this chapter is to identify features of the current reform, legally constituted in LOGSE, as it affects teachers – the opportunities it opens up and those it closes, for whom and in what manner – attempting to show how the reform will affect teachers in each stratum, and the role of the unions. Sociologically, the ideas covered by this chapter emerge from studies of professionalism and analyses of the work process, which look at the integration of professionals into professional associations and unions acting as channels for participation and representation in negotiations and processes of reform.

THE TEACHING PROFESSION: TECHNICAL AUTONOMY AND INTERNAL HIERARCHY

For analysis of the professional character of an occupation the dominant paradigm in sociology is the functionalist, which takes medicine and law as an ideal-type defined by a range of characteristic features, and then identifies those occupations which comply with these prerequisites as professional.

In the field of education the existence of differentiated educational activities, fundamentally divided between the public and private networks and by the educational cycles at primary, secondary and university levels, is a measure of different degrees of autonomy, marked as much by the length and specialization of training (three-year diploma, five-year degree and doctorate) as by the character of their teaching functions (contractual or tenured position) and procedures for access to them. Consequently it can be said that each educational body or level within each schooling network constitutes a stratum of the teaching profession, with particular training and competencies. Recall the differences in contractual or operational character and teachers' involvement – or to what degree – in processes of their own reproduction, i.e. in the training and selection of new faculty members. Teachers in private education possess less autonomy than state school teachers, in being more dependent in their work on the decisions of proprietors of schools and other educational enterprises. State school teachers consider themselves, in this respect, freer, and they also participate in the processes of selection of new members of their professional bodies (*cuerpos*), although primary teachers have less involvement than secondary, and both are less involved than university teachers. In every case, the administration, by establishing the content and procedures of competitive access examination, and by hiring an important proportion of new teachers on a temporary basis, manifestly interferes in teacher autonomy, above all at pre-university levels.

At the corporate level, only the *Colegio de Licenciados* has regulatory jurisdiction, albeit modest, over the teachers of private secondary education; teachers in state schools come under civil service statutes. There is no corporate body of this kind for primary education.

Thus, to speak of the teaching profession requires consideration of its internal stratification, the extent to which each teacher group is characterized by a distinctive quantity and mix of academic, social and administrative capital, in relation to training and autonomy of practice. These strata coincide with the educational cycles of primary, secondary and university levels, and with their respective administrative or working arrangements (including the dual network of public schools or private, with or without state aid), and are therefore characterized by different educational and social requirements, evaluated hierarchically, and integrated through salary scales. It is not just a question of label (*maestro* or *profesor*). In the Ministry of Education and Science there are different departments for each stratum, and unions themselves recognize the distinctions, having distinctive secretaries, federations, platforms and elected deputies, carefully differentiated by one or another stratum or sector. As a result, educational policies relate differently to each stratum, which respond differently to the different situations in which they find themselves (corporate restructuring, teaching career, salary structure, etc.). Each teaching stratum, in turn, is internally splintered by the dynamics of gender and age which classify and group teachers as male and female, older, younger or intermediate, and situate these in different positions within their own stratum.

SALARY AND STATUS: THE TEACHING CONDITION

In the most recent past, union demands on behalf of teachers have centred on the system of remuneration, the working day and the teaching career, demanding a new and more just system of remuneration similar to that of comparable sectors, a more rational working day and expec-

tations of a professional-style career. All this is with the object of revitaliz-
ing the teaching profession, which is considered to be at a very low level
in terms of money and prestige.

Up until now, the remunerative structure for teachers has been very
homogeneous, with small differences between strata, inclining towards an
overall uniformity and narrow salary range. The common elements are
the basic salary, common to all members of a corpus or stratum; the
complementary payment, specific to each individual corpus or stratum;
and the seniority payment, which is a measure of length of service. The
absence of career structures for teachers, besides, accounts for the fact
that the ratio of salary on retirement to the salary on entry has never
been more than two to one. Further, the differences between the different
corps and strata of the teaching hierarchy are maintained within that
range. Thus, currently and through gross salaries without seniority payments, the salary range between the *magisterio* (primary teachers) and
the university professors is 1:1.774. At the same time the ratio of private
to state teacher payment oscillates between 1:1.236 in FP and 1:1.53 in
EGB, increasing to 1:1.193 in BUP, according to data referred to in the
1992 Budget and the current General Agreement on Private Education.

Within the reward structure, an important element is accounted for by
payments to those who take on specific additional jobs, above all in state
education. While these have been growing in monetary significance in
recent years, in response to the reluctance of teachers to take on such
jobs, they have had limited powers of incentive (according to MEC data,
40 per cent of state school head teachers had to be installed by ministerial
nomination, in the absence of voluntary candidates).

Since the start of the 1990s a process of evaluating teaching and
research productivity has been introduced at university level, which
increases salaries and which might be seen as a nominal compensation,
in name, and monetary compensation, in magnitude, for the old *quin-
quenios* and *sexenios* (seniority) payments. The significance of such measures, general in the case of evaluation of teaching, and rather more
complex in the case of research, is that in addition to opening up the
salary range they have served to create the mirage of meritocratic distinction and, indirectly, to justify the control which is exercised over teacher
productivity and attitude by means of in-service training – through the
CEPs (teachers' centres) – and research grants.

In relation to the working day, it has to be said that the problem is
most keenly felt in the private sector and among primary teachers who
in effect have a working week of 30 hours' physical presence in the
school [in 1992: made up of 25 hours' teaching contact and 5 hours' time
for 'complementary' activities (eds)]. Teachers in state secondary schools,
on the other hand, rarely spend more than 21 hours. In state primary
schools, although there has not been a formal reduction, the falling of
the ratio of children per class and the incorporation of support teachers

and of specialists in physical education, music and special education have had the effect of alleviating the teaching load, although perhaps only for the one-third of teachers who teach the older age groups at this level (i.e. the upper cycles of primary education which benefit most from specialist teaching). The real issue, nevertheless, persists in being the 'continuous day', although that has already been achieved in practice by state BUP teachers for whom the social function of *guarderia* (watching over children) exercises less pressure. None the less, for these teachers the problem seems to be the function of *tutoria* [i.e the pastoral and related tasks undertaken by form teachers at secondary level (eds)], something which seems to remind them of their primary colleagues and which clashes with their professional ideals.

The issue of career structure is a clear example of the tensions generated by the internal hierarchy of the teaching body. If for primary teachers the ideal career would presuppose a unified professional body covering all teaching from pre-school to university, for BUP teachers this ideal would extend only from their own level to university. Such dynamics of inclusion and exclusion are meticulously represented, as demonstrated by the last great teachers' strike.

TEACHERS AND UNIONS: A PROFESSIONAL SYNDICALISM

The participation of teachers in unions is not extensive but it is important, given the struggle on the part of their negotiators for the unions, characterized by plurality and the existence of corporatist and class orientations, to be legally recognized (achieved in 1988). This syndicalist position owes much to the prohibition under Franco of all union activity outside the official unions, which created an apathetic attitude towards affiliation, aggravated by the slow legalization of the unions during the transition to democracy, the generation of divisions between unions and the denial to unions of practical experience (the right to collective bargaining for civil servants was not conceded until 1990). The left–right polarization and their respective divisions were the sources of a split into five representative bodies at state level[1] and with it a lack of confidence and a poor image for all the teaching unions, given their disunity, lack of transparency and politicization. The strength of the teaching bodies developed throughout these years by means of *coordinadoras* (pre-union, self-organizing groups which achieved a measure of success in their struggle for professionalization, gaining stability in the employment of temporary teachers, whose numbers had increased significantly following the implementation of the 1970 reform).

Studies exist of levels of union membership which demonstrate the hybrid character which teacher unionism has currently acquired. A first group of studies calculates membership rates as varying between 12.3 per cent (Guerrero, 1991a) and 23.3 per cent (TE, 1992), passing through 16 per cent (CIDE, 1985) and 22 per cent (Ortega and Velasco, 1991). A possible arithmetic mean would situate it at 18.4 per cent of the total number of teachers, a figure well above the national average of 7 per cent, and above the 10 per cent average for the higher professions and the 15 per cent average for the middle-ranking professions, calculated by CIS in 1990 (REIS), (p. 49). The figure could even be considered comparatively high, indicating, in any case, a degree of achievement beyond the more primitive forms of organization – the *coordinadoras* – which formerly enjoyed such prestige. A second group of studies (Taylor and Mitchell, 1988, and Guerrero, 1991b) is concerned with the comparability of the objectives of different kinds of union and the extent of their convergence in negotiating positions, and these studies identify existing forms of teacher organizations as representing a kind of hybrid 'professional syndicalism', defending at one and the same time both syndicalist and corporatist positions.

Together with determining historical factors, an explanation for this pattern of membership and for the plurality of unions may be found in the two-way directionality common to low-status professions, situated at the mid-point between proletarianization and professionalization. As potential professionals, they exercise a strategy of exclusion which separates them from their nearest, and more numerous but lower-status, competitors. As threatening proletarians they demand to be included among the smaller and better rewarded strata represented by those professionals who are above them in the social hierarchy. At an empirical level, one or other tactic is reproduced at the heart of the teaching profession and even, to be more precise, at the heart of each stratum. Those teachers who belong to the higher bodies practise exclusion with respect to those who belong to the lower bodies. Reciprocally, the latter grow ambitious to be included in the positions immediately superior to theirs. Look, for instance, at the negotiating dynamic of private education, which seeks homogenization with state or public education, whose teachers in turn seek homogenization with respect to equivalent-ranking members of the civil service. Observe, likewise, how the demand for a unitary body has only been supported by teachers of primary or of private education, while it is rejected by the rest. But even within primary education it is supported with greater conviction by certain sectors (e.g. men, seniors, graduates) who consider that they are particularly likely to benefit from a process of unification with the secondary teachers.

TEACHERS AND REFORM: A CONTINUING RELATIONSHIP

Teachers believe that the degree of their participation and consultation in the reform process has been minimal and rhetorical. On the other hand, small groups associated with the more progressive sectors or with movements of pedagogic reform have participated and have put into effect their previous experiments. For some schools, involvement in reform has given them additional support teachers (above all, in schools which have adopted policies of 'integration' for special needs pupils), and an influx of materials and resources, at least where they have managed to avoid the wholesale removal of some classes. But the teaching profession as a whole, with demonstrations of collective foreboding, does not consider that it has contributed as such to the reform. Nor, to be fair, does it expect great things of the reform, for the majority believe that for teachers, as for education, things will go on much the same.

What is surprising, however one looks at it, is that such forceful opinion should have developed at all, given the allegations of teacher ignorance about the reform. In one study of primary teachers in Madrid, four out of every five maintained that they had not read LOGSE in detail, the legal high point of the reform; a third claimed that they had only read 'some parts' of it (34.5 per cent), with a further third having read it only 'superficially' (38.9 per cent). In hardly any of the schools studied had there been formal discussion within the *claustros* [bodies representing all teachers within each school (eds)].

THE PROCESS OF REFORM AND PARLIAMENTARY NEGOTIATION OF LOGSE

Whether acting through individuals or as members of *claustros*, those who have participated most of all in the experimental phase of the reform and who had the most influential voice in direct negotiations with MEC or in the *Consejo Escolar del Estado* [major state-wide representative and advisory body for education (eds)] have been the unions, albeit with unequal intensity and fortune: firstly, in the phase of the *Libro Blanco* (government White Paper), later during the parliamentary passage of the legislation, negotiating concrete features to be incorporated into the text of LOGSE, and now, after its approval, negotiating its regulatory implementation.

The concerns of the unions have centred on the issues which directly affect teachers and their contractual conditions: the configuration of the teacher guilds (*cuerpos*), which is especially problematic at secondary level; initial access and training; and teachers on temporary contracts. The confederated unions have placed their emphasis on those aspects which directly affect the quality of teaching, that is to say, on conditions of schooling (the educational character of infant schooling, the length of compulsory education and various ratios). CCOO, in particular, has presented alternative legislative proposals, together with financial projections.

The results, encoded in specific, significant agreements (including solutions to the problems of temporary contracts and mobility between different teaching bodies or between schools), have not carried with them the unanimous support of all the unions. In some cases, this has been because of problems of identity or ideological constraints (e.g. in the case of ANPE and CSIF, which are opposed to the abolition of the guild of *catedráticos* – secondary school professors), in others because the reform, recognized as an advance, has not gone as far as had been hoped (e.g. CCOO and UGT, which object to the absence of a financial plan and which, with STE, lament the lack of any movement towards a unitary body of teachers). What is clear is that there has not been firm, committed union support for reform. At the moment of parliamentary approval there was a testimonial photograph of the union secretaries of CCOO and UGT, Gutierrez and Redondo, with the Minister of Education, Javier Solana. None the less, while the first decrees for the implementation of reform are being negotiated, and while the unions assess the negative implications for school construction and staffing of the cuts resulting from the neo-liberal policies of the Socialist Government, it is as if the 'photo' had never taken place and naturally the attitude of the unions has turned harder and less neutral, the 'class' unions demanding that those elements of the law which they consider most progressive be implemented.

INCIDENCE OF REFORM AMONG TEACHERS

It is to be expected that such a general reform of the educational system should profoundly and comprehensively affect its most important and established components – the teachers themselves. The reform systematically introduces four significant innovations for teachers: new *cuerpos* (guilds), new schools, new students and new curricula.

Modification of phases and teaching guilds

The change in the structure of compulsory education from three to two cycles and the reduction of the age of completion of primary education from 14 to 12 bring with them a general restructuring of teaching bodies, reducing the age range and, with it, the field of responsibility of the *magisterio*. Equally, their internal features are changed, as in the case of the new specialist categories of *maestro*: infant, primary, musical education, foreign languages, physical education, special education and language and listening.

On the other hand, for the most qualified sectors of the primary teaching body [e.g. for those who hold five-year degree *licenciaturas* (eds)], the possibility is held out of accession to the guild of secondary teachers – with the added possibility of acquisition of the status of professor (*catedrático*) – which brings together the old guilds of BUP and FP teachers, now serving the age group 12 to 14. What some previous BUP teachers regard as historic retribution for what they consider the misappropriation or disappearance of the 'elementary *Bach*' by means of the 1970 law of general education, others, those with shorter memories of the system, regard as the standardization of *enseñanzas medias* by means of the total comprehensivization of the age group 12 to 16, and of the predicted avalanche of graduate primary teachers into this cycle. As a new BUP teacher suggested in one discussion group: 'Now the Ministry would like to see all of us in secondary education as primary teachers.' This is an example of the dynamics of inclusion–exclusion between EGB (primary) and EM (secondary) teachers.

School reorganization

In a parallel process the schools, and especially the state schools, must be restructured to take account in their design and resourcing the new phases of primary and secondary (at least in the case of mainstream schools). In the short term, there is a real possibility (given the politics of austerity and of 'convergence' in the wake of Moncloa and Maastrich) that this may take the form of a recycling of existing schools, with nominal changes in title. Of the current population of EGB schools, therefore, some will become primary and others will become compulsory secondary schools. Of the current BUP institutes, some will become post-compulsory secondary schools specializing in academic studies while the FP colleges will be assigned responsibility as secondary schools specializing in techno-logical and professional studies [reflecting the different specialist routes through the new *Bachillerato* that will be available (eds)]. Every case will involve the integration of teachers from different levels and different guilds to teach in the new or recycled schools (which will thus be affected by the corporatist dynamics which we have already discussed).

In all schools the institution of the post of administrator and a redefi-nition of the functions of head teacher are pushing management away from a democratic model towards a bureaucratic model, possibly tending in the direction of a more 'European' style of school with more marked managerial features. In compensation, the specialized services of pro-fessional educational psychologists can discharge many support functions for teachers and help them to be more professional. Similarly, some problems of responsibility and competence, arising over the new tutorial role of teachers, towards which secondary teachers, especially, have expressed measured opposition, may be resolved.

New students

Even so, the students will be different. The old BUP teachers will now receive and have to teach *all* students, not just the best 60 per cent which the filter of *graduado escolar* currently allows through. FP teachers, on the other hand, will be the 'winners', receiving 'better' students than they previously have had. Such changes have clear and immediate implications for methods and rhythms of learning and, very concretely, for problems of discipline and level. Perhaps for that reason and in order to smooth the way, LOGSE establishes quotas on the numbers of students per class, now that the demographic decline allows such fine tuning.

In addition, the raising of the age of compulsory education to 16 years, as Ball (1981) observed in Beachside Comprehensive in the UK, will incorporate in greater measure – by raising the participation rate of these age groups by 100 per cent – the anti-school adolescent sub-culture which, in itself and together with the conflicts among teachers and between schools, will constitute the Gordian knot of the reform in its pure teaching sense.

In any case and *a priori* it would seem ingenuous to think that the egalitarian principles and the social engineering implicit in the comprehensive formula of LOGSE are going to *guarantee* that students of different social origins are going to share the same building, given what I have argued above and given the existence of the private network. Equally, it remains to be seen whether they are going to share the same classroom (even if they do share the same building), given the demonstrable consensus of teachers – under pressure to maintain academic quality – which favours compartmentalization according to achievement (applied in English comprehensive schools under the label of 'streaming'). But in the final analysis it is difficult to envisage, even if they do indeed share both building and classroom, that they should share similar destinies, taking into account the dynamics of differentiation (brought about both by teachers, through assessment, and by the attitudes of students) and polarization (brought about by students themselves in the wake of differentiation) arising from the formation of pro-school and anti-school sub-cultures (Lacey, 1970 and Fernández Enguita, 1988). It is the practice of comprehensive schooling more than the rhetoric which affects the experience of schooling and students' expectations of the future, and that practice is conditioned by the pressure exercised by the teaching culture and by external social expectations, which are concretized through the criteria of discipline and level (Ball, 1981).

The new curricula

The new subjects and curriculum areas (technologies, physical education, music) in primary education, and the new types of *Bachillerato*, are superimposed upon methodological innovations (globalization – or integrated curriculum planning – in primary, and comprehensivization at secondary) and on the organizational changes already discussed. Comprehensivized levels and curricula, but divided into the four modalities of the *Bachillerato*, prefigure some new hierarchies among teachers: compulsory secondary as opposed to *Bachillerato* secondary, technology to pure science, etc. All this will be aggravated by the publication of school results, which will have an overall and unintended effect of bringing about a classification and hierarchization of schools, as already exists in the Anglo-Saxon countries from which the reform was imported. None the less, diversity and plurality of teachers among school staff, always assuming that these are furnished with the necessary resources, allows the possibility of rotation and welcome relief from teaching timetables.

One significant feature is the scope for adaptation of the DCB or common national curriculum to the environment of individual schools and the social environment in which they are located. In principle it seems like a measure which favours the professionalization of teachers and which gives them greater autonomy. Its true significance remains to be seen, especially in relation to what MEC understands by the 55 per cent of the curriculum fixed by LOGSE and the problems that can be created for teachers by what Apple calls 'intensification' (Apple, 1989). From that point of view one could imagine a pattern whereby current curriculum plans get photocopied from year to year, without ever really being practised in the majority of schools.

From experience of the development of all these reforms in practice, we can establish the extent to which teachers are affected, whether they will experience an increase in professionalism arising from greater autonomy and participation in curriculum design or whether, on the contrary, they have to put up with mixed-ability pupils, a loss of hierarchical position or deprofessionalization, whether they suffer a reduction of social status or an increase. Very probably there will be a process of 'intensification' at least while there is adaptation to reform. What is completely certain is that the reform is going to be accompanied by a substantial increase in salaries. Just as the first attempt to reform public administration took the form of a bribe in the form of holidays known as *moscosos* [after Moscoso, the minister responsible (eds)], now there has been a concession to teachers in the form of the *sexenios* payments in line with seniority. With these a payment is made that is proportional to length of service and which concedes a big increase to the longest serving who are, in principle, the most strongly opposed to the reforms, thus neutralizing their resistance. The *sexenios* may yet be remembered as *solanas* [after the Minister of Education, Javier Solana (eds)] so that what is left of the reform is a bribe which, as with the *moscoso*, would be a symptom of failure if not of collective prevarication. This would conceal the unequal fortune of the various elements of the reform in the hands of the different strata of the teaching profession.

EDITORS' POSTSCRIPT

A 1993 survey of 1,500 non-university teachers at all levels reported broad satisfaction with working conditions, with the changes introduced by LOGSE and with teacher training. Teachers were most likely to complain of the lack of social recognition for their work, low pay, inadequate scope for promotion and poor materials, and to want better and more up-to-date in-service training (77 per cent had taken in-service courses in recent years). Teachers appear in this survey as a stable social group with a defined civil status; religious beliefs (75 per cent describe themselves as Catholic); a higher-than-average level of professional membership; politically central with little support for political extremes but inclined towards disenchantment with Spanish society; with a high regard for their profession; and conscious of their personal and social responsibility. They are rarely absent and their average age is 38 years (only 4 per cent are under 25 and 20 per cent are older than 46) (Gonzalez-Blasco and Gonzales-Anleo, 1994). A study of teachers in the País Vasco, based on 1989 and 1992 surveys of 500 of the community's 1,200 teachers (Barquín and Barceló, 1994) found that most teachers were women, originating from the lower-middle or working classes, whose parents had low levels of academic achievement. Their average age in this study is 35. Sixty-nine per cent of them had a permanent position. Over half described themselves as left of centre (but not extreme left). They had confidence in methods of assessment, did not like the growing influence of parents or students in decision-making, and had faith in textbooks and the didactic methods embedded in them. Pedagogy and finance were two of the areas of strongest controversy among them. The majority believed in learning based on investigation rather than memorization. They worried about pupil motivation and the influence of the mass media.

NOTE

1 From the Francoist *Servicio Español del Magisterio* (SEM) emerged the *Asociación Nacional del Profesorado de EGB* (ANPE) and the *Federación Estatal de Sindicatos de Profesores de EGB* (FESPE, today incorporated into CSIF together with other ex-corporatist secondary level associations), orientated towards the Conservative party (AP) and Centrist party (UCD), respectively. From the opposition to Franco emerged the *Federación de Trabajadores de la Enseñanza de UGT* (FETE), orientated towards the PSOE; the *Federación de Enseñanza de CCOO*, orientated towards the PCE; and the *Union Confederal de Sindicatos de Trabajadores de la Enseñanza* (UCSTE) of extra-parliamentary orientation. In private education one has to substitute for the first two acronyms the confessional union (FSIE) and the moderate FESITE-USO.

REFERENCES

Apple, M. (1989) *Maestros y Textos*. Barcelona: Paidos.
Ball, S. (1981) *Beachside Comprehensive: A Case Study of Secondary Schooling*. Cambridge: Cambridge University Press.
Barquín, J. and Barceló, F. (1994) *El Profesorado de Euskadi. Estudio de sus planteamientos didácticos*. Bilbao: Departamento de Educación del Gobierno.
CIDE (1985) Encuesta a profesores no universitarios de la enseñanza pública, *Revista de educación*, no. 277, pp. 207–37.

Fernández Enguita, M. (1988) El rechazo escolar: alternativa o trampa escolar?, *Politíca y Sociedad*, no. 1, pp. 23–37.
Gonzalez-Blasco, P. and Gonzalez-Anleo, J. (1994) *El profesorado en la España actual*. Santa Maria: La Fundacion.
Guerrero, S. A. (1991a) Maestras y maestros: autonomía, practica docente y sindicación en una profesión subordinada. Unpublished doctoral thesis.
Guerrero, S. A. (1991b) Los movimientos profesiónales y sindicales en la enseñanza: un sindicalismo profesiónal, *Documentación Social*, no. 84, July–September, pp. 141–59.
Lacey, C. (1970) *Hightown Grammar: The School as a Social System*. Manchester: Manchester University Press.
Ortega, F. and Velasco, A. (1991) *La profesión de maestro*. Madrid: DIDE.
Revista Española de Investigaciones Sociologicas (REISs) (1990) 'Datos de Opinion', no. 49, *Enero-Marzo*, p. 311.
Taylor, C. and Mitchell, D. (1988) *The Changing Idea of a Trade Union*. Philadelphia: The Falmer Press.
TE (1992) Estudio sobre las condiciones de trabajo, no. 131, III Epoca, *Marzo*, pp. 3–22.

15 The teachers' centres*

Sara Morgenstern de Finkel

Since 1972 the universities have been entrusted with the training of future teachers. Teachers for EGB (and now for primary education) were required to take a three-year course at 'university schools'. Secondary teachers have had to complete a five-year course leading to a Licenciatura *in a particular discipline, followed by a one-year course providing pedagogical training. There was a common entrance examination open to holders of the* Bachillerato *for the university schools, and this had a pass rate of 95 per cent, with no interviews. The university schools enjoy relatively low prestige (by contrast with the prestigious university faculties) and conduct little research. For holders of the* Licenciatura *wanting to enter state (but not private) secondary teaching it has been necessary to take a one-year course, heavily academic and traditionally containing relatively little teaching practice, leading to a Certificate of Pedagogical Aptitude (CAP), offered by the Institutes of Education and Science (ICEs) (Morgenstern de Finkel, 1991). Plans for primary training approved by the* Consejo de Universidades *in 1991, and awaiting legislation, propose seven core subjects in education, plus teaching practice, together with subject training and corresponding teaching methods. The long delay in implementation of reform of initial training has been accompanied by the promotion of in-service education, under the particular charge of the teachers' centres since 1984. In this chapter, Morgenstern de Finkel offers a critique of the teachers' centres, with particular reference to the recruitment of personnel, the degree of their commitment to reform and the programmes that they offer.*

INTRODUCTION

The education programme of PSOE in 1982 expressed many of the democratic aspirations that were nourished in the last years of Franco's dictatorship and the first moments of the transition. The programme took as its point of reference the policies put into practice by social-democratic governments some twenty years previously – that is to say, extension of

---

* This chapter translated by Oliver Boyd-Barrett

schooling, improvement in the quality of education, comprehensivization, emphasis on compensatory education – principles which later inspired the 1990 law of educational reform.

Clearly, to put into practice a reform of this importance required the active consensus of the teachers, recognized as a critical factor by the Socialist Government from the beginning. The problem was not simple. On the one hand, almost all teachers at primary level had been trained and socialized in authoritarian institutions, whose curricula were designed by experts close to *Opus Dei*, and teachers at secondary level received only a precarious professional preparation by means of the much criticized 'course of pedagogic suitability' (CAP). On the other hand, in-service education was reproducing the same pattern as initial training, its principal contents based on key theories of behaviourism, taxonomies of objectives, programmed instruction, Taylorist school organization, etc., to which were added a characteristic Spanish twist expressed as 'personalized education'.

During more than ten years of government with an absolute majority, the PSOE delayed reform of initial teacher training, without doubt one of the most urgent tasks. The new study plans which have yet to be put into action have not resolved many of the most important problems (Morgenstern de Finkel, 1993). The delay in reform of initial teacher training was a conscious option, based on purely economic considerations, as the Minister considered that in-service education was more productive, 'given the youth of the Spanish teaching force, whose average age is appreciably less than that of other countries' (MEC, 1987, p. 9). Thus was put into motion, rightly or wrongly, a policy of teacher retraining, principally through the teachers' centres.

In the public sector, in-service training is entrusted to different authorities, be they provincial, regional or UNED (the national distance-teaching university), or to the Ministry of Education itself. In this chapter we refer exclusively to the teachers' centres which are within the jurisdiction of the Ministry, not only because their activity affects a greater number of teachers but also because they were explicitly created as reforming institutions, destined to prepare the teaching profession which must engage with the reform of the educational system.

THE CREATION OF THE TEACHERS' CENTRES

In the last decade of the dictatorship some sectors of the teaching profession began to recognize the necessity for changing the basic features of Francoist schooling. Slowly, from the first Summer School of Barcelona, there began to flourish various experiments throughout the country, which were organized under the generic title, 'Movements of Teaching Reform' (*Movimientos de Renovación Pedagógica*) (MRP). Despite their heterogeneity, underlying all of them was an anti-authoritarian ethos. They all defended the state school and they all shared a secularizing attitude towards social life in the extent to which they believed that educational reform and political reform were two facets of the same process.

There is no research which enables us to estimate the actual influence of the MRPs on the teaching profession, but it can be affirmed that their activity was sufficiently extensive that it was of concern to the dictatorship. In reality, the MRPs were part of a great civic mobilization, led by the workers' movements, which embraced neighbourhood associations, university professors, students and artists. From 1982 when the socialist party won the elections, this mobilization was gradually extinguished, in part because some of its demands were already on the political agenda and also because many of its leaders had been incorporated into government posts.

The creation of the teachers' centres in 1984 was received with enthusiasm by the MRPs and the class-based trade unions – the *Comisiones Obreras* and the *Union General de Trabajadores* – because fundamentally it was a recognition of the professional maturity of teachers in the sense that it legitimated their capacity for autonomous management of their own training. Although some MRPs refused to be incorporated into the teachers' centres because they considered that institutionalization would lead to a loss of autonomy and a creeping bureaucratization there was, overall, a cordial understanding between the Ministry and most of the reformist movement (Martinez Bonafe, 1992; Domenech i Francesch and Vinas Cirera, 1992).

Until the creation of the teachers' centres, the greater part of public resources for the retraining of teachers was directed to the Institutes of Education Sciences (*Institutos de Ciencias de la Educación*) (ICEs) in the universities, where the mass of teachers at the primary and middle levels had not the least influence over the activities designed for their own in-service training. With few exceptions, the ICEs conformed to a technocratic model, removed from the real problems of the classroom and based on courses of short duration. At its most negative the system was a lottery of dubious morality where teachers obtained certificates for their merely passive presence at courses which had no relevance, and the ICEs were converted into machines for the issue of bureaucratic credentials. It was no accident that the most critical teachers or at least those most committed to the improvement of teaching rejected this official model and felt more at home with the voluntary activities organized by the MRPs.

The decision to create the teachers' centres was without doubt an act of political valour, which signified the rerouting of the considerable funds which had been available to the ICEs, generally controlled by conservative sectors, to certain new institutions managed by the teachers themselves. The concerted reaction of the educational right-wing did not delay in coming, and counted on the decided support of the conservative press and many university teachers, up until then the most influential forces behind the ICEs. The fact that the new Sub-Director of Teacher Training was a secondary teacher, a syndicalist and, in addition, a woman, was a symbol of the new times.

In 1985 the first fifty-six teachers' centres began to function, situated in the territory which was under the direct jurisdiction of the Ministry of Education (representing 63 per cent of the national total in terms of geographical area and 40 per cent in terms of population). The network expanded until it reached its current total of 113 centres. The autonomous regions of Andalucia, Valencia and the Canary Islands also created their own teachers' centres, while Cataluña and the País Vasco developed other systems of further training.

The teachers' centres were born at a historical moment which was without doubt favourable to their implementation. On the one hand, while there existed strong expectations with respect to the educational change promised by the PSOE, the right-wing could offer only a traditional rhetoric, based on the defence of the privileges of private education. On the other hand, while the ICEs still had little credibility among the teachers (MEC, 1986, pp. 34–6), the teachers' centres were presented as a modern alternative, sufficiently tested in the United Kingdom, and supported by a theoretical framework which exalted the professionalism of the teacher.

The creation of the teachers' centres in 1984 signified much more than a legal act (Royal Decree 2112/1, 1984, pp. 33921–2 through which is regulated the creation and functioning of the teachers' centres). The Administration had generated a significant change in the conceptualization of continuous training, whose central points could be summarized as (a) the facilitation of the teacher–researcher, (b) the emphasis on qualitative foci, both in evaluation and in research, and (c) the constructivist conceptualization of learning. The Administration promoted extensive dissemination of these theories and in the pursuit of this objective it spared neither efforts nor resources in the arrangement of seminars and publications to lend legitimacy to this new model. For the teachers who aspired to work in the teachers' centres, the Ministry organized specialist courses that were manifestly informed by the new philosophy.

In theory, the organization envisaged for the teachers' centres signified a break from the framework within which continuous training of the teaching force had traditionally taken place. An attempt was made to break down the typical isolation of teachers by means of group work among teachers of different levels and subjects. If this is difficult in general it is even more difficult in the Spanish context, where membership of different teaching corps has reinforced both individualism and the struggle for the monopoly of knowledge. Besides enabling inter-level and inter-disciplinary activities, it put into question the usefulness of a training based on short courses. The teachers' centre would offer other, more consistent alternatives, involving active participation, the production of materials for the classroom, interchange of experiences and, of course, theoretical reflection. In order that all these aspirations should materialize, there had to be created the conditions that would involve teachers in educational research, which was considered to be a fundamental aspect of the institutional development of the teachers' centres.

PERSONNEL

Although there is not sufficient historical perspective for an analysis of the evolution of the teachers' centres, it seems obvious that it must be interpreted in the context of the social changes experienced by Spain in the past decade. The question is: up to what point do the apathy and demobilization which are characteristic of civil life today affect institutions which were explicitly created for the purpose of change, as were the teachers' centres? It is obvious that an institution of this kind will have social influence to the extent that it is supported by the voluntary participation of broad sectors of the teaching force and if in 1984 many expectations and hopes were fostered, that is no longer the case today.

Nevertheless, it would not be right to exaggerate the weight of the crisis, because a good share of the problems which the teachers' centres currently face arise from a lack of coherent planning, as much on the part of the Ministry as on the part of the centres themselves. This general assertion is based on evaluative research of the first fifty-six teachers' centres, which has yielded significant results (Morgenstern de Finkel and Martin Rodriguez, 1992). It remains to be said that, given the brevity of this chapter, we cannot look into very much detail, but will limit our remarks to those aspects which are considered most worrying.

One of the most symptomatic changes in the evolution of the teachers' centres can be seen in the recruitment of personnel. In 1984 many of the old fighters for democracy in education were incorporated into the teachers' centres, as an extension of the work which was being undertaken in the unions or by the MRPs. Although many were also militants for the party now in government, it was rare for teachers in any given region to question their suitability as promoters of educational innovation. Of that 'pedagogic vanguard' very few currently remain in the teachers' centres, in line with the increasing disconnection of the CEPs from the reform movements.

If we look at the professional biographies of personnel who currently work in the teachers' centres it can be said that they represent a sector very much separate from the initiatives of educational innovation which have taken place in Spain. In addition, practically none of them has participated in civic organizations, suggesting that even in the best cases their horizon is limited to the classroom. Only one-third of the advisers began their work in the centres because they identified with the mission which these represent; for the rest, the reasons have been strictly individual, not least connected with the search for personal promotion.

Very few advisers have assumed a new professional role and, what is worse, most do not feel themselves respected by the teachers of their respective zones. They believe themselves to be perceived as minions of the Administration, or mere disseminators of the reform, which suggests that the centres lack credibility as autonomous institutions destined to improve educational practice. The rejection is much more marked among the secondary teachers, who are in general the most reluctant to participate in training activities and the most indifferent in the face of the change on which the reform of the educational system is premised.

We do not have the evidence to evaluate how far this image is real; in any case the research on which we draw analysed only the general characteristics of the fifty-six teachers' centres and certainly there are notable exceptions. Nevertheless, taking into account the overall data, it can be said that the majority of the current personnel of the centres do not represent suitable role models for the kind of teacher that the reform is attempting to create. The time which they dedicate to self-development is negligible and, in the few cases where some kind of research task is undertaken, this takes up on average between two and four hours a week. The conclusion is almost self-evident: despite the rhetoric, training and research are left for others.

DISTORTION OF THE MODEL

Although it is true that a good proportion of the current personnel do not present an adequate role-model for the training of other teachers, the exclusive responsibility for the crisis which the teachers' centres currently face cannot be placed on their shoulders alone. Owing to the fact that the Administration has left unclear which themes the teachers must prioritize in order to meet the curricular requirements of the future reform, each centre has organized its own offer of in-service education in isolation from the others. While the statistics of the Ministry of Education with respect to in-service activities are not very trustworthy and must be carefully interpreted, it is obvious that if we look at the content and the type of these activities there exist significant imbalances which reflect the lack of rational planning at the global level (MEC, 1991).

Among the most important imbalances must be mentioned the disproportionate weight which is enjoyed by the so-called 'new technologies', especially the concentration of resources in two particular projects (*Atenea* and *Mercurio*), which were managed directly by the Ministry for the development of informatic and audio-visual media in schools. To give an idea of the extent of disequilibrium that favours the new technologies, it is sufficient to note that in recent years the rate of activity in this sphere has more than doubled that of the areas of mathematics and natural sciences put together. From any perspective, it is an absurd situation where the new technologies should be so fashionable at the expense of a solid training in the scientific principles which underlie them. The disequilibrium would be certainly greater if it were possible to discriminate better between the data, given that Physics is included within Natural Sciences while the category of new technologies combines many activities which have little to do with technological knowledge.

It is precisely in the area of technical education that there has been the greatest improvisation in the training of specialist teachers. Although it is true that the Ministry has established some one-off programmes, these have affected only a very small number of teachers. The problem is all the more serious because these teachers have neither the specialized training nor are they abreast of the technologies which are required by modern companies. It is difficult to understand how LOGSE can attempt to eliminate the second-class and working-class character of the current *Formación Profesional*, strengthening the technical culture of compulsory secondary education and creating a specialized *Bachillerato* in professional technical education (*Enseñanzas Técnico Profesionales* (ETP)), without training a competent teaching force. To judge by the extent of the training activities so far accomplished (2 per cent of all teachers of technology in compulsory secondary education, and less than 4 per cent of teachers of ETP) the least that can be said is that there has been an underestimation of the strategic importance which these teachers have for the success of the reform, contrary to the declarations of the Ministry itself, which in 1989 estimated that it would be necessary to undertake a major effort for the requalification of a collective totality of 8,500 teachers for the future ETP (MEC, 1989, p. 213).

While retraining in the different technologies is difficult, given the facilities which the teachers' centres have available, they have not recognized that the problem forms an essential issue for in-service education in their respective zones.

Another major problem, insufficiently addressed until 1990, is the preparation of specialized pre-school teachers. Very few have a specialized initial training, and to a significant extent activity at this level of education is in the hands of unqualified personnel in private nurseries. The lack of planning is surprising given that LOGSE made provision for the development of pre-school education in the public sector.

In general, and with the exception of the area of language and literature, very little weight has been given to retraining in the central areas of the curriculum, in primary as much as in secondary. This situation is particularly worrying in the smallest teachers' centres located in the least urbanized zones, where there are obviously fewer opportunities to broaden the cultural horizon of the teachers.

The general scenario demonstrates that the current training of the teaching profession has been developed without prioritizing criteria. Even in the year 1992–3, which has seen a correction to some of the worst problems, there persists a failure to make clear the disciplinary fields or themes which most require provision or even to concentrate on the training of those teachers who are at the forefront of the reform. When the resources are scarce, and the necessities great, the Administration cannot pursue a low-profile policy. Although it seems strange in a country with a tradition as centralist as that of Spain, the reality is that continuous training of teachers has been organized up until now on the basis of a chance balance between voluntaristic demand and spontaneous supply.

From an Anglo-Saxon perspective this situation could be interpreted as a reaffirmation of the professional autonomy of teachers who supposedly choose teachers' centre activities in accordance with their own interests. But in the Spanish context this is not the case. Many teachers, especially those in secondary education, attend these activities simply for the certificates which the centres issue, given that these constitute precious credentials in the competition for promotion or transfer. The Administration has even exalted teachers' centre courses over other, more established, routes to training, including university courses and doctorates. Of course, such artificial strengthening does nothing for the institutional development of the centres, rather it reinforces the bureaucratic–credentialist model which is the very opposite of the philosophy which informed the creation of the centres.

In these circumstances it is no accident that the short course should be the training activity that predominates in the teachers' centres, around half of them lasting fewer than 20 hours, that is to say, about a week. In such a limited period it is not possible to go much further than some pragmatic recipes, without the minimum foundation which a process of serious reflection would require. But worse, the short course is precisely the method which favours isolation of the teachers in so far as it does not demand team work. That is perhaps one of the principal reasons why activities which have an inter-disciplinary character have such a low profile in the teachers' centres.

It is difficult to assess up to what point teachers' centres have the potential to change the traditional frameworks of teaching, but certainly it is the case that they have done little to counterbalance the individualist models of work which the teachers have internalized. The point of reference continues to be the individual teacher and rarely are activities planned for teams of teachers from the same school or for the school as a whole.

In many respects the development of the teachers' centres has disappointed those who had entertained justifiable expectations that the centres would offer serious and democratic alternatives for empowering the professionalism of teachers. Considerations such as the ones just discussed demonstrate that there exist strong tendencies towards bureaucratization, credentialism and, especially, improvisation. There is little that can contribute these days to the generation of an active consensus for the success of the reform.

EDITORS' POSTSCRIPT

The May 1994 editorial for an edition of the professional journal *Aula de Innovacion Educativa*, dedicated to in-service training, noted that negative evaluation of the work of the teachers' centres was widespread, and located the principal reason for this in an insufficiency of training for the teachers recruited to run the centres, and inadequate recognition of the specific skills involved in developing in-service work and stimulating school-based innovation and development.

In 1994, the teachers' centres were amalgamated with the network of resource centres which hitherto had principally served rural schools, to form *Centros de Profesores y Recursos* (CPRs). The resource centres had principally served rural schools, and some of their functions were transferred to the *Colegios Rurales Agrupados* (groups of small rural schools which, in combination, share resources and act collaboratively as an alternative to the closure of village schools). CEPs have tended to focus on primary rather than secondary needs. Since 1984 they have generated 1,400 publications and reports, forty-five magazines and thirty-three information bulletins. But dissemination of the results of CEP-sponsored projects leaves much to be desired (Garcia Alvarez, 1994).

REFERENCES

Domenech i Francesch, J. and Vinas Cirera, J. (1992) Movimientos de Renovación Pedagógica, in *Cuadernos de Pedagogía*, no. 199, January 1992, pp. 72–81.

Garcia Alvarez, J. (1994) Los Publicaciones de los CEPs, *Comunidad Escolar*, 25 May 1994.

Martinez Bonafe, J. (1992) Diez años de renovación pedagógica organizada, in J. Paniagua and A. San Martin (eds) *Diez años de educación en España* (1978–88). Diputación Provincial de Valencia, Valencia de la UNED, Centro de Alzira, pp. 337–50.

Ministerio de Educación y Ciencia (Subdirección General de Formación del Profesorado) (1986) *Encuesta al Profesorado de los niveles de Educación General Básica y Enséñanza Medias*. Formación Permanente del Profesorado. Madrid: Centro de Publicaciones, MEC.

Ministerio de Educación y Ciencia (1987) *Proyecto para la reforma de la enseñanza. Educación infantil, primaria, secundaria y profesional. Propuesta para debate*. Madrid: MEC (Prólogo del Ministro, José María Maravall).

Ministerio de Educación y Ciencia (1989) *Plan de Investigación Educativa y de Formación del Profesorado*. Madrid: Centro de Publicaciones, MEC.

Ministerio de Educación y Ciencia (1991) *Memoría de Actividades de Formación Permanente del Profesorado. Curso 1989–1990*. Dirección General de Renovación Pedagógica. Subdirección General de Formación del Profesorado. Madrid: MEC.

Morgenstern de Finkel, S. (1991) The Slow Reform of Teacher Education in Spain, *European Journal of Education*, vol. 26, no. 3, pp. 239–49.

Morgenstern de Finkel, S. (1993) Teacher Education in Spain: a postponed reform, in T. S. Popkewitz *Changing Patterns of Power. Social Regulation and Teacher Education Reform*; New York: State University of New York.

Morgenstern de Finkel, S. and Martin Rodriguez, E. (1992) *La evaluación de los CEPs. Analisis de su Contribución a la reforma educativa.* Madrid: CIDE, Centro de Publicaciones, MEC.

Royal Decree 2112/1 (1984) *Boletín Oficial del Estado* 24 November.

16 Church, State and educational reform*

Juan José Sanchéz de Horcajo

Private providers are responsible for the education of approximately one-third of all schoolchildren in Spain, although the percentage varies considerably across phases, and across the different autonomous communities. Most schools providing privately for the compulsory education of children are dependent on state funding, and cannot charge fees for such education. The Catholic Church is the single largest provider in this category. Since 1990, Catholic schools have established their own representative body, Confederación de Centros de Educación y Gestion *(CCEG), independent of the* Confederación Española de Centros de Enseñanza *(CECE), which had previously represented almost all private schools. In a move to concentrate church interests further, CCEG has helped to establish a separate negotiating committee to focus solely on the interests of the direct-grant sector of the private sphere in which most church schools are located. Now subject to state regulations governing community participation in school management, freedom of conscience and of education, the social power of the Church through schooling is much less significant than it was during the Franco regime. This chapter outlines the struggle for education between Church and State over the last two centuries, but with particular reference to their respective positions in the debates leading to legislation under the PSOE Government, especially LODE (1984) and LOGSE (1990).*

The question of responsibility for education is an ancient and universal debate. Who should educate? Who has the right to teach? Sometimes the question has been posed even more crudely: who owns the child? The general view today is that the child belongs to himself and responsibility for the child's education falls to everyone, but above all to its parents as a right and a duty inherent to parenthood. But without entering into deeper philosophical or juridical reflection, we can say that Church and State have bitterly disputed the ownership of education and that they continue to do so.

In societies that are primarily confessional in nature, both institutions

* This chapter translated by Pamela O'Malley.

have laid bitter claim to rights and interests which they have then attempted to exercise, not just happy with competition but in a struggle for monopoly. In these societies, and such is the Spanish case, the powers of Church and State have engaged in dialectic struggle for education, with historical persistence, since education is one of the most efficient vehicles for the transmission and exercise of power. Education is the most subtle and manageable instrument for inculcating and achieving the objectives of power. The formal involvement of Church and State is thus inevitable.

In Spain, the struggle for power in education between Church and State is persistent and unresolved. It can be said that since the very formation of the modern Spanish State there has been strife between the two institutions as to which should dominate and predominate. It is possible to say on reflection that a dialectically articulated dual tradition is to be found which resurfaces with any change in the dominant ideology, and under a variety of different guises and denominations, be it progressive–conservative, revolutionary–reactionary, reformist–integrationist.

This alternating ideology is clearly reflected in the development of education in our country. Education has become the site and the strategy for ideological and political change in the social and economic structure of the nation. Thus, Spaniards of the Age of Enlightenment in the eighteenth century infused their dynamic concept of education with the task of economic transformation. The reactionaries of that century, meanwhile, with a static vision of education, attributed to it the capacity for conservation of society, through transmission of traditional values.

Again, in the nineteenth century the confrontation over education between the two ideological–political positions was clearly manifest. For the liberals, education played a forceful revolutionary role in promoting democracy and progress. This concept inspired educational legislation in 1813, again in 1821, and then again in the educational philosophy of the Second Republic. On the other hand, for the conservatives and moderates, historically, education was the vehicle for maintaining the established social order and the social orders of the past. The conservative tradition was represented in the education plan of 1836, in the Moyano Act of 1857 and during the epoch of the radical Republicans in the conservative phase of the Second Republic, 1933–6.

The Church has always considered education as a means of indoctrination and mediation for the exercise of its power. It uses diverse strategies of approaching and retreating from state power, according to the degree of harmony between their respective interests; but it always maintains a direct influence on education. From this political–educational perspective, it can be said that the Spanish Catholic Church has kept in line with the most conservative policies and ideologies.

In reviewing the role of Church and State in present-day Spanish educational reform, we are simply bringing up to date the positions, established views and interests of both powers in the field of education, while adding some new trimmings.

THE STATE CLAIM TO EDUCATION

The State discovered its interest in education rather late. For as long as education was restricted to the minority, it was delivered for centuries by voluntary social groups. Its social significance with respect to its potential for personal growth, or in relation to the reproduction of privilege, went unperceived. Gradually, the powerful social function of education was revealed and integrated into the agenda of the modern state, to the point of being considered one of its essential tasks. In most states there was a progressive intervention in education to the point when it came to be considered a basic public service.

The strongest arguments in favour of the setting up of state education had their origin in the ideas of the Enlightenment on the one hand, the intention of extending culture to all social strata; on the other, the consideration of instruction as one of the rights and liberties of the individual, whose guarantee became an essential obligation for the State. Because it was opposed to Enlightenment ideas the influence of the Church had to be repressed, and this could only be achieved through an institution which was equal to it in power – the school.

Apart from these philanthropic motives, there were economic interests which recommended the establishment of an education system. Industrial development required a sufficiently skilled work force in order to increase productivity. Such transformation was strongly believed to require a process of concentration and unification of education. Only the State could impose such conditions.

Purely political demands must also be added to this process. The State recognized education as the most beneficial and necessary instrument for proposing and carrying out its objectives. Education became the vehicle by means of which state policy could be directed and reinforced. The State tried to supplant the Church in educational power. In this sense, all during the nineteenth and twentieth centuries the dispute over freedom in education and its secular or confessional nature was prolonged.

The various arguments still used today to defend the State's hegemony in education start from consideration of education as a demand for continuity and coherence and as a guarantee of equality among citizens, and go on to present education as the only reliable means of empowering citizens to exercise their rights and freedoms. In this way the modern State tries to control all educational activity through what is known as the educational system.

THE CHURCH CLAIM TO EDUCATION

The arguments of the Catholic Church in relation to education derive from ancient times, and rest on the premises of its divine origins and its role as spiritual father to its members (Gil de Zarate, 1991, p. 127).

Since Vatican II, there has been increasingly less frequent reference to these principles by the Catholic hierarchy in favour of principles of human dignity, and freedom of conscience and of religion. Reference is made to the universal recognition of every person's right to an education and to free choice of education, which the Church extends to the freedom of parents to select a school for their children and to freedom for the establishment of confessional schools, as indispensable conditions for the carrying out of these fundamental principles (Pio XI, 1929).

The Church also supports its position with reference to the declarations of principles in international organizations and pacts. Official church documents support the principles of the Universal Declaration of Human Rights of the UNO (1948), of the International Pact of Economic, Social and Cultural Rights (1966), the European Parliament's Resolution on the Freedom of Education (1984) and other international pacts and agreements.

The educational claims of the Church are essentially threefold:

- Recognition of the identity and values of Christianity in the general field of culture;
- Participation of the Church in schools to exercise its responsibility for the religious education of its members; and
- The right to establish and manage schools according to its own confessional character.

Church declarations and documents, at both national and international levels, defend the following positions:

- The right of those baptized to receive an education in their faith;
- Respect for the pupil's conscience in educational processes and activities;
- Religious education, forming an integral part of general education, should be provided in all schools, both public and private, where Catholic pupils are taught;
- Schools are an appropriate place for the development of faith, and, therefore, for religious education. The Church must provide religious training wherever believers are being educated;
- Given the scientific nature of religious knowledge, religious teaching should be integrated into the curriculum. It must also be recognized that Christian education is exercised through the transmission of culture;
- The church hierarchy should decide on the content of religious edu-

cation and it should be delivered by persons who are recognized as believers and who are willing to carry out this service;

- The right of the Church to provide all types of teaching in its own schools, established and managed by the Church itself, with its own specific identity; and
- The right of church schools to state subsidies on equal footing with the state schools.

(Concilio Vaticano II, 1989)

CHURCH EDUCATIONAL POLICY

The Church in its declarations defines education as a public service or uses other expressions such as a service to the community, a service of social initiative, services of general interest . . . thus putting state and non-state schools on the same level, and declaring that all schools should be considered as forming part of a joint social educational enterprise. All schools should be at the service of society under equal conditions and without any discrimination between pupils.

The Church emphasizes the confessional school as an open service which offers admission, help and progress, in conformity with its role as a public service, since teaching, as a social function, may be offered by state and non-state entities, which guarantee different options and pluralist schooling.

Church educational policy is not in favour of a uniform state school system, but rather of the establishment of a unified school system of homogeneous quality and level, and without any discrimination in facilities, means, teachers or content.

While recognizing the responsibility of the State for guiding and regulating education in conformity with national demands and needs, the Church maintains that it is not the role of the State to establish the model of teaching and learning which is to inspire the school system. The obligation of the State, says the Church, is to guarantee that all citizens can claim their right to education, to redress any discrimination or inequalities that may exist, to establish the general conditions and to control quality while respecting the autonomy of each school, and to promote the setting up of schools where educational needs have not been adequately met by voluntary initiative.

Finally, the Catholic hierarchy refers to the Agreements between the Holy See and the Spanish State of 3 January 1979, which recognize that educational activity should respect the principle of religious freedom and the fundamental right of parents regarding the moral and religious teaching of their children in schools. Also, the education given in state schools shall demonstrate respect for the values of the Christian ethic (*Consejo General de la Enseñanza Católica*, 1989).

SOCIALIST EDUCATIONAL REFORM – ANTECEDENTS

After Franco's death on 20 November 1975, a period of political transition commenced, during which two events of great significance stand out: restoration of the monarchy, and the passing of the Bill for Political Reform, which was submitted to referendum on the 15th December 1976. The importance of this Act resides fundamentally in the fact that it established:

- A new structure of Parliament, comprising two houses: the House of Deputies and the Senate;
- A new procedure for constitutional reform; and
- The setting up of basic principles for an electoral Act, which would permit the people to make known their support for the different political parties.

The bill of 23 March 1977 established the electoral norms, constituted the Parliament and commissioned the drawing up of a draft constitution. The politics of consensus, as it was called, had begun.

The Moncloa Pact (October 1977) included in its nine ample chapters a variety of measures (economic, political and social). The fourth established the principles and criteria which were to orientate educational policy and, in synthesis, were the following: (a) democratization of the educational system, (b) progressively free education, (c) introduction of vernacular languages.

Throughout 1978 the text for a new Spanish Constitution was prepared to include the aforementioned aspects and others designed to give shape to the educational system. The Constitution was approved by Parliament on 31 October 1978 and ratified in referendum on 6 December 1978. Article 27 of the Constitution, referring to education, was one of those which caused greatest conflict, and tried to reconcile two different concepts of education, along lines similar to those of the 1931 Constitution.

Article 27 expresses the political orientation of the educational system and the broad ideological principles which have come to be accepted as the basic values underlying action, although later the education policies of different political groups tended to privilege one ideological interpretation over another. It expressly recognizes:

- The right to education and the freedom of education;
- State guarantee of the right of parents to have their children receive religious and moral instruction in accordance with their convictions;
- Basic education is compulsory and free;
- Guarantee of the right to establish schools and to participate in their management;
- The Public Administration will inspect and homogenize the school system, so as to guarantee respect for legislation; and

- University autonomy is recognized.

Article 27 was the result of a complicated negotiation between the parliamentary right and left, with considerable pressure from the Church and other social agencies to achieve a difficult balance between the principles of equality and freedom of education. While the left placed greater emphasis on the principle of equality and consequently on the right to education and to participation and intervention in management by the school community, the right insisted on the principle of freedom, centred mainly on the creation of private schools and confessional education. The Centre party accepted the principle of community participation in the control and running of schools maintained by public funds.

As can be appreciated, a precarious balance was reached in the Constitution between two old political ideologies of education: the principles of educational equality and of freedom. Clearly this constitutional pact was going to be difficult to put into practice, as we shall see. The decade of the 1980s was characterized by a lengthy argument about how to express these constitutional rights in legislation, reproducing the traditional ideological and political cleavages. Once more the ideological battle was fought out between the left and the right during the parliamentary debate on the *Ley Orgánico del Estatuto de Centros* (LOECE), which was intended to develop article 27 of the Constitution. This law was directed mainly towards the right of private initiative to create and manage schools, and their right to establish their own ideological identity.

For the socialists, LOECE upset the constitutional balance between the principles of equality and freedom by placing excessive emphasis on the freedom of education, understood in a limited way as the freedom to set up schools, while other freedoms, such as the freedom to participate in school management, freedom of conscience, freedom in teaching, control of the grants given to private schools, etc., were marginalized. In this way the Act supported and protected the rights and interests of the proprietors of private schools, but did not protect the interests of the other members of the school community, teachers, parents and pupils. The bill was passed on 19 June 1980. But the Socialist party presented a constitutional appeal which, in part, was upheld by the sentence of the Constitutional Tribunal of 13 February 1981.

The other important project which was to develop section 10 of article 27 of the Constitution was that of university autonomy. The first texts were drawn up during the Government of UCD (*Unión de Centro Democrático*), but the debate was frozen until, under a socialist government, the Bill of University Reform (LRU) was passed on 15 July 1983.

As soon as the PSOE (socialist party) came into power, it gave priority to education and embarked on corresponding legislation.

In the words of the new Minister of Education, José María Maravall, in Spain, contrary to the situation in other countries, the State has taken a long time to assume the responsibility for education. Education has been in the hands of private initiative, especially the Church, which has considered that the public authorities should exercise only a subsidiary role with respect to private initiative (Corral, 1980). According to the new Minister, it was up to the Socialist Government to carry out profound educational reform as a channel for social change because, in his opinion, many of the problems of the country stemmed from the deficient organization of the educational system and from the enormous power which the Catholic Church exercised over it.

With the constitutional framework as a basis for educational organization, the PSOE proposed to carry through their educational reform. Their electoral programme was based on two essential premises: guarantee of the right to education and elevation of the quality of the teaching process. The first premise was interpreted as inflecting education as a public service, reinforcing the school system so as to eliminate any social inequality. The second premise was intended to present ample numbers of school places in conditions of equality, and to raise the quality of provision.

According to Maravall himself, 'the constitutional pact signified a reorientation of educational politics'. The educational principles of the socialists did not now differ substantially from those supported by the radical liberals of the last century or from those of the socialists of the Second Republic. In the Extraordinary Congress of the socialist party in 1931, the ideological lines upon which the present reform is based were already drawn up: nationalization of education, lay or religiously neutral schools, defence of the single school (unified school system) and the need for a single body of teachers.

The Socialist Government set in motion various programmes and measures in order to carry out its educational proposals:

- The programme of compensatory education, approved by Royal Decree in 1983, mainly directed towards marginal sectors of the population in the fringes of urban areas and in rural zones;
- The programme of adult education, directed principally towards wholly or functionally illiterate people; and
- The programme of special education, promoting the integration of disabled students within mainstream school and life.

The University Reform Bill (LRU) should also be counted among the first educational reforms. In this the University is considered as a public service, although this does not prevent the creation of private universities, organized in a similar way to the public ones. The University is considered as an autonomous service, with statutory, academic, financial and institutional autonomy. Departments, considered as units of both teaching and research, are the basis of university organization.

In parallel with the drafting of the University Reform Bill (LRU), the

Socialist Administration prepared the *Ley de Ordenación del Derecho a la Educación* (LODE) which, from an ideological point of view, attempts to develop the educational clauses of the Constitution, especially with respect to the delicate balance between the rights and freedoms of education.

Although the Constitution acknowledges the principle of freedom of education, this has more than one interpretation among the interested social agencies. The Catholic Church, fearful of losing its power and influence in education, once more sustained a dialectical and social struggle, lobbying the conservative political parties and organizing public demonstrations, pushing for regulations in accordance with its interpretation of the freedom of teaching in the ideology and practice of education, both with respect to the right to set up and to manage private schools and the right to their own ideological identity, as well as wanting public subsidies for private schools – demands which, in the opinion of the Church, give practical effect to the principle of freedom in education.

LODE

Although passed in Parliament on 15 March 1984, LODE was not immediately sanctioned, because the conservative opposition appealed on the grounds that various articles of the Act were unconstitutional, referring in particular to the criteria for the admission of pupils to schools sustained by public grants, to the owner's right to establish the ideological identity of a private school, to the system of school grants and to the powers given to governing bodies in schools.

A co-ordinating committee for Freedom in Education, representing all the private school organizations, opposed the system of grants for private schools right up to the last minute, to the point of opening up serious tensions within the ecclesiastical hierarchy which finally inclined, on balance, to the acceptance of the grant system for private schools.

Even following the judgement of the Constitutional Tribunal, the *Federación Española de Religiosos de la Enseñanza* continued to express its disagreement with LODE, stating on 3 July 1985:

Some of the Act's ambiguities have been dispelled. There remain, however, dark areas which may become the source of severe conflict in grant-aided schools. The Act continues to be a socialist Act, whose underlying philosophy is contrary to the vision of man and society propagated by Christian humanism. Declaring it to be constitutional does not make it a good Act.... There are still grey areas with respect to the harmonization of the rights of the school proprietor to manage with the rights of the school community to participate in the control and administration of schools maintained by public grants, which will require progressive clarification by means of appeals to the Courts of Law.

(Fere, 1985)

The socialist political proposals for educational reform required a general reorganization of the school system at the level of pre-school, basic education and secondary education.

A gradual process of experimentation and consultation with all sectors concerned with education was initiated. The motives which inspired this general reform were expressed in the prologue of the *Proyecto para La Reforma de la Enseñanza: Propuesta para Debate* (Proposals for the Reform of the Education System: an invitation to debate). These are to redress inequalities, and overhaul the obsolescent existing curriculum and the backward teaching techniques and methods derived from unsatisfactory processes of teacher training and selection processes (*Educadores*, 1985, pp. 329–59).

The document summarized the proposals for educational reform which the Ministry of Education had offered to the entire educational community and to Spanish society in general. It was at one and the same time a definition and an invitation to debate. It presented a diagnosis of Spanish problems and their appropriate remedies. Once a broad-ranging social debate had taken place, the Ministry of Education and Science edited five volumes containing a transcription of the various points of view. In the synthesis of all these contributions, with diverse shades of meaning and positions, as we shall subsequently demonstrate, a basic consensus is revealed favouring reform of the school system, as well as an acceptance of the fundamental objectives of this reform.

The Minister of Education and Science, Javier Solana, published the *Libro Blanco para la Reforma del Sistema Educativo* (White Paper on the Reform of the School System), which served as a basis for the initial draft of the bill and the Reform Act itself. The specific objectives of the reform are defined as being:

• Attention to infant education up to 6 years;
• Extension of basic education from 6 to 16 years, eliminating early selection and enhancing social integration; and
• Improving quality of teaching by means of co-ordinated and appropriate use of all relevant resources: curricular design, teaching staff, materials, etc.

The draft bill was presented to the public on 12 February 1990, and reproduces all the basic components of the White Paper. It also includes various sections devoted to adult education, compensatory education and the teaching of art and music.

THE CHURCH VIEW OF LOGSE

The position of the Catholic Church with respect to LOGSE follows the same practical and theoretical lines to which we have referred throughout this brief historical account, reflecting its traditional ideology of education and teaching. This position is maintained by the Church both through the ecclesiastical hierarchy and through the institutions directly linked to education (the General Council of Catholic Education, the Spanish Federation of Religious Order Schools, the Catholic Confederation of Pupils' Parents) with multiple and varied shades of argument; all, however, always centred on the demand for freedom to establish and manage schools with their own identity and on the right to have religion taught in all schools where Catholic pupils attend.

The debate between State and Church throughout the reform process has certainly been intense, although there appeared to be a convergence of interest between both parties on the need for reform to improve the democratization of education and the quality of teaching.

The main points of disagreement centre on these three arguments:

1 Holistic education (including spiritual values);
2 Freedom in education; and
3 Religious teaching in schools.

The Church considers that LOGSE does not deal adequately with these three fundamental points.

1 The Act considers that education should be inspired by the values of the Constitution and by respect for human rights, but it should also base itself explicitly on transcendental human values.
2 The Act assumes that there is freedom of education, regulated by LODE, but it does not envisage total freedom for infant education [i.e. there is no provision for direct grants to private providers for this age group (eds)], so that the principle of freedom at this level of education is compromised: warning is given of the difficulty of achieving economic viability for schools established by private initiative at this level.
3 Although the Act formally acknowledges the Agreements on education between the State and the Holy See, recalling that it is compulsory for schools to offer classes of religion, attendance at which is voluntary for pupils, there is no requirement that ethics should form a compulsory alternative for those who do not choose religion.

The first collective reaction against the reform within the Church appeared in the Study Sessions of 28 and 29 December 1987, organized by the General Council of Catholic Education. These argued the 'need for an integrated education and a balance between an education in values, a humanistic formation and a technical preparation'. There was a demand for 'true freedom' in education, which should be free from infant education up to 18 years. It was stated that religious teaching should form an integral part of the subjects within the common curriculum and an alternative subject should be offered. It was demanded that the State should not dictate infant education and that the necessary resources should be provided to permit existing schools to be adapted to the requirements of the reform (MEC, 1987).

The Episcopal Education Commission had already warned on 30 March 1987 of an ethical and moral vacuum and a deficiency in the conceptualization of man and society.

The Plenary Assembly of the Episcopal Conference of 18 April 1988 continued to denounce the hidden laicism of the proposed bill. By consensus it denounced the failure of the State to use the educational system to impose a concept of humanity or a system of values on society. The State's obligation was to guarantee parents the possibility of educating their children in accordance with their ethical and religious convictions. This right demands a plurality of schools.

Again, the Plenary Assembly of the Spanish Episcopal Conference on 10 April 1989 insisted, with regard to educational reform, that religious–moral formation should occupy an area of its own within the new school system, on equal grounds with other areas. This would also involve the offer of alternatives for those pupils who did not wish to receive a specific religious formation.

Once the White Paper on the reform was published, the General Council of Catholic Education pointed out that, although religious teaching appears to be included in primary and secondary education, there is still no alternative offered to religion. Infant education is not going to be free nor are the modules of vocational education at level 3, resources for the adaptation of private schools are nor guaranteed, not is there a proportionate share-out of resources for in-service training of teachers.

In their document *Catholics and Education in Spain* (CGEC, 1989), both the Episcopal Education Commission and the General Council of Catholic Education once more expressed their disagreement with the legal, ideological, economic and moral treatment of the reform which failed to resolve in a satisfactory manner, from their point of view, the problem of education in Spain. They expressed a preference for an education pact similar to that established in Belgium, a country which possesses a similar religious structure to that of Spain.

When, in February 1990, the Ministry of Education and Science sent the bill of LOGSE to all relevant social agencies, including the Church, once again the Spanish Episcopal Conference thundered its negative judgement of the excessively technical and pragmatic mentality of the reform bill, which does not take into account the transcendent and moral dimension of the person and relegates the teaching of religion in schools to a peripheral clause, with a mere mention of the Agreements with the

Holy See, while diminishing the principle of freedom of education, which demands that it be possible to establish schools and to choose any type of education without discrimination. The bill not only creates difficulties for the setting up of new schools but also for the maintenance of those existing voluntary schools.

The General Assembly of the Spanish Federation of Religious Schools, to which most church schools belong, in March 1990 expressed an identical view, affirming the diminution in the concept of humanity, claiming discrimination in infant education on the grounds that the offer of such education would not necessarily be free, and protesting the restriction of voluntary schools in the new secondary sector, the denial of grants for additional years, the lack of subsidies for the adaptation of schools and the lack of guarantees for provision of in-service training to private school teachers (CGEC, 1989).

On 17 May 1990 the Permanent Commission of the Episcopal Conference, in special session devoted to the study of the educational situation, recognized that LOGSE had introduced improvements in the recognition of moral values, but had not set up the means to put into effect this recognition. The bill continued to make difficulties for the setting up and continuity of voluntary schools. They expressed the fear that 400,000 Catholic school places might be lost with the implementation of LOGSE.

On 24 May the Spanish Episcopal Conference, the General Council of Catholic Education in collaboration with the Spanish Federation of Religious Schools, published some observations and proposals for modification of the LOGSE bill, reaffirming these frequently reiterated positions.

LOGSE was passed on 3 October 1990, although one cannot say that opposition and struggle for power in education between Church and State have terminated; rather it can be said that a genuine dialogue between the two institutions has not occurred; in fact, each has turned a deaf ear to the other's arguments, and the old ideologies and concepts of education remain latent.

Even before LOGSE was put into effect, the Spanish Federation of Religious Schools did not hesitate to sustain its protests:

> The Minister of Education has tried to present the new Act as being the fruit of a wide political and social consensus, but in reality LOGSE has been passed with most of the opposition voting against it, in face of the criticisms of the church hierarchy and of the majority of educational associations of the Catholic Church ... LOGSE is not, therefore, an Act of consensus, but rather an Act which has been imposed with very little support and which does not reconcile the Spanish people on a matter of such importance for the future of our country, namely education. Once more a historic opportunity has been lost. They persist

in considering that LOGSE imposes restrictions on the freedom of education, bordering on the unconstitutional and creating serious problems for the voluntary schools. In spite of everything, FERE states the Catholic schools are preparing themselves so as to take full advantage of the Act. The curricular plans make assumptions about the separation of Church and State. They are no longer inspired by a Catholic concept of life, as was the General Education Act of 1970, but rather they mainly follow a neutral line, when it is not actually contrary to that concept. Consequently Catholic schools will be obliged to take into account the values of their own Christian educational mission in drawing up curriculum plans for each school. In this way LOGSE offers Catholic schools the great opportunity of underlining their special identity and contribution to national education. . . . The restrictions imposed on the freedom of education and the difficulties created for religious and moral education of the pupils of state schools may also be an occasion for Catholics to rethink their strategy of involvement in schools.

(FERE, 1990)

More recently FERE has maintained its resistance to the development of the Act. Referring to the new pupil ratio, in their journal *Educadores* of January–March 1992, they state:

The constant harassing by the Socialist Administration of private schools, especially confessional ones, is attempting a new victory in its ambition to reduce to a minimum the expression of Christian values in Spanish society by imposition of lay values. For this they use power and coercion, rather than the force of reason or conviction. FERE predicts that by the end of the period of implementation of LOGSE, Catholic schools will have lost 275,000 pupils, 15 per cent of their present numbers, not as a consequence of the decline of the birth rate nor of the lack of confidence of Spanish families, but because of the impositions of the Socialist Government. Through subtle undermining of the right to education, of parental freedom to opt for the education and school of choice for their children, the Socialist Government goes against the Spanish Constitution and against the principles of freedom of education, clearly declaimed in the LUSTER Resolution of the European Parliament, passed on the 14th March, 1984. We have not provoked the education battle. The Socialist Administration has provoked it by apparently choosing to ignore what the Spanish Constitution recognizes: freedom in education, a subject still pending in Spanish democracy, although it is the basis of many other freedoms.

(FERE, 1992, p. 599)

THE TEACHING OF RELIGION IN SCHOOLS

One of the central claims, and one which is most controversial for the Church in the reform process, is the teaching of religion in schools. It is taken for granted, as a natural and unquestionable fact, that religion is taught in those private schools promoted or managed by the Church itself. Taking into account the different official curricular frameworks, responsibility for how and when religion is taught is practically left open for each school to do as it pleases. But the struggle about the teaching of religion in public schools has been virulent.

The position and guidance offered to teachers by the Catholic hierarchy for religious teaching in schools has oscillated between two options: (a) formative catechism-type instruction; (b) educative and cultural teaching.

The Agreement between the Holy See and the Spanish State of 1979, as well as the Document of the Episcopal Education and Catechism Commission of June 1970, consider that religious teaching should be integrated, as a right deriving from the individual's freedom of conscience and the recognition of the value of a religious culture as forming part of society's historical–cultural heritage. As a result, the teaching of religion should be incorporated into the model of the whole curriculum, as a theme which will inform the whole curriculum across curricular areas, and as one more subject, common to all pupils.

This was the model which the Episcopal Education Commission presented to the Ministry of Education in February 1989. On the other hand, the Ministry proposed an extracurricular model, which, essentially, stated the advisability of instituting schooling as a socializing and homogenizing agency, rather than as the defender of particular interests, one of which is religion. Religion should not form part of the core curriculum because there are matters which do not form part of the common heritage of the Spanish people (Solana, 1990).

This is the model which is expressed in LOGSE. An alternative to religion is not offered, only a study period. The model respects the letter both of the Constitution and of the Agreements with the Holy See, and the international treaties and pacts, but does raise questions as to its implications; and in any case, does not satisfy the hierarchy of the Spanish Catholic Church, which feels that Catholicism has a public and general presence in Spanish society.

The Catholic hierarchy continues to argue about the demand for religious education, based on a view of religion as an integral cultural aspect of the full development of the human personality and on the respect for beliefs and convictions of pupils and their families. It considers the teaching of religion not as a response to an individual's exercise of a subjective right that is the property of each pupil, but as a compulsory provision which the school should undertake, giving pupils diverse and optional ways of exercising that right, always respecting the freedom of conscience and of expression (EDICE, 1980). Confessional religious culture is considered by the Spanish bishops as a form of teaching which contributes to the character of secular culture, and fits into the characteristics of a modern, pluralist society. They opt, therefore, for the inclusion of religious teaching within the general curricular framework; and within this framework the teacher of religion should operate to the same criteria as other teachers.

EDITORS' POSTSCRIPT

In 1994 a judgment of the Constitutional Tribunal declared null certain clauses in the *enseñanzas minimas* (conditions governing basic educational provision) allowing for additional tuition in other curriculum subjects for students who opt out of religious education classes, on the grounds that this would constitute a privilege that would favour the academic records of pupils opting out. The MEC has subsequently proposed that schools should offer alternative classes of similar duration only in subjects that are not included in the *enseñanzas minimas*. The Spanish bishops are still opposed to such measures. They would like alternatives such as ethics or religious culture.

REFERENCES

Concilio Vaticano II (1965) *Declaración 'Gravisimum educationis'*. 28 October, Madrid: BAC.

Consejo General de la Enseñanza Católica (CGEC) (1989) *Los catolicos y la Educación en España, Hoy*. Madrid: CGEC.

Corral, C. (1980) *Los acuerdos entre la Iglesia y el Estado en España*, Madrid: Editorial Católico.

EDICE (1980) Documentos del Episcopado Español (1979) *Orientaciones pastorales sobre la enseñanza religiosa*. Madrid: EDICE, June.

Federación Española de Religiosos de la Enseñanza (FERE) (1985) Sentencia del Tribunal Constitucional sobre la LODE, in *Educadores*, no. 153, January.

Federación Española de Religiosos de la Enseñanza (FERE) (1990) Declaración final de la Asamblea General de la FERE, *Educadores*, no. 156, April–June.

Federación Española de Religiosos de la Enseñanza (FERE) (1990) Indiferencia e inquietudes ante la entrada en vigor de la LOGSE, *Educadores*, no. 158, October–November.

Federación Española de Religiosos de la Enseñanza (FERE) (1992) 'La nueva ratio' y la libertad de Educación, *Educadores*, no. 161, January–March.

Gil De Zarate, A. (1992) De la instrucción pública en España, Madrid, 1855, in M. de Puelles (ed.) *Educación a ideología en la España contemporanea*. Barcelona: Labor.

Maravall, J. M. (1984) *La reforma de la enseñanza*. Barcelona: Laia.

MEC (1987) *Proyecto para la reforma de la enseñanza: educación infantil, primaría, secundaria y profesional. Propuesta para debate*. Madrid: Centro de Publicaciones, MEC.

Pio XI (1929) Enciclica *Divini Illius Magister*.

Solana J. (1990) *Rueda de prensa de 30 Marzo, 1990, Ideal*, 31 June.

17 Education and the languages of Spain

Oliver Boyd-Barrett

A distinguishing feature of Spain's democratic emergence from Franco's forty-year period of dictatorship has been the restoration of community political and cultural structures. The country is now divided into seventeen autonomous communities, each with its own community parliament. There are still (1994) significant differences between these communities in the extent to which powers have been transferred to the various community administrations from Madrid. The language issue in Spanish education reflects both the aspirations of community governments to establish and further promote the use of Spanish languages other than castellano *and the response of successive central governments to the issue of regionalism through enabling legislation and regulation. This chapter attempts to locate the language issue within the historical and political contexts of regionalism, trace the main characteristics of plurilingualism in contemporary Spain, identify the major phases in the development of community policies for bilingualism through education, examine the principal models of provision for bilingualism that have been established, and review a range of issues to which they give rise.*

REGIONALISM

The forty-year period of Franco's dictatorship, especially in its earlier years, was one of centrist consolidation, the reformulation of Spain as one indivisible, unified nation in which all but the most politically neutral symptoms of regionalism were ruthlessly suppressed and deprived of legitimacy, and in which there was only one official language, *castellano* or simply Spanish as the term is commonly understood. This process extended even to the redefinition of national geographical and cultural divisions of long standing, so as to exclude politically sensitive appellations from the map of Spain. The predictable result was a smouldering resentment that was easily fanned into flame upon first light of democracy by hitherto clandestine or simply dormant regionalist parties or community branches of national parties (although tentative moves in a more liberal direction had already occurred well before Franco's death).

Resolution of the language question in education has been a salient issue in the process of regionalization for those communities where there are substantial numbers of people who speak languages other than *castellano*. This process has been construed by its proponents as politically liberating for community cultures and educationally liberating for children whose mother tongue is the community language. It has also been in some senses a burden: for some of those children who live in or have moved to these regions but whose mother tongue is *castellano*; for teachers required to master the language of the region in which they work; for the educational administrations that have had to provide for bilingual pathways through a curriculum which is itself in the process of reform.

The political impulse to regionalism and to the maintenance or even the resurrection of community languages (and their elevation to co-official status) is premised on two related aspects of a regionalist reading of Spanish history: that Spain has never truly been an undivided, monolithic nation and, secondly, that the Francoist imposition of *castellano* as the sole officially recognized language of the nation was a violation of historical reality and of the self-esteem of large constituent populations.

A PLURILINGUAL STATE

Gispert and Prats (1978) speak of four major ethnolinguistic groups: *galaicó* or *gallego* (spoken mainly in Galicia in the north-west, but extending into Portugal), *castellano* (more commonly called español, 'Spanish', not only by non-Spaniards but also by most Spaniards in *castellano*-speaking regions), *euskaldun* (also often referred to as *euskera* or *vascuence*, in the Basque provinces) and *catalán* (in the regions of Cataluña, Valencia and the Islas Baleares, and extending into France). *Castellano*, *galaicó* and *catalán* all have Latin roots, while the origins of *euskaldun* are unknown.

In 1970, according to estimates quoted by Gispert and Prats (1978), more than 25 per cent of the total Spanish population covering 40 per cent of the territory spoke maternal languages other than *castellano*. Of the nine million non-*castellano* speakers, six million spoke *catalán*, two and a half million spoke *galaicó*, half a million spoke *euskaldun* and several thousand spoke dialects of *aranés* (in the province of Aragón) and *portugúes* (close to the borders of Portugal and among immigrant workers from Portugal), with possibly as many as 800,000 speaking *asturiano* (spoken in Asturias). These broad estimates disguise important complexities. They are also out of date: the political climate has since become considerably more favourable for community languages, and the figures pre-date the process of 'linguistic normalization', which includes the teaching of community languages in schools, teaching through the community languages and the adoption of community languages as the languages of educational administration.

Gregorio Salvador (1987), Professor of Spanish Language at the University of Complutense, Madrid, argues that there are eleven languages in Spain. These are *español (castellano)*, *gallego*, *vizcaíno*, *guipuzcoana*, *alto navarro meridional*, *bajo navarro occidental*, *bajo navarro oriental*, *alto navarro septentrional*, *labordano*, *aranés* and *catalán*. Of Salvador's eleven languages it is notable that seven are basque languages (he believes there are 25 *euskera* varieties altogether). Equally noteworthy is the exclusion from his list of varieties of *castellano* or *catalán* such as *valenciano*, *andaluz*, *asturiano (o babel)*, *astur-leonés*, *castúo*, *portugúes*, *aragónes*, *panocho*, *mallorquín* and *ibizenco*.

FEATURES OF A PLURILINGUAL SOCIETY

Castellano dominance

Spain is clearly a plurilingual state, even if the nature of the divisions between its languages are in dispute. The pattern of language variation has been determined by patterns of invasion (especially the invasion and occupation by the Romans), political struggle (e.g. the conquest of Valencia by Cataluña) and the mobility of peoples (Siguan, 1988). Nevertheless, for the majority of Spaniards *castellano* is the mother tongue and the sole language of use, and *castellano* is the language of Spain widely regarded as the one with the greatest political and economic weight.

Variations between and within regions in use of community languages

Within those communities which have two official languages, there are many citizens who cannot or do not speak or understand the community language, and the proportions vary between one community and another. Siguan (1988) reports that *catalán* is mother tongue for some 50 per cent of the six million population of Cataluña, and that another 30 per cent speak or at least understand it. A 1987 survey (*El País*, 17 September 1987) found that just fewer than 10 per cent of persons resident in Cataluña still did not understand *catalán*: 64 per cent could speak it, 60 per cent could read it and 31 per cent could write it. There were still some areas, however, where *catalán* was spoken only by small minorities of local communities. In Santa Coloma de Gramanet, for example, 28 per cent spoke *catalán*, 28 per cent could read it and only 9 per cent could write it. In some parts of the metropolitan area as many as 80 per cent still speak *castellano*.

In Valencia and the Islas Baleares between 50 and 70 per cent of the population can be considered to speak *catalán* (sic) as their native language (Siguan, 1988), although it is usually restricted to family use. *Valen-*

ciano speakers accounted for more than 50 per cent of the population in 18 of the 22 districts of Castellon (one of the three provinces that make up the autonomous community of Valencia) in 1983–4; more than 50 per cent in eleven districts of the province of Valencia; and in Alicante province, *valenciano* speakers accounted for more than 50 per cent in ninety-six districts (*Consellería de Cultura, Educació I Ciencia*, 1984).

In Galicia, of the three million population some 80–90 per cent speak or understand *gallego*, though it is used predominantly in rural and family settings (91 per cent understand it, 84 per cent can speak it, 47 per cent can read it and 33 per cent can write it – *El País*, 20 October 1993). Only 25 per cent of the two million inhabitants of the País Vasco speak *euskera*, and as little as 10 per cent of the neighbouring community of Navarra, population 450,000.

A 1981 municipal census covering the provinces of Vizcaya, Guipuzcoa and Alava of País Vasco estimated variations in understanding of *euskera* from 13 per cent in Alava to 57 per cent in Guipuzcoa, from 11 to 53 per cent in the proportion who could speak it, and from 9 to 39 per cent in the proportion who could write it (Vila, 1986). The same source refers to a 1984 Navarra poll which found only 7 per cent of the population speaking *euskera* and 16 per cent who could understand it (although a 1977 poll indicated sharp variations between low *euskera*-speaking numbers for Pamplona and relatively high numbers – up to 63 per cent – of school children in some other areas). Vila concluded that in the País Vasco *euskera* was relatively stable, while in Navarra it was declining. Siguan (1988) is more optimistic, arguing that within a few years nearly 40 per cent of the País Vasco population will be able to speak *euskera* habitually and a further 30 per cent will have some understanding.

Political and social support for community language policies

Despite substantial numbers who do not themselves speak the community languages, there is widespread support for policies of bilingualism in these areas, although there have been and continue to be pockets of sometimes fierce opposition to certain aspects of the process of 'normalization' of community languages, and in particular to measures involving education *through* rather than simply *in* the community language.

The prevalent tolerance is enshrined nationally by the Constitution, by the national decree on bilingualism of 1979 and by subsequent recommendations of the Ministry of Education and Science (1981) which provide the basic model for the implementation of bilingualism in educational contexts.

The 1978 Spanish Constitution refers to the 'national' character of the Spanish state. Article three (clause 1) declares that *castellano* is the official Spanish language 'of the State', and that all Spaniards have the duty to know it and the right to use it. The other Spanish languages are also official in their respective autonomous communities (clause 2). This measure goes some way in itself towards meeting the promise of clause 3 – that the distinct language traditions of Spain represent a cultural heritage which will be the object of special respect and protection.

The principles of the Constitution are given effect by the statutes of autonomy which govern the transfer of powers from central government to the autonomous communities. There were eight communities in 1988 whose statutes referred to languages other than *castellano*. These were Asturias, Aragón, Cataluña, Comunidad Valenciana, País Vasco, Galicia, Islas Baleares and Navarra. In most cases the statutes refer to the right but not the duty to know and use the community co-official language, and they seek to promote its normal and social use.

The 1978 Constitution does not expressly allow for teaching *in* the community languages, but it is generally understood that this is implied (cf. Bosch and Diaz, 1988). These matters are addressed through community laws of 'linguistic normalization'. In Cataluña the law of linguistic normalization makes provision for the progressive use of *catalán* in all levels, grades and courses, to make *catalán* the 'normal vehicle of expression, both in internal activities, including those of an administrative nature, and in external ones' (Webber and Strubell i Trueta, 1991). Catalonia in particular demonstrates the potential contradiction between the drive towards establishing the language of the community as a 'vehicle of teaching' and the constitutional commitment to co-officiality of languages.

Despite the large number of non-*euskera* speakers in the País Vasco discussed by Vila (1986), this source contends that 'the greater part of the population wants a society in which the basque language would hold a place of some importance'. The place of *euskera* in schooling has a strong champion in the *ikastolas*, private schools established specifically to promote and protect the use of *euskera*. In the neighbouring province of Navarra, where *euskera* is much less widespread, 93 per cent of parents of state school children in Pamplona, the capital, wanted *euskera* to be a subject in the school curriculum even though fewer than one in ten of the population spoke the language.

In Cataluña, a high proportion (up to 50 per cent in the early 1980s) of the population is formed by immigrants from less industrial and less prosperous parts of Spain, who moved there during the 1960s and 1970s, and whose mother tongue is *castellano* (Siguan, 1984). *Castellano* may still have the 'greatest political and economic power' and the highest visibility in the media, but *catalán* is the mother tongue of the socio-economic élite, a mark of resistance to Madrid centralism and a badge of upward mobility for many immigrants.

In Galicia, the majority of the population understand *gallego* without difficulty but there has been a decline in its use, especially among the young (CE, 6 December 1989, *El País*, 20 October 1993). A report of the *Real Academia Gallega* indicated an 'alarming reduction' in the use of *gallego* and complained of weak enforcement of the Law of Normaliz- ation (CE, 9 November 1994). But some 55 per cent of the adult popu- lation supported the progress of '*galleguizacion*' in schools, while 45 per cent were opposed. There was stronger support for a mixed system of education which used both *gallego* and *castellano* in teaching than for a system of primarily *castellano* or primarily *gallego* instruction (CE, 11 October 1989). All political parties supported the 1983 *Ley de Normaliza- ción Lingüistica*.

Support for bilingualist provisions is sustained by folk memories of Francoist language repression. In Valencia, a 1984 community planning paper (Consellería de Cultura, Educación I Cienca, 1984), which talked of '*La Escuela Valenciana*' as the primary objective with instruction of children in their maternal language, cited the previous exclusion of *valen- ciano* from schools as a cause of high failure rates. The report condemned the 'decades of marginalization, abandonment and persecution . . . humili- ating treatment' to which the community language had been subjected. Marginalization of *valenciano* had resulted in generations of people illiter- ate in their own language, 'establishing a systematic process of linguistic colonization in the school, much aggravated by the exclusive use of *castellano* in the social means of communication and the total absence of *valenciano* in the administration'. Students experienced an education that seemed disconnected from their interests and environment.

Progressive standardization

Catalán was completely standardized, thanks to a strong tradition of literary culture, well before the establishment of community autonomy (Siguan, 1988). Important varieties of *catalán* have been identified as separate community languages, as in the case of *valenciano* which them- selves have been subject to processes of standardization.

Euskera batua is the form of basque as standardized by the Academy of the basque language and which is taught in schools of the basque provinces, but Salvador (1987) derides it as a 'laboratory' language, one which is not understood by a great many basque-speakers. In the edu- cational context there is considerable convenience in having a standard- ized form for teaching, teacher training and school texts, especially for a relatively small population. The elevation to official status of several languages might also weaken the impression of cultural unity which helps to underwrite community autonomy and demands for further autonomy. *Euskera* does not have the same solidity of literary tradition and cultural institutionalization as *catalán* and use of the language itself is less wide- spread. The language has been less subject to modernization than *castel- lano* and borrows from *castellano* for many modern concepts. Its linguistic structure is also quite separate from *castellano*, whereas *catalán* can inter- weave more flexibly with *castellano*.

In Galicia, where *gallego* is widely spoken or understood, there has been less of a history of separatist sentiment, and there has not been as strong a literary tradition in *gallego*. The language has recently been standardized by the *Real Academia Gallega* and the *Instituto de la Lengua Gallega*, whose norms were adopted by the community parliament in 1983. These norms have not acquired full consensus in the practice of writers, linguists or teachers. There is a division between those who prefer the standardized version and those who prefer a version which is closer to Portuguese.

Status and use

The community languages relate in different ways to structures of social status. In this respect *catalán* is the best integrated because it is the language of the social élite. For immigrants, *catalán* can improve their chances of integration and help them to overcome social or occupational discrimination, directed not so much against *castellano* as such, but against *castellano* as a symbol of 'foreign' and in particular andalucian culture. Siguan (1988) refers to *catalán* as an example of 'reverse diglossia', where the (until recently) persecuted and marginalized language, *catalán*, actually enjoys higher status than the dominant national language, *castellano*. He considers that *castellano* still enjoys greater political, economic and media power. He notes that *catalán* and *castellano* are often used interchangeably. But whereas most *catalán* speakers are also competent *castellano* speakers, fewer than one-fifth of *castellano* speakers were fully competent in *catalán* in 1981–2 (Arnau and Boada, 1986).

A similar situation pertains in the Basque provinces where *euskera* enjoys a high political if not necessarily social status. Parents who supported the *ikastolas* in order for their children to acquire *euskera* had to pay for the privilege. But *euskera* is much less widely used than is the case with *catalán* in Cataluña, and is most common in rural domestic contexts. In other words, a situation of common diglossia pertains, as is the case in Galicia, Valencia and the Baleares.

STAGES OF IMPLEMENTATION

The different communities have followed a similar model in their implementation of policies for the promotion of community languages in education. The various overlapping stages may be summarized as (a) mobilization; (b) legislation; (c) language as subject; (d) language as vehicle. Only the fourth of these is subject to major controversy.

Mobilization

The process begins with consciousness-raising and the introduction of voluntary education programmes as part of a general campaign to revitalize the community culture. The process may pre-date democracy, either through clandestine activity or officially tolerated initiatives of private schools (Tusquets and Benavent, 1978) as in schools established by co-operatives of teachers and parents, sometimes with church blessing, which helped to nurture *euskera* and *catalán*.

Legislation

During this initial stage the community government begins to identify those districts which are predominantly *castellano*-speaking, those where the community language is in the ascendant and those which are mixed. This is accompanied by attempts to standardize the language where this has not already happened. Laws of 'linguistic normalization' establish norms for language use in the fields of state administration, education and culture.

Language as subject

Once legislation is in force, teaching of the community language becomes compulsory. All students are required to study it successfully as a subject in order to pass their basic education and to gain access to a community university. Such measures were introduced in the period 1978 to 1984 for the communities of Cataluña, País Vasco, Galicia and Valenciana.

Language as vehicle

There then follows a process of creating and extending opportunities in and through the community language, and its introduction as the language of use in educational administration and communication. The trend towards immersion programmes is, however, constrained. The Constitution enshrines the right of children to become competent in both the official language of the nation and the official language of their community; it gives parents the right to choose an education for their children; it offers protection against discrimination on the basis of language. Another important constraint has been the supply and commitment of teachers. There are differences between the communities in their commitment to parental choice with respect to language. Major areas of controversy and litigation appear to relate to provision or the lack of provision for a diversity of models for bilingualism; the imposition of the community language as the language of educational administration and teaching; and new linguistic qualifications required of teachers.

Opposition, where it occurs, is provoked not so much by a community government's commitment to community language as such, as by policies of positive discrimination in favour of the community language. This may be perceived as contrary to the constitutional guarantee of co-officiality of languages. Positive discrimination derives from the observation that while most speakers of community languages speak *castellano*, the reverse does not hold: speakers of *castellano* within the regions do not necessarily know the community language. Moreover, teaching of the community language only as a *subject* to *castellano*-speakers has generally proved ineffective in achieving linguistic competency in both languages.

Accompanying these various stages is an extension of provision of language training for teachers. Classes may be provided for teachers outside contract hours. Attendance may be voluntary for existing teachers, but for new candidates a qualification in the community language can be a requirement for employment within the region or within certain schools or districts within the region.

MODELS OF DIVERSITY

Valencia

In the Comunidad Valenciana a decree of the provisional government in 1982 had already established the obligation of teaching *valenciano* in the *valenciano*-speaking communities at pre-school, primary and secondary levels, and it authorized the progressive introduction of *valenciano* to *castellano*-speaking areas. The same decree established the academic qualifications which teachers must possess to be able to teach *valenciano*. Regulatory orders followed in February and July of 1983. That of July laid down the basic curricular structure for the teaching of *valenciano*, established the post of co-ordinator for the preparation and support of teachers of *valenciano* and regulated the creation of a department of *valenciano* in each centre. A 1983 circular suggested that *valenciano* should be obligatory for three hours each week at secondary level. The 1984 *Libro Blanco* talked of what was seen as the necessity to introduce *valenciano* to *castellano*-speaking areas, and to establish study pro-grammes for teaching in *valenciano* in *valenciano*-speaking areas.

In this, as in many other areas, the promises of the Valencianan *Libro Blanco* were quickly realized. Even as early as December 1985 a total of 600,000 students were studying *valenciano*, and 138 schools were teaching in *valenciano* to a total of 6,000 students, while a further 3,000 were being taught through *valenciano* in some but not in all subjects. During 1983–4, 12,613 teachers had taken classes in *valenciano* on a total of 553 courses (*Papers*, December 1985). By April 1987, 100 per cent of *valenciano*-speaking students and 58 per cent of *castellano*-speaking students studied *valenciano* (*Papers*, April 1987). The number of schools teaching in *valen-*

ciano, in whole or in part, had increased to 209 by 1989, affecting 34,000 students, roughly one in ten of the total number of students in EGB education (*Papers*, September 1989). These numbers are likely to increase as teaching through *valenciano* spreads to more schools, affecting more areas of the curriculum and more age-groups of children within schools.

By September 1987 the educational authority was ready to offer all parents the choice of having their children educated either in *valenciano* or in *castellano*, subject to the students' linguistic competence ('in order to guarantee the proper transmission of knowledge'). Where parents wish their child to be educated in an official language other than that currently provided at the school or planned for that child, they must write directly to the head within the first fortnight of the school year so that necessary steps can be taken. Although not all schools are likely to teach in both languages, all must teach both languages as subjects on the school curriculum. The administration attempted to require that all schools should teach at least one curriculum area through *valenciano*, namely *experiencias* (a type of integrated science), but this measure was revoked in 1987 in response to heated opposition. Schools may adopt the measure voluntarily where teachers and parents agree. In reviewing the legality of quasi-immersion programmes, the *Audiencia Territorial de Valencia* (community judicial body) endorsed by the *Tribunal Supreme* (National Constitutional Court) has concluded that it is legal for a school to teach only in *valenciano* (provided of course that *castellano* is taught as a subject).

The requirements to learn *valenciano* may be burdensome for children living in areas where *castellano* is the language of the majority, or for children who have moved into the region from other parts of Spain or from abroad. Community policy allows that children moving out of the community to another community or country need not suffer the indignity of a record of a negative grade in *valenciano* appearing in their academic report.

Galicia

In Galicia the 1983 Language Law recognized *gallego* as the official language of teaching and a compulsory subject. In September 1983 it was decreed that the same number of hours would be assigned to the study of *gallego* and to *castellano* as subjects. In August 1987 it was established that teaching would be in *gallego*, at the very least in the area of *sociales* (a mixture of history and geography) for the middle and upper cycles of EGB, and in at least two disciplines within BUP and FP.

This order provoked controversy (CE, 6 December 1989) when in November of the same year the Council of Ministers in Madrid submitted a requirement to the local administration for the modification of four articles of the said order, on the grounds that they were contrary to the principle of co-officiality in their designation of *gallego* as the appropriate language of educational administration and the language of normal expression in schools. The disputed order had been approved by the community government, then under the control of *Alianza Popular*, the leading opposition (conservative) party. Later, the community government changed complexion, being controlled by the socialists (PSOE) in alliance with two nationalist parties. This created the appropriate context for an understanding between central and community governments, both now socialist, and in March 1988 a new order was approved which upheld the previous order, albeit with some modifications. The extension of the use of *gallego* to areas of the curriculum other than the subject of *gallego* itself now became 'permanently unalterable'. Demonstrations organized by unions and movements of teaching reform and nationalist parties against the original obstruction by central government included an independent organization, *Associación Gallega por la Libertad del Idioma* (AGLI), which championed the right of parents to decide the language in which their children should be educated.

The *Dirección General de Política Lingüística*, a local government body set up by the 1983 law of normalization, has acknowledged the lack of reliable data on teaching in *gallego*. It is known that teaching of the community language is widespread, but as for its use in other areas or subjects, the data are partial and not published. Their estimations are that 60–75 per cent of EGB schools use *gallego* in the teaching of *sociales* and that 45–60 per cent of BUP institutes use *gallego* in at least two subjects other than *lengua gallega*.

These examples from Valencia and Galicia illustrate a number of interesting features: (a) considerable variation in approach to the development of community languages as vehicles for education; (b) tensions between what policy-makers expect to happen and what actually does happen; (c) involvement of the courts as arbiters in policy disputes; (d) significance of political balance between community and central governments.

The 1981 MEC guidelines have not been sufficient to allay controversy and anxiety. These guidelines recommended that both languages (*castellano* and community) should everywhere be used as media of instruction, that policy should allow for different patterns of provision for bilingualism, that there should be parental choice between the modes of provision, that education should be initiated in the child's mother tongue and that any EGB school should be prepared to admit children irrespective of their mother tongue.

Cataluña

Progress towards the re-establishment of *catalán* in education in Cataluña began at least as early as 1975, six years before full community autonomy, when a royal decree permitted the introduction into schools of 'native languages' on a voluntary basis for three hours a week. In that year, an office was established for this purpose within the community's department of education. A royal decree of 1978 made the teaching of *catalán* compulsory at all non-university levels. In 1978–9, 73 per cent of schools had introduced *catalán* as a subject, rising to 85 per cent by 1981 and nearly 100 per cent by 1985. The 1979 statute of autonomy stated that the community administration would 'guarantee the normal and official use of both languages'. Not until 1983 did the *Ley de Normalización Lingüistica* establish *catalán* as 'the language of instruction in Cataluña', although this has not meant in practice that all schools use *catalán* as the vehicle of instruction. Neither the availability of teachers nor the attitudes of parents have permitted it, although the government of Cataluña is committed to progressive generalization of *catalán*. It is the relative strength of the determination of the community government to achieve eventual generalization of *catalán* as the language of instruction that accounts for the increasing evidence of unrest among *castellano* speakers against this policy.

In Cataluña the government was faced initially with a population many of whom had immigrated to the region from other parts of Spain. This had implications also for the supply of teachers sufficiently qualified and confident in the use of *catalán* to teach the subject or teach through the language. In 1971–2, 40 per cent of teachers in Cataluña came from outside the region, and 52 per cent came from areas where no *catalán* was spoken. Of the non-natives, 63 per cent could understand *catalán* but did not speak it; 19 per cent neither understood nor spoke it.

The number of *catalán* speakers among teachers increased from 36 per cent to 41 per cent in the period 1978–81 alone, an intense time of activity in the promotion of awareness and use of *catalán*, in the period leading up to assumption of full community powers for education in 1981. Numbers of teachers taking courses in *catalán* provided by the community government increased from 7,700 to 18,600 in this time. This was achieved on a voluntary basis, involving the sacrifice by these teachers of two or three hours a day after normal class work. Very few teachers reported that they felt pressurized into taking these courses.

Such efforts notwithstanding, most teachers (73 per cent) still lacked qualifications in *catalán* and a high proportion had still not asked to be admitted to courses. Of those who had taken courses, '*Castilian*-speaking teachers do not come out with a good command of *Catalán*' (Arnau and Boada, 1986, p. 112). Since 1981, teachers from other areas of Spain seeking to acquire school posts in Cataluña have been obliged to obtain a qualification in *catalán* after the second year in post. This has tended to reduce the numbers of teachers looking for work in the region. By 1988, more than 10,000 of the 42,000 public sector teachers had taken *catalán* courses organized by the Department of Education or by the university institutes of education.

Policy in Cataluña in the late 1980s has been summarized (*Comunidad Escolar*, 5 May 1988) as follows: students have the right to start their education in their mother tongue; both *catalán* and *castellano* shall be taught in all classes and at all levels of education; in all classes and at all levels both *catalán* and *castellano* are to be used as media of instruction in at least one subject; students should have mastered both *catalán* and *castellano* by the time they have completed EGB; all teachers are required to know the two languages; teachers and students of higher education have the right to use either official language (almost half of all university courses are taught in *catalán*); the administration cannot separate students into different schools solely on the basis of their language.

Where *catalán* is taught primarily as a subject, it is timetabled for three to four hours a week from pre-school through to the end of EGB, with four hours of *catalán* language and literature in BUP (three hours in *catalán* language at COU), with two hours required in the FP curriculum. In addition, the teaching of social studies (*Sociales*) and general sciences (*naturales*) in EGB is required to be taught through *catalán* from the second or middle cycle. By 1987, over 3,000 schools, public and private, were teaching almost a million students through *catalán*. Some of these schools taught *catalán* at all levels, while others had a policy of progressive introduction of *catalán* from the first levels. A full immersion programme was offered by 613 EGB schools to 53,140 students. At secondary level, the incidence of teaching in *catalán* was less marked, although more *catalán* was used in BUP than in FP.

Schools in Cataluña may be distinguished between those whose teaching is mainly in *catalán*, those where teaching is mainly in *castellano* and those where teaching is in both languages (mixed). In '*catalán*' schools a minimum of three hours a week must still be dedicated to courses in *castellano* and literature. Siguan (1984) reports that in these schools, *catalán* is also the principal language for extra-curricular activities and educational administration. These schools were estimated to account for 15–20 per cent of the school population in 1982–3. Writing later, Siguan (1988) estimated that *catalán* schools taught 20–25 per cent of the school population in 1983–4, although no official data were available (but see next paragraph). In '*castellano*' schools, *catalán* is taught merely as a subject, and *castellano* is otherwise the language of instruction. Such schools accounted for 60–70 per cent of all pupils in the early 1980s. The remaining schools, in the 'mixed' category, fell between '*catalán*' and '*castellano*' schools. Siguan (1984) identified four different types of school in this category: those which aim to provide a truly bilingual education, dividing up the curriculum between *castellano* and *catalán* as the respective languages of instruction; those which are basically '*castellano*' schools, but which endeavour to provide a greater measure of teaching of and in *catalán* than is the norm for such schools; schools which are on their way to becoming '*catalán*' schools; and those schools in which it has proved impossible to reach consensus as to language policy, and whose day-to-day teaching reflects an uneasy but practical compromise.

Agell (1987) considers that since 1983 the schools of Cataluña have been converging towards a single type, where *catalán* will be the language of instruction at the lower level – for pupils of 5 to 8 years of age – and its use as a language of instruction at other levels will be stepped up and extended. To accomplish this aim, the department of education has extended provision of immersion programmes in areas where few children speak *catalán*. A report on the '*Programa de Inmersion al Catalán*' (CE, 7 March 1990) suggests that this development has been successful. Starting in 1984–5 with 408 state schools and affecting 30,000 children, it had grown to include 702 state schools catering for 70,000 children by 1989–90. This report noted that 41 per cent of all children in pre-school and initial EGB classes were now incorporated within the immersion programme, and that if children learning through *catalán* outside the immersion programme were included, the proportion rose to 70 per cent of all teaching at these early levels.

INSET provision for teachers prior to their involvement in immersion programmes typically involves an intensive half-day meeting with community advisers some days before the start of the school year. Teachers also receive printed support materials and during the school year they attend regular meetings with advisers. Schools offering immersion programmes benefit from the assistance of support teachers (of whom there are now a total of 1,117): each immersion class can expect to receive up to five or six hours a week of such additional teaching support. There are also eighty-five peripatetic 'conversation assistants' and seventy specialist community advisers.

The language policy adopted by any particular school is determined by the school's governing body (*consejo escolar*) in consultation with the teachers' body (*claustro*) and parents, with the approval of the administration. Arnua and Boada (1986) note that schools generally choose a single teaching model regardless of the language used by children at home. Teachers prefer not to divide children by language group when they start school, and most *castellano*-speaking parents of children attending *catalán* schools do not actually assert their right to have the children educated in their mother tongue to begin with, provided that the pedagogical programme is coherent and cohesive. The 1990 report (CE, 7 March 1990) notes that many such parents are andalucian in origin; they want their children to acquire *catalán* in order to avoid the discrimination which they, the parents, had experienced.

Nevertheless, there have been cases of parents resigning from governing bodies in protest against immersion policies. *Castellano*-speakers are especially sensitive to evidence that some *catalán* teachers hold a low opinion of *castellano* and of *castellano* (especially andalucian) culture, even though they are formally trained within the immersion programme to allow children to develop their understanding and use of *catalán* at their own pace. Problems of cultural tension may essentially reflect problems of social class. They can be exacerbated by lack of choice: in the city of Tarrassa, there is now only one (1990) state school which does not practise an immersion programme.

In 1993, a group claiming membership of 4,000 parents in Tarragona, *La Coordinadora de Afectados por La Defensa de la Lengua*, was established to denounce the directors of five colleges of Tarragona and two of Barcelona whom they accused of not respecting the right to education recognized in the Constitution, and of having suppressed the lines of teaching in *castellano* in those schools (CE, 6 October 1993). The group wanted to see the maintenance of two separate language routes, and they opposed the system of immersion: they proposed that children should be taught in *castellano* up to the second cycle of EGB and that from the third cycle all subjects should be taught in *castellano*, except classes in *catalán*.

The Counsellor for Education in Catalonia, Joan María Pujals, commented that while parents were entitled to receive primary teaching in the maternal language, this did not necessarily mean in separate classes – in other words, that schools did not have to provide linguistically distinct lines of study. Schools can decide how many subjects they wish to teach in either language, but they must make it possible for children to acquire competence in the two official languages. At infant level, and in the first cycle of primary education, children have the right, said Pujals, to be taught in their maternal language, but they must have sufficient exposure to both languages in order to be able to learn through either language by the second cycle. He reminded his audience that numerous studies had shown that *castellano*-speaking children only achieve stable competence in *catalán* if they have been subjected to immersion, while immersion does not impair either their learning of *castellano* or the learning of *castellano* by *catalán*-speakers. The decision on how to deal with *castellano* is a matter for the school governors but the Department of Education signals that 'normally, *catalán* will be the language of teaching' which does not mean, says Pujals, that it is exclusive, or obligatory, and does not affect the individual rights of students.

High teacher turnover, insufficient knowledge of *catalán* among teachers and lack of will on the part of *claustros* can bring about changes in school policy from one year to the next. Unions and teacher associations are seeking guarantees of continuity from the administration, together with safeguards against minority groups or individuals who wish to subvert collective decisions in favour of *catalán*ization.

The movement towards *catalán*ization, as we have seen, is regularly subject to litigation. Most judgements of the courts up to 1993 have upheld the view that the requirement that teachers should learn *catalán* is not a violation of any constitutional right, and that teaching through *catalán* in *catalán* schools is fully legal provided it does not prevent children acquiring their first teaching in their mother tongue where parents so wish. *Castellano*-speakers have sometimes secured judgements favourable to their interests from the *Audiencia de Barcelona* (Community Appeal Court), only to see these judgements overruled by the *Tribunal Supreme* (National Appeal Court).

The Tarragona case quoted above first went to the *Tribunal Superior de Justicia de Cataluña* (TSJC). Its first judgement, in December 1993, rejected the parents' argument that the children should be educated exclusively in *castellano* in separate classes; but it required the educational administration to provide individualized attention to children below the age of 7 whose parents wished them to be taught in *castellano*. The case was forwarded to the *Tribunal Supremo* which coincidentally had asked the *Tribunal Constitucional* to pronounce on the possible unconstitutionality of three articles of the *Ley de Normalización Lingüística de Cataluña*. These raise fundamental issues of potentially grave significance for the relationship between the autonomous community and the Central State Government (CE, 5 January 1994).

Article 14.2 of the law of linguistic normalization says that children have a right to receive education in their mother tongue, whether *catalán* or *castellano*. The *Tribunal Supremo* warns that this could be unconstitutional if interpreted to mean that they do not have the same right at later stages of education, which would be against articles 1, 9, 10, 15 and 27 of the Constitution.

Article 14.4 of the law says that all children of Cataluña, whatever their maternal language at the beginning of education, have to be able to use, normally and correctly, *catalán* and *castellano* by the end of their basic studies. The *Tribunal Supremo* warns that this would impose on children the duty (in addition to the right) of knowing an official language other than the language of the State, which would be contrary to article 3 of the Constitution.

Article 15 of the law says that a student of basic education cannot be deemed to have graduated if he or she has not acquired sufficient knowledge of both *catalán* and *castellano*. The *Tribunal Supremo* opines that this could be contrary to article 149.1 of the Constitution which protects against discrimination on account of language. The *Trubunal Supremo* also worries that article 20 may be questionable, as this requires that *catalán* should be 'the vehicle of normal expression', which would thus seem to relegate *castellano* to a secondary place (CE, 23 February 1994).

The chief prosecutor of the TSJC, on the other hand, expressed the view that there does not exist a single Spanish language, but several, and that *catalán*, like other community languages, is subject to special protection by the Constitution and that there is a right and duty to know it. The two languages, he claimed, should be taught equally and not separately. The Catalán Administration was justified in protecting *catalán* from the consequences of the historical impediments which it had suffered (presumably a defence of measures of 'positive discrimination'). But the same source also indicated that the administration, in the wake of the greater curriculum flexibility allowed by LOGSE, had failed to take precautions to guarantee that *castellano*-speakers would continue to be taught in their mother tongue where this was desired (CE, 2 March 1994).

Political sources within Cataluña have been quoted (CE, 2 March 1994) as saying that a judgement 'adverse' to *catalán* would call into question the viability of the Constitution. Indicating perhaps the extreme sensitivity of the issue, the President of the Constitutional Tribunal diplomatically offered an opinion that he did not think there existed a right of *not* knowing *catalán*. The Minister of Education considered that the rights of all citizens must be protected, including the rights of *castellano* speakers, but was not in favour of segregated education.

In December 1994 the *Tribunal Constitucional* upheld the existing language law of Cataluña. It judged that it is constitutional that catalán should be the vehicular language of education in Cataluña and its 'centre of gravity' within a bilingual model. The law does not exclude the employment of *castellano* as a teaching language. There is no right to opt for just one of the two co-official languages of Cataluña. The State and the autonomous community determine the application of the two co-official languages in education. The judgement does not define what must be the balance between the two languages provided that children are enabled to achieve competence in both.

País Vasco and Navarra

In the autonomous communities of País Vasco and Navarra, the three major different kinds of bilingual schooling that have emerged in Cataluña are formally recognized as different models of provision, but without the drive towards an eventual unitary model as exists in Cataluña. Recent regulations for Navarra (CE, 19 June 1988) formally distinguish between a *Zona Vascofona* (where there is a high proportion of *euskera* speakers), a *Zona Mixta* and a *Zona No Vascofona*.

Teaching of *euskera* is obligatory in *Zona Vascofona* save for temporary residents who (as in Cataluña) may apply for exemption. In this zone there are three different models for language teaching. (Identification of these models is taken from those provided throughout País Vasco.) In Model A, the school teaches *euskera* as a subject only, with *castellano* acting as the vehicle for teaching of other subjects. However, at the request of parents and students, and provided there is a sufficient minimum number of students, *euskera* can be used as the vehicle of instruction in a subject or subject area of the third or final cycle of EGB, and in one or two areas of BUP, COU or the first cycle of FP, subject to the permission of the administration, and taking into account the language capabilities of the students, the school's *plan del centro*, and available human and material resources. In Model B, the school teaches in *euskera* and *castellano* is a separate curriculum subject taught at all levels and as the language of instruction in one subject or area during the initial and middle cycles of EGB and in one or two areas of BUP, COU and the first cycle of FP. In Model C, finally, teaching is entirely in *euskera*, except that *castellano* must still be taught as a separate subject.

Whatever the model and its form of application, the administration guarantees the parents' right to elect for their children the education they think best. The Administration determines which model or models should be taught within a school in the light of parental requests as collated by school management. Where necessary, students are educated in the nearest alternative school available (with the support of grants for transport, meals or residence if appropriate). There must be a certain minimum number of students per model in any given school for that model to be considered viable. Once a model is established in a given school, its continuance is guaranteed up to the end of schooling for those students affected. Students must normally continue with the chosen model up to the end of their schooling.

In the *Zona Mixta*, *euskera* is taught as a subject only where sufficient numbers request it. But the option of teaching through *euskera* is also open where sufficient numbers request it. In the *Zona No Vascofona* the administration merely undertakes to provide appropriate facilities for the learning of *euskera* where this is requested by parents. In summary, the Government pursues a policy of obligation in the *Zona Vascofona*, at least with respect to *euskera* as a subject, a policy of voluntarism in the *Zona Mixta* and solely one of promotion in the *Zona No Vascofona*.

In Navarra as a whole only a small part of the population, up to 16 per cent (CE, 6 December 1989), speaks *euskera* and only in those areas where *euskera* is widely used is there much general sympathy for teaching in *euskera*. In País Vasco the number who speak *euskera* represents a larger part of the population (25 per cent) and the figure is thought to be increasing. Yet in 1983 only 11 per cent received a bilingual education or education primarily in *euskera*. Most (59 per cent) simply learnt the language as a school subject, while as many as a third (30 per cent) received no instruction in *euskera*.

Siguan (1988) quotes community statistics showing that among the school population, some 15 per cent speak *euskera* as their mother tongue, yet are taught primarily in *castellano*, 10 per cent speak *castellano* and are taught primarily or partly in *euskera*, 33 per cent speak *castellano* and are taught mainly in *castellano* with some *euskera* instruction and 30 per cent receive no systematic instruction in *euskera*. But more recent statistics (CE, 20 September 1989) show that by the 1988–9 school year, 31.4 per cent of students attended schools which taught primarily in *castellano*, 31.4 per cent went to schools teaching primarily in *euskera*, 36 per cent went to mixed schools and only 1 per cent received no instruction in *euskera*. This suggests there may have been significant progress during the 1980s in the provision of quasi-immersion or partial education in *euskera*. Progress in teacher training in País Vasco has been more challenging than in Cataluña, given that it is more difficult to train adults to competency in *euskera* than it is to train them to competency in *catalán*, as *catalán* and *castellano* share common Latin roots whereas *euskera* and *castellano* do not.

CURRICULUM AND PERFORMANCE

One consequence of provision for bilingualism is that a higher proportion of the curriculum is dedicated to language study than otherwise would be the case. Of the total number of teaching hours per week, namely 25 at EGB, in the *Zona Vascofona* of Navarra, for example, eight or 32 per cent are devoted to the '*area de lenguaje*' (regardless of which language is the vehicle of instruction) in the initial cycle, and nine or 36 per cent in the next two cycles. Of these hours, four must be devoted to *castellano* and four to *euskera*. There is an additional hour in the middle cycle to help reinforce learning in one of the two languages. In the third cycle, three hours each are reserved for *castellano*, *euskera* and a foreign modern European language. In the first cycle of BUP, four hours are devoted to *castellano* language and literature and four hours to *basque* language and literature, with three hours for a foreign modern European language. Maths and Natural Sciences, incidentally, get four hours apiece. In the second cycle of BUP, the time devoted to *castellano*, *euskera* and a foreign modern European language remains the same (eleven hours) with an additional three hours for Latin. Chemistry, Physics and Maths get three hours each. Thus 14 of the 29 hours or 48 per cent of the BUP timetable are dedicated at this level to the study of language and literature.

These calculations pre-date the process of curriculum reform represented by LOGSE, which will result in earlier introduction of a modern European language (from the age of 8), provision for the study of two modern European languages at secondary stage and greater flexibility for community and school-based modifications of the curriculum to take account of local needs. The process of reform highlights the issue of the availability of textbooks and general works of literature printed in the various community languages. Multilingualism increases production costs, reduces market-size for given texts and may increase cover charges. In Galicia there did not exist any reading books in *gallego* until the mid-1980s. *Gallego* had not been used as a literary language for several centuries, only as the language of peasants, and treated with indifference by the educated classes. Children who are taught through their community language may not receive much assistance from parents whose mother tongue had no official status under Franco, who possibly did not acquire literacy in either tongue or who in any case would not have had access to literature in their mother tongue. This consideration also needs to be contextualized with reference to relatively high rates of illiteracy (by northern European standards), especially among the older age groups. In Valencia, for example, 7 per cent of adults identify themselves as illiterate and a further 25 per cent as functionally illiterate, while a much larger proportion have been unable to reach the minimum standards of language proficiency that are necessary to pass through EGB (*Papers*, May 1985). Levels of reading of newspapers and books are significantly lower in Spain than in northern European countries.

Provision of teaching through a community language is of considerable significance, contributing to equal opportunity for those children for whom a community language is mother tongue, and thus accounting for a substantial proportion of the population. But there does not appear to be any firm evidence that bilingual education has actually contributed to greater overall academic success in the community. What evidence there is tends to address issues of language performance rather than general academic performance. The topic is under-researched and merits further research funding.

The issue of equal opportunity is complicated by the fact that some parents of children whose mother tongue is a community language prefer their children to be educated through *castellano* because they perceive *castellano* to be more useful to their child's future. In a situation of diglossia, in other words, teaching through community languages could conceivably limit career opportunities, even if it improved overall academic performance, in the absence of simultaneous reforms aimed at removing those features of language discrimination which had given rise to diglossia in the first place.

In Cataluña there is some evidence that '*catalán*' schools obtain very good results in both *catalán* and *castellano*, while '*castellano*' schools do not achieve satisfactory results among students whose mother tongue is *castellano*. Even *castellano* speakers in '*catalán*' schools achieve satisfactory levels of *catalán* and *castellano*, as do *catalán* speakers in '*castellano*' schools. But it is the *castellano*-speakers in '*castellano*' schools who do less well in acquiring catalán. They may come to understand written and spoken *catalán*, but are generally not able to use it actively, either orally or in writing (cf. Siguan, 1984 and 1988 for more detailed summaries of the relevant research).

Expert opinion on the benefits of *catalán* immersion programmes for *castellano*-speakers in Cataluña is divided. Critics of immersion programmes point out that in the years of the dictatorship, educators who wanted to be able to teach through *catalán* had stressed the negative effects for *catalán*-speakers of having to be educated through *castellano* from the moment they first went to school. Yet these same educators seem quite content today that *castellano*-speakers should be encouraged to submit their children to education solely through *catalán*. The response to this criticism is that whereas *castellano* was imposed inflexibly upon *catalán*-speakers, no child in the *catalán* immersion programme is forced to speak *catalán*. Teachers are told not to correct children who speak *castellano*. Their use of *catalán* is to emerge gradually, in imitation of the teacher's example. Furthermore it is alleged that children in the immersion programme whose mother tongue is *castellano* will learn to read first in *catalán*, but that this automatically gives them access to *castellano*, as it has all the phonemes of *castellano* whereas the reverse is not true.

There are many variables to take into account in assessing the academic implications of bilingual policies for education, including the language patterns that prevail in the area in which a given school is located, the numerical strength within the school of the different language communities, and the relative social status of the respective groups (in Cataluña the *castellano*-speakers often have lower status).

In País Vasco, the education department considers that where *euskera* is taught only as a subject, the results in *euskera* among students whose mother tongue is *castellano* are unsatisfactory. It has extended the use of *euskera* into physical education and art as a minimum basis for improvement (CE, 16 March 1988). It is these findings that have encouraged community administrations to promote the use of community languages as vehicles of instruction in one or two subjects even where teaching is predominantly in *castellano*. Most people who speak community languages also speak *castellano*, whereas those who live in these regions but whose mother tongue is *castellano* are much less likely to speak the community language. Schools which teach primarily through the community language but which are based in areas which are predominantly *castellano*-speaking may find that the language of the playground is still *castellano*. (Conversely, schools in areas in which the community language is predominant may find that the language of the playground is the community language even where teaching is primarily through *castellano*.) Such factors may support arguments for 'positive discrimination' even at the risk of seeming to sail close to the wind of constitutional provisions against language discrimination. A survey of teachers in País Vasco (Barquín and Barceló, 1994), however, found that many teachers, especially those teaching in *castellano*, considered the methods of '*euskaldunización*' ineffective. Eighty per cent of all teachers considered that the school alone could not recover the *basque* language as the language of normal use: 'The schools cannot compensate for all that the family cannot manage, society does not allow, the economy determines, and history has bequeathed' (Barquín and Barceló, 1994). But bilingualism was viewed positively.

REFERENCES

Periodicals

CE: *Comunidad Escolar* is a weekly newspaper published for the national educational community by the Ministry of Education and Science, Madrid.
El País is a national daily newspaper published in Madrid. There is an internal weekly supplement dedicated to education.
Papers is a monthly newspaper published for the educational community of the Comunidad Valenciana by the Consellería de Cultura, Educació I Ciencia of the Generalitat Valenciana.

Articles and books

Agell, J. G. (1987) Linguistic normalization of education in Catalonia, *Prospects*, vol. XV11, no. 2, pp. 297–330.

Arnau, J. and Boada, H. (1986) Languages and School in Catalonia, *Journal of Multilingual and Multicultural Development*, vol. 7, nos. 2 and 3, pp. 107–21.

Barquín, J. and Barceló, F. (1994) *El Profesorado de Euskadi. Estudio de sus planteamientos didácticos.* Bilbao: Departamento de Educación del Gobierno.

Bosch, F. and Díaz, J. (1988) La Educación en España. Una Perspectiva Económica. Barcelona: Editorial Ariel, SA.

Consellería de Cultura, Educació I Ciencia (1984) *Libro Blanco de la Educación en la Comunidad Valenciana.* Valencia: Generalitat.

Gispert, C. and Prats, M. (1978) *España: Un Estado Plurinacional.* Barcelona: Editorial Blume.

Salvador, G. (1987) *El Español y Las Lenguas de España.* Barcelona: Editorial Ariel, SA.

Siguan, M. (1984) Language and education in Catalonia, *Prospects*, vol. XIV, no. 1, pp. 107–19.

Siguan, M. (1988) Bilingual Education in Spain, in C. B. Paulston (ed.) *International Handbook of Bilingualism and Bilingual Education.* Westport, Connecticut: Greenwood Press, pp. 449–74.

Tusquets, J. and Benavent, J. (1978) Linguistic and Cultural Unity and Diversity in Spanish Education, *Compare*, vol. 8, no. 1, pp. 101–11.

Villa, I. (1986) Bilingual Education in the Basque Country, *Journal of Multilingual and Multicultural Development*, vol. 7, nos 2 and 3, pp. 123–45.

Webber, J. and Strubell i Trueta, M. (1991) *The Catalan Language. Progress Towards Normalization.* Exeter, UK: The Anglo-Catalan Society Occasional Publications, no. 7.

18 Vocational education in LOGSE: a new model for the future?*

Diego M. Justicia

This chapter assesses the extent to which LOGSE promises to transform provision for vocational education and training, and should be read in conjunction with Chapter 19 (Gil Padilla) which deals with the same subject but from a more critical perspective. Diego Justicia sketches the historical context, summarizes the major changes introduced by LOGSE and offers a tentative evaluation.

On 13 September 1990, Parliament approved LOGSE. This law attempts to correct the dual structure which currently exists at the end of EGB (primary education to age 14), namely BUP (*Bachillerato*) for those who pass their EGB, and FP (*formación profesional*, vocational education) mainly for those who do not.

In the preamble to LOGSE, it is stressed that the law 'undertakes a profound reform of FP'. It attempts to eliminate the dual structure of FP, to jettison the conception of FP as a second-class destination for the failures of compulsory education. Equally noteworthy, the design and structure of the new route to vocational education includes a 'phase of practical training in the work-place' and 'encouragement for the participation of social agencies'.

VOCATIONAL EDUCATION TODAY

In the 1970 law of education, FP is constructed in two levels: FP at Grade 1 and FP at Grade 2. The first grade continues for two years and can be taken upon completion of EGB and attainment either of *Graduado Escolar* (pass) or *Certificado de Escolaridad* (not passed). Successful completion of FP at Grade 1 leads to the qualification of *Técnico Auxiliar* and can be followed either by employment or by further study. FP at Grade 2 takes three years, and can be entered either after BUP or after FP at Grade 1. It leads to the title of *Técnico Especialista* and can be followed either by employment or by study at the level of the *Curso de*

---

* This chapter translated by Oliver Boyd-Barrett

Orientación Universitaria (COU: this is a one-year continuation of secondary schooling which normally follows the *Bachillerato* and precedes university entrance, but which is due to be phased out with the implementation of LOGSE), or university schools [i.e. colleges, including teacher training institutions, which give diplomas after three years (eds)], or by study for FP at Grade 3.

FP in its existing form, therefore, constitutes a distinctive route, quite separate from the academic line which leads from EGB to university by way of BUP and COU. By and large, those who pass EGB go on to take BUP, and the 'failures' proceed to FP.

VOCATIONAL EDUCATION FOR THE FUTURE

Legally, the new system of FP will comprise *FP Reglada* and *FP Ocupacional*. *FP Reglada* is to be managed by the Educational Administration and *FP Ocupacional* will be managed by the Labour Administration. The law requires mutual co-ordination between the two. In practice, it sanctions a separation of the two subsystems.

FP Reglada is geared to young people, and attends to their initial training, always within the framework and structure of the general educational system. *FP Ocupacional* is directed towards persons of working age, attending to their placement in, or adaptation to, the world of work, and embedded within the structure of employment policies.

FP Reglada

FP Reglada (under LOGSE) comprises the following levels: foundation level and specialized level. Specialized FP, in turn, is divided between medium and higher levels.

Foundation FP begins in compulsory secondary education. It is present across the compulsory 12–16 curriculum area of Technology. It also forms part of the *Bachillerato*, ages 16 to 18, throughout one of the four optional modules, also entitled Technology. The other three modules of the *Bachillerato* are Arts, Natural and Health Sciences, and Humanities and Social Sciences.

For young people who do not pass their compulsory secondary studies there will be specific 'social guarantee' programmes which will reintegrate basic training with vocational training, to prepare them for work or for continuation of study. All those who obtain the qualification of *Graduado en Educación Secundaria* can choose between continuing on to the *Bachillerato* or progressing to medium-level specialized training.

FP Específica

'Specialized training will comprise a group of training courses organized in modular fashion, of variable duration, constituted by areas of theoretical and practical knowledge relating to a variety of professional fields. The training will be organized into middle and higher levels' (article 30.4 of LOGSE). These are short training courses of modular duration of between 1,000 and 2,000 hours (one or two years). At medium level, modules lead to Level 2 qualifications (module 2) and at the higher level, modules lead to Level 3 qualifications (module 3) according to the nomenclature agreed by the Council of Europe, 16 July 1985. Level 2 modules require entry qualification of *Graduado en Educación Secundaria* or otherwise a special examination must be taken. On successful completion of this level, the certificate of *Técnico* is awarded. Entry to Level 3 modules requires attainment of the *Bachillerato* or otherwise a special examination must be passed, for entrants up to the age of 20 years. There exists no continuity or line of access from Level 2 modules to Level 3 modules.

The most significant feature of this new academic arrangement is the implantation of Foundation FP in secondary education, with the concomitant disappearance of the old duality between BUP and FP. Another significant feature is the conception of Specialized FP as a passage or gateway to the world of work. In the autonomous community of Madrid a series of Level 3 modules is being offered to COU students as part of the priority that is being given to reducing the overcrowding of Madrid's universities.

1 DISTINCTIVE FEATURES OF THE NEW FP

In addition to the new academic structure, LOGSE introduces two other new features. In the context of the design and planning of Specialized FP, there is the participation of social agencies (e.g. employers, trade unions). In the context of the development of the curriculum of Specialized FP, there is practical training in places of work.

The formula for the participation of social agencies in the text of LOGSE has the effect of sanctioning what has already been a fact since the signing of the Economic and Social Agreement of 1984 between Government, employers and workers. The fruit of that agreement was the creation of the General Council of FP, an institution created by law in 1986, on which are represented the Administration, workers and employers. Its functions are consultative and advisory, but also include the co-ordination and development of a National Plan of Vocational Education.

The other novelty is similar, coming as it does from the Programme for Sandwich Training, which was introduced in the year 1983–4 for the purpose of making work experience available for students of *FP Reglada*. The origin of this programme is the framework of agreement between the Ministry for Education and Science, the Ministry of Labour and the

Spanish Confederation of Enterprises in 1982, later ratified in the Economic and Social Agreement of 1984.

The whole system of training will be evaluated by the National Institute of Quality and Assessment (INCE), defined in article 62 of LOGSE.

In the process of consultation leading up to the drafting of LOGSE, the unions, with the support of *Izquierda Unida* (national left-wing political party), negotiated the introduction of an additional clause which committed the government to the development of a National Plan for the prediction of labour needs. This plan will include a programme of assessment of employment demand, and establish a permanent watchdog to monitor the development of occupational change. No interest is served by vocational education in the absence of adequate vocational training or, what is more important, an effective system of co-ordinating supply and demand in the labour market.

DEVELOPING LOGSE

In order to develop FP, which is dealt with only sketchily in LOGSE, the Ministry of Education and Science has developed a plan for the reform of FP. This reform plan has to address a complex territorial problem deriving from the division of Spain into autonomous regions. Currently (1992) there are seven autonomous regions which control education directly and the remaining regions depend upon the Ministry. The scope of the reform therefore varies from one region to another. Some autonomous communities must undertake their own development of FP, derived from LOGSE. This requires an articulation of the different plans for FP that have been developed in the various autonomous territories, and in order to bring about a co-ordination with *FP Ocupacional*, administered by the Ministry of Labour, the General Council of FP has to provide a national programme of FP.

The reform plan for FP

According to the new model of FP designed for LOGSE, the plan of reform for FP summarizes its action-objectives into three stages:

1 a single system of 'general' training and 'basic professional studies' taught in secondary school;
2 a specialized quality FP which offers preparation for vocational work, relevant to current conditions and to the future; and
3 an integrated system, with the participation of social agencies and responsive to demand for requalification of adult returners to work.

Developing the reform of FP: objectives and actions

With respect to the first objective, we have already described its reali-zation briefly, particularly the role of professional orientation, above all in the second cycle of compulsory secondary education and in the *Bachillerato*, encouraging students towards the work option most in accordance with their level of scholastic achievement.

We will look in more detail at what is happening in relation to the second objective. Two measures are already being put in place aimed at renewing the contents of *FP Específica*: the development of a new list of FP qualifications and the development of a system which guarantees the continuing adjustment of FP qualifications to occupational change.

Responsibility for the implementation of the plan for FP provision, adapted to its socio-economic environment, falls to the new provincial FP committees in the territory for which the Ministry is directly respons-ible, drawing upon representatives of workers, enterprises and adminis-trators both for education and for employment.

A curious feature of the creation of a system for the selection and training of teachers to deliver FP is that the minimum qualification for FP teachers is the same as that for secondary teachers, yet a further, additional *cuerpo* or guild has been established for the technical teachers of FP. Thus in the field of FP one encounters teachers of diverse statuses, even including 'specialist teachers' temporarily contracted from compan-ies. At the present time of budgetary constraint for the Ministry this new teaching force has been formed by the conversion of secondary school teachers and from teachers of the old FP, which means that the offer of new public jobs is rather scarce: 564 places for teachers of technology, out of a total of 5,000 places for secondary education, and only 200 places for technical teachers of FP, to cover a territory of 27 provinces (out of a total of 51) which represents 38.98 per cent of the total population of the country.

Measures for the updating of equipment and teaching material in FP colleges are likely to be deferred due to the economic recession and the extensive public deficit which challenges the current government. Systematic evaluation of the adaptation of training to the needs of employment and of quality implies a continuing improvement in the employment and professional development of FP graduates. Other mea-sures to improve quality include the provision of training in distance mode, provision of FP for students with special educational needs and the development of 'social guarantee' programmes.

As for the third objective, developmental measures include the intro-duction of collaborative training between colleges and places of work for training in places of work, in the manner described, which is considered to be a key feature of the new FP. The articulation of *FP Reglada* and *FP Ocupacional* to ensure that the new FP curriculum focuses on professional competence (activities and professional capacities relevant to each module) which can be 'capitalized' by each worker (young or adult) and which can be turned into varied training credits so as to qualify for the corresponding award. There is recognition of the professional qualifications whose awards, according to a CE (Community of Europe) directive, are:

- Diplomas (post-secondary training of less than three years' duration, like that of *Técnico Superior*);
- Certificates (secondary training equivalent to the higher *Bachillerato*) like the *Técnico*; and
- Certificates of *competency* (training of less than six months' duration) as in the case of those obtained in *FP Ocupacional*.

The plan for the reform of FP, as it says in its own summing up, is already a fact and has been piloted and put into practice over some years. LOGSE merely sanctioned something which was already a reality. None the less, the great handicap which impedes its general application and full development is the budgetary reduction which both the Ministry of Education and the Ministry of Labour have suffered as a result of the economic crisis and of the costs of adjustment to the requirements for a United Europe.

To the plan for the reform of FP must be added the respective plans of the autonomous communities of Andalucia, Canarias, Cataluña, Galicia, Navarra, País Vasco and Valencia, which have educational responsibility for the development of LOGSE up to this level. The reform will be truly completed upon co-ordination of the diverse reforms of the different communities into a national plan of FP.

Co-ordinating the reform FP

In June 1992 the General Council for FP debated the foundation for a national programme. In commenting on this provisional document one should observe that the 1986 law which created the General Council for FP gave this body a mandate for the development of just such a national plan. From 1986 to 1990, while the Ministry for Labour has worked on a plan for training and work placement, the Ministry for Education has developed LOGSE. In the wake of these initiatives there has at last appeared a new project for the co-ordination and integration of policies for FP that takes account of the needs of profit generation, employment, regional and local economic development, and the single European market.

THE NATIONAL PROGRAMME OF FP

This programme is regarded as flexible, adaptable to the two administrative subsystems (of labour and education), as well as to the different administrations which must manage it and the different autonomous communities with responsibility for education. It establishes priorities and a calendar of application, and creates the means and the organizational structures for its co-ordination and operation. As a corollary of this, it also provides for a restructuring of the representative composition of its own General Council of FP.

Developing the national programme of FP

The following objectives have been established for the reform of FP provision:

1 *Content*: updating; establishing an integrated and relevant system; the creation of a national system of qualifications and a catalogue of degrees and professional certificates.
2 *Planning*: identification of 'families' of similar professions; training courses, modules and work-place experience, calculated for each region by the *Comisiones Provinciales* (regional committees of the MEC), the *Observatorio Permanente de las Ocupaciones* (occupational review body) and the social agencies (e.g. unions, employers, etc.).
3 *Administration*: substitution of academic frameworks (geared towards acquisition of knowledge) by a structure of modules for the acquisition of competencies, with the objectives of capitalizing on and validating the acquired competencies, and opening up the educational system to the adult population.

In order to address the identification of demand, the following groups have been targeted: (a) people of school age and (b) the active population. To fulfil the commitment of LOGSE (eighteenth additional provision) to a 'Programme for the Calculation of Labour Demand', it is considered important to identify and classify total demand for employment. Finally, it is proposed that criteria for prioritization be set for attending to the various existing collectivities, and for establishing the annual quota of likely possible job offers.

Responsibilities for provision are allocated thus:

1 The educational administration will be responsible for *FP Reglada*, for young people and adults, and the programmes of 'social guarantee', i.e. the basic general training for those seeking their first job and for those already active (whether in or out of work).
2 The labour administration will be responsible for *FP Ocupacional* for the unemployed, those looking for first employment and those with special needs.

3 Quality control is addressed through teacher training, provision of equipment, professional/career orientation, system evaluation, research and innovation, by means of a network of centres for training, innovation and development of FP, and the establishment of centres for work experience.

4 Homogenization with European qualifications and the free mobility of workers, through the establishment of a uniform co-ordination of qualifications.

5 Continuing training of workers (there are more than nine million active, salaried employees): this depends on the outcome of an agreement with the large centralized unions, *Comisiones Obreras* and *Union General de Trabajadores*.

SUMMARY

1 The model that has been presented for the future is a development from the existing system, but with improvements that eliminate the old conception of FP as an inferior alternative to BUP, incorporating workplace training in its design, involving the participation of social agencies and establishing mechanisms of co-ordination, although the two subsystems of FP continue in existence: *FP Reglada* and *FP Ocupacional*.

2 Foundation or basic FP is absorbed within secondary education.

3 Specialized FP in modular form is more open. Adoption of this approach represents a rejection of the current educational system as too academic, too bureaucratic and excessively rigid. The modules are organized in such a way that they are an invitation to abandon the educational system, in order to reduce overcrowding of classes in institutes and universities. They offer an education less regulated, less formal and a little less diffuse.

4 The programmes of 'social guarantee' are a key to the resolution of the significant problem of scholastic failure in the educational system, which expels without certification more than a third of young people at the basic levels. Can there be more effective measures of prevention and optimization in order to avoid this failure before it actually occurs?

5 The notion of professional competence and its realization, at the heart of the modular design, is a significant advance on account of its flexibility.

6 The policies of co-ordination and adjustment to regional, economic and social development hold out considerable promise and raise expectations.

7 Transition programmes preparing 'social guarantee' students for their entry into the world of work are not clearly defined.

8 Continuous training (for nine million salaried employees) is more noted for its scarcity. Beyond *FP Reglada* (850,000 young people) and *FP*

Ocupacional (300,000 beneficiaries in 1990, from a collective total of 2.5 million unemployed), continuous training continues to be the great educational challenge.

9 Continuous, universal education for adults is conceived not only and principally as developing individual potential for productivity, but also as developing the social dimension – education for participation, for leisure, for retirement, etc. – from a perspective of change and of socio-cultural interaction with the environment in which we live, which is absent from the existing educational system.

Finally, a caution: is this model, which tries to adjust to the laws of supply and demand in the labour market, well designed for the purpose? It attempts to lift many workers to middle-range professional qualifications (second-level modules, programmes of social guarantee, occupational training), yet sociological analysis of the labour market of our country predicts the destruction of a large number of jobs at this level of qualification and an increase in jobs requiring higher-level qualifications, although in less measure than those at the lowest level of qualification, which are also increasing.

EDITORS' POSTSCRIPT

In 1994 the Government announced planned expenditure of 83,500 million pesetas (about £417 million) on FP over the period 1994–7, co-financed by the European Social Fund. This same year the Government approved the revised list of training qualifications, and anticipated further expansion in the light of the 'map of labour supply' still in the process of design. In the period 1994–7 it is anticipated that all teachers of the new professional courses will have had 200 hours of training, complementing existing in-service courses of 70 and 90 hours' duration, and that there will be training programmes launched by the new centres for FP training, innovation and development – of which it is planned there will be one for each professional 'family'. Numbers of places on 'social guarantee' programmes will increase from 4,000 to 15,000 in the same period. These are regarded as essential for the future of less academic pupils in the transition to the new system of compulsory secondary education (CE, 11 May 1994).

19 Training and employment*

Antonio José Gil Padilla

Gil Padilla's chapter combines strong approval for the theoretical directions established by LOGSE for vocational training with extreme scepticism about the ability of the Administration to achieve these in practice. Such scepticism finds more than an echo in a 1994 assessment by Julio Sanchez Fierro, Deputy President of the Escuela de Negocios. *He writes:*

> *For many years training has received insufficient attention in Spain, despite its strategic importance for companies, economic competitiveness and for society generally. Lack of cultivation has yielded a pernicious harvest of problems among the most important of which are problems of design; professional training that is conceived as something parallel to but distinct from and without interconnection with conventional education (secondary and university), without opportunities for practice nor measures for relating it more closely to economic conditions nor to ensuring continuity; poor quality leading to low prestige; problems of finance, depending on scarce resources that are not always applied according to clearly established criteria and priorities; difficulties of organizational management on account of the fragmentation of responsibility (MEC, Defence, etc.), lack of procedures for adequate co-ordination, and the virtual non-existence of economic or tax incentives to companies or workers.*
>
> *(Sanchez Fierro, 1994, p. 3)*

He notes that company training is concentrated in the service sector, in the most capitalized industries, and the larger companies. Average spending on training in 1992 was 4,600 pesetas (about £23) per worker in the service sector, contrasting with 3,600 pesetas (about £18) in industry and 1,000 pesetas (£5) in construction. Training provision in educational institutions, despite recent extension of the range of courses and qualifications, is still too concentrated in the fields of administration, automobiles, electricity and health, while only a relatively low proportion of students achieve qualifications. Padilla makes a number of observations about the plight of

---

* This chapter translated by Pamela O'Malley

those institutions which were involved in earlier experimental reforms, and which continue to offer certificates that will soon be over-taken by LOGSE. In the MEC-administered regions, 11,395 students followed vocational modules in experimental ESO schools in 1992–3.

MALADJUSTMENT BETWEEN EDUCATION AND PRODUCTION IN SPAIN

A principal mission of education in any country is to equip its citizens with a vocational or professional training which will satisfy the present and future needs of production. This training component should be clearly differentiated from general education of a more scientific and/or human-istic nature and should appear in the latter years of any given system of education. However, in our country, both at university level and at other levels, specific vocational training is confusingly combined with general training throughout. The 1983 *Ley de Reforma Universitaria* (Law of University Reform) (LRU), even in its experimental stages, has not brought any improvement in this respect. The situation is exactly the same, currently, at the level of secondary training. The application of the recently promulgated *Ley de Organización General del Sistema Edu-cativo* (Law of the General Organization of the Educational System) (LOGSE), to which we will make further reference, modifies, at least in theory, the present situation.

I believe that this lack of concern for educational planning in relation to professional preparation is caused, in our country, by the fact that education, taken in its widest sense, is considered to be an end in itself. This attitude is strongest in relation to university levels. Parents' greatest aspiration and, through their influence, that of students also, is for students to commence university studies and, if possible, finish them successfully. Concern about finding a job or a professional career begins only when the studies have been completed.

The divorce between education and production is manifest both in curricular design and in its application. It never in the past occurred to designers of university study programmes to take into account the reality of the country's production, nor to define training programmes in accord-ance with the needs of the labour market. Nor had students at this stage of education any contact whatsoever with the real world of work at any point during their entire period of studies. If in addition we take into account the nepotistic manner of recruitment and contracting of teaching staff at this level of education – they are largely selected from among the students who graduate from the very same school or faculty – then we may conclude that the educational system and the world of work are seen within the universities as separate watertight compartments.

Provision of vocational training at secondary level, in terms of edu-cational content, reflects the needs of the universities and currently represents a parking lot within the system for students who have performed poorly in their studies or for those who come from families with low economic resources.

On the other hand, Spanish employers have never concerned themselves with planning their labour requirements in relation to available human resources nor, consequently, with defining the professional profiles most appropriate to labour conditions. On the contrary, they have adopted the nomenclature belonging to the educational system, and offers of work are made, in the majority of cases, in accordance with the degrees and certificates conferred by the Ministry of Education and Science.

Such longstanding lack of communication between the organizations responsible, and the élitist attitudes which accord high regard to matters of an artistic and intellectual nature but show only contempt towards manual labour and towards anything that pertains solely to work, have generated a lack of harmony between the needs of the production system and the training given by educational institutions. This imbalance between the two systems and the lack of resources for research within education logically translate themselves into deficient vocational preparation for our older students who are, after all, our future workers and professionals.

While these are not the only problems, such factors contribute decisively towards industrial weakness, low profitability in certain sectors, the disappearance of specialist firms and their absorption within multinational companies, and our ever-increasing technological dependence on neighbouring countries.

THE EVOLUTION OF NON-UNIVERSITY VOCATIONAL TRAINING IN SPAIN

In the previous section I dealt with vocational training as a component of education and I have referred both to the training imparted at university levels and at non-university levels. From now on I shall refer, exclusively, to the non-university cycles or stages of vocational training.

I do not wish to go back as far as the origins and circumstances of workers' training in Spain. I will carry out a brief analysis, beginning with the great education reform represented by the *Ley General de Educación* (General Education Act) (LGE) in the year 1970.

Prior to the appearance of this Act, there existed in Spain vocational training centres known as *Escuelas de Maestría Industrial* (Schools of Industrial Craftsmanship) and, as their name indicated, these limited their instruction to the sector which, outside agriculture, at that time was predominant and which employed the greatest number of workers. The training was carried out at two different levels: skilled workmen and master craftsmen. The first qualification corresponded to skilled labour and the students were given basic training in the use of machine tools and other means and implements appropriate to contemporary technology.

The master craftsman was a higher level and required a more extensive technical knowledge and especially a more profound theoretical training. At this level the object was to provide the necessary requirements for jobs involving responsibility for the co-ordination of teams of skilled workers, without the need for the involvement of an engineer.

The training which developed in this epoch maintained a certain relationship with the real world of work which, unfortunately, has subsequently been lost.

The 1970 reform transformed the *Escuelas de Maestría Industriales* into *Centros de Formación Profesional* (vocational training schools), giving them a wider educational brief. The training was no longer limited to the industrial sector but was extended to the service sector. A greater number of professional trades appeared and specialization was increased. In this way separate specialisms such as mechanics, electricity and electronics, along with trades related to the service sector such as administration, health work and many others, developed, although in time their presence was more nominal than real. Vocational training within the regular school system was created with a clear mission of service to the production system as a whole and two different levels were established: *Formación Profesional de Primer Grado*, FP1 (first-level vocational training) and *Formación Profesional de Segundo Grado*, FP2 (second-level vocational training) which in turn corresponded to two different levels of professional qualification.

This reform attempted to unify vocational training which was dispersed across a multitude of institutions and training centres of different kinds. However, this was not fully achieved, since sectors such as agriculture and fishery continued to maintain their own schools and education programmes.

For the first time, the 1970 Act contemplated the possibility of a professional rerouting, through FP2, of those students proceeding from the *Bachillerato* or secondary education who did not wish or were unable to gain access to higher education. But what was originally created (FP2) with a view to offering a period of relatively brief general study (two academic years) for access to employment rapidly became the exceptional route. Vocational training became a second-class education, parallel to the *Bachillerato*, and constituted of the two aforementioned levels of FP1 and FP2. The main stream of students into FP2 come from FP1 and not from the *Bachilleratos* as had been anticipated. On the other hand, the viability of FP1 as a route into the labour market has also been questioned, since the majority of students who complete this level of education, instead of going into work, transfer automatically to FP2 as though they were passing from one academic year to the next one within the same cycle.

One important defect in the reform of vocational training which emerged from the 1970 Education Act was that it did not build upon the participation of representatives of the labour market, so that the law itself remained unfamiliar to employers for many years. It was developed by the Ministry of Education as a purely theoretical exercise, drawing upon the consultancy support of the educational specialists who taught in the universities.

It must be recognized, in all fairness, that following a series of temporary labour difficulties, FP2 has come to be recognized by the labour market and has experienced growing popularity in the decade of the 1980s. The growing demand for students with this qualification has meant that FP2 within this period has accomplished the role for which it was originally intended; that is, it has been used as a bridge between the *Bachillerato* and the labour market. New specialisms related to electronics and informatics have helped to attract students away from the *Bachillerato* route.

The greatest failure of present-day initial vocational training, which is organized by the Ministry of Education, has been the absence of workers in the classrooms of the state schools. Neither the syllabus nor the timetable have given workers the opportunity to update and/or to extend their knowledge through formal education, leaving this fundamental task to the vocational training courses organized by the *Instituto Nacional del Empleo* (National Employment Institute) (INEM), an organization which is controlled by the Ministry of Labour and also, nowadays, by the autonomous communities.

VOCATIONAL TRAINING IN LOGSE

Vocational training as it is contemplated in LOGSE arises from a critical analysis of present-day regulated vocational training. It attempts to correct the most manifest defects which have been identified, and to achieve those aims which were not achieved through the application of the 1970 Act. Although the budgetary situation in both cases are analogous, the procedures for implementing the established aims are significantly different.

LOGSE proposes two different components of vocational training: basic vocational training (FPB) and specific vocational training (FPE). The former will adopt a broad multi-disciplinary approach and forms a part of the common core of compulsory secondary education, that is, in the *Educación Secundaria Obligatoria* (ESO), and of the new *Bachillerato*. Specific vocational training (FPE) is organized into modules or educational blocks which respond to the training needs of groups of occupations and which are articulated through intermediate and higher training cycles (taken after ESO). Each training cycle is composed of a group of modules which respond to the requirements of a particular job, characterized by a job profile. It is estimated that when the design process is completed, the number of training cycles will be approximately 300. Each cycle will be made up of 6 to 8 modules approximately.

A number of training cycles, defined in a somewhat haphazard manner, are currently offered in pilot form. The formal process of design has commenced, for which a methodology elaborated by the Ministry itself is being used. The pilot is being carried out in particular sectors of activity or families of occupation and it is intended that the experimental phase should be complete by the end of 1993.

Process of definition and characterization of the new specific vocational training (FPE)

Unfortunately, in Spain we do not have organizations or institutions such as the National Council for Vocational Qualifications (NCVQ) of the United Kingdom, the French CEREQ or the Italian ISFOL, which undertake analysis of the production system and establish corresponding work qualifications. In order to define with a certain degree of precision the higher vocational training which the labour market currently requires, it has been necessary to set up an agreement between the Ministries of Education and Science and of Labour for the carrying out of sectoral studies of production activity. This study, carried out by the National Institute of Employment (INEM), is the starting point for design of the new basic vocational training.

The Ministry of Education has set up professional working parties (GTPs) whose task is to advise and collaborate with the Ministries' own advisers in charge of implementing the reform project. In their initial stage, these working parties are composed of experts from the most representative firms of each one of the production sectors being studied. The working parties' task in this initial stage is to define the most relevant job profiles in each sector of activity. The job profiles are made up from a group of related activities, which are to be expressed in terms of abilities rather than concrete tasks in specific jobs. Each job profile, in short, has a generalized (transferable) character and should correspond, from a labour point of view, to a group of different occupations.

Once each one of these job profiles in a specific sector has been decided upon, the working party exchanges its labour experts for educational experts. The main task in this new stage is to define the most appropriate training for each one of the job profiles so that the students may develop their skills and acquire the necessary knowledge which will enable them to carry out the actions demanded by the production process.

There is a vocational certificate which is also an academic qualification corresponding to each job profile, issued by the Ministry of Education. In order to obtain this certificate it will be necessary to pursue a basic course lasting more or less a calendar year. As we have already mentioned, each course or cycle is made up of a group of modules, each one of which has a particular significance and value for the future employment.

These vocational modules are specifically committed to vocational training; that is to say, they do not include a general humanistic or scientific education (such matters should have been covered previously in the core curriculum of compulsory education). The principal advantage is that each separate module has value in itself and a student may obtain the corresponding certificate over a longer period of time than the normal academic year. The Ministry of Education and Science intends to bring vocational training closer to the workers and not just to the students who are already part of the educational system, by converting training into a useful tool for in-service training and promotion. This system also allows for the study of one or various modules that make up a vocational cycle, without having to follow the cycle in its entirety. In this case the Administration will issue a vocational certificate which guarantees the student's proficiency in the content of the module or modules in question.

To sum up, the vocational training promoted by LOGSE attempts to bridge mainstream general education (ESO and the *Bachilleratos*) and the labour market. They are training cycles of short duration (approximately a calendar year) composed of specific training modules, each one being an end in itself, which may be studied independently and which consequently has value in itself.

FPE is intended for students coming from compulsory education who do not wish or are unable to continue into higher education and also for all those workers who wish to extend or update their knowledge. It is thus intended to become a powerful instrument which will, to a large extent, replace the occupational training provided by traditional institutions or by those entities which, taking advantage of resources deriving from the European Social Fund, operate such training on a business basis to earn substantial profits.

Training on the shop floor

One of the most outstanding characteristics of the new FPE is the training to be carried out within the work-place (FCT) as to which I wish to make special reference.

FCT refers to the period which a student who is in the basic cycle spends in a work-place in order to complete his or her training. It is regarded as one more module and as such involves a final assessment of the student on termination.

Through FCT it is intended to familiarize the student with specific work experience and enable him or her to manage and study the machines or installations which, because of their high cost or rapid technological evolution, it is impossible to house in the training centres.

The duration of the FCT module will be approximately 300 hours and a tutor overseer will be nominated within the firm where the work experience is offered. This person will be in permanent contact with the training centre and will play an important role in the student's assessment.

Current experimentation in the training cycles

The process of reform and experimentation throughout the new education system has proven to be long and complex. The path followed has been somewhat tortuous and at times uncertain. In reality, it may be said that three different forms of education coexist in Spain: the regulated system deriving from the 1970 Education Act; that which is contemplated in LOGSE and which will have replaced the former entirely by the year 2000; and another, intermediate model, which constitutes the beginning of reform and is limited exclusively to secondary education. The principal intention of the latter was to prolong compulsory schooling to the age of 16 and replace the present secondary education (BUP and FP) with five secondary modalities, similar to the French model, which include industrial technology, and administration and management. These two latter modalities are the main alternatives to present-day vocational training. In order to facilitate access to the labour market for those students who wish to leave the educational system on completing this stage, a series of more specialized basic cycles were created on the basis of the *Bachilleratos*. These basic cycles were created in 1986 in rather precarious circumstances, counting on the participation of a very small number of people and starting out with very limited job-related knowledge. Subsequently, the Ministry of Education and Science has gone on to create more cycles under similar circumstances, with the sole purpose of offering possibilities of continuity to those students who were involved in other areas or stages of the experimental process.

Consequently, there are a few FPE cycles in an experimental stage, set up before approval of LOGSE, which have very slight possibilities of survival. Without any doubt all of them should be revised and the majority eliminated when the final catalogue of training certificates is drawn up, at the end of the current experimental process.

The present experimentation is not providing useful data and is therefore not proving a source of information for the definitive design. Initially, the Education Administration maintained contact with the experimental schools, organized study sessions, carried out visits and supplied teachers with supporting material. Now, however, the experimental schools have been totally abandoned in spite of the fact that the experiment goes on year after year and becomes stronger as new cycles or new schools are added to it. In reality the process continues more for political than for practical reasons. The basic cycles, precariously and provisionally defined, are being used to provide a way out to students who have finished secondary education and cannot find a university place or in order to substitute for certain specialisms of the present regulated system of vocational training which is attracting very few students.

Among the many problems which affect the experimental schools, it is worth mentioning those related to FCT work experience. The responsibility for finding firms in which to carry out the work experience falls on the teachers of the school and they encounter very serious difficulties in guaranteeing all their students an opportunity for work experience. Most students end up doing jobs which have nothing to do with the job profile of the cycle they are studying. Moreover, the follow-up and assessment of the work experience does not match the requirements stipulated by the Ministry of Education and Science itself.

VIABILITY OF THE PROPOSALS FOR THE REFORM OF VOCATIONAL TRAINING: A CRITICAL ANALYSIS OF THE PROPOSAL AND ITS IMPLEMENTATION

The present model of vocational education proposed by the Ministry within the framework of reform bears very little resemblance to the model that was initially proposed. The Spanish Ministry of Education and Science has a clear academic bias and has never proposed, up to now, an adjustment of its vocational training to the training requirements of the production system. The change which has come about and the reason for it are reflected in the terms in which LOGSE presents these proposals, and correspond, incredible as it may seem, to the pressure of certain advisory teachers drawn from industry who managed to convince the educational authorities of the need for a transformation of vocational training to enable our students and workers to train in accordance with educational tenets similar to those of other countries within our immediate geographic and economic neighbourhood.

The model for the design and development of future vocational training is theoretically sound but, given the tradition and evolution of our educational institutions in this field, the marginal concern of industry for the vocational training of its workers and for the definition of job profiles most appropriate to production needs, and, finally, given the traditional divorce between education and work, I believe that serious difficulties will be encountered both in the project and in its application, which may well derail an initially sound proposal. These difficulties may well be exacerbated due to the existence of other problems such as the diversity of organizations currently involved in the organization of vocational education; the existence, in our country, of a weak and disorganized labour structure; the lack of firm, determined decision-making procedures on the part of the Education Administration for the exercise of profound reform; the present state of the teaching staff; and the lack of social prestige accorded to vocational training.

244 Antonio José Gil Padilla

THE MAIN PROBLEMS ENCOUNTERED IN THE DESIGN PROCESS

In the first place, the Administration should have opted for a model in which all basic training would be unified in one institution, but unfortunately it did not do so. This would have meant that curriculum design and the issue of qualifications could have been centralized in one single state institution. At present, the following institutions have responsibility, both for the design and the issue of qualifications: various ministerial Departments of Education, Labour, Industry, Agriculture and Fishery, etc. The Ministry of Education and Science has the power to issue official certificates which authorize access to higher studies, but the other organizations may issue certificates which permit certain professional or working activity, while in some cases authorization for carrying out particular jobs can be obtained only from the Ministry of Industry.

In relation to the process of curricular design itself, the participation of industrial experts in determining job profiles is proving to be less effective than hoped for. The majority of companies in our country have not defined the tasks of their employees and skill levels are typically calibrated by the certificates issued by the Ministry of Education. The experts therefore lack criteria and, when it comes to expressing their needs, they make continuous reference to the official certificates handed out by the Ministry of Education rather than to the skills and knowledge which arise from the working conditions of their respective firms.

In summary, the design of the resulting job profiles in each area of activity has been left to the teaching advisers selected by the Ministry of Education who, in the majority of cases, have not had the required work experience.

In the field of curriculum design for training, finally, starting from the definition of the most relevant curricular components (objectives, content and learning activities) corresponding to the job profiles established in the first stage, substantial difficulties may arise, especially if it is intended that a constructivist concept of learning be adopted. This mode of understanding the training of our students demands knowledge of certain techniques and methods, and of their application, for which the academic authorities of our country have never considered it necessary to prepare the advisers with whom they would collaborate in the project of reform.

MAIN PROBLEMS OF IMPLEMENTATION

The application of an innovative model such as the one proposed demands that the Administration takes a firm attitude to decision-making, implying in the first place a precise design and, in the second place, appropriate training provision that corresponds with the social and economic contexts of those institutions which are to provide the new vocational training.

This should allow access to workers, appropriate allocation of space, technological and didactic resources, a profound transformation of teacher training and, fundamentally, the facilitating of relationships with the production system for adequate communication so that the reciprocal services provided by both institutions (education and production) may be fruitful.

For all these requirements to be taken into account we need, in addition to a will for firm action on the part of the Ministry of Education (which we do not believe exists), a generous slice of the budget. The putting into practice of the Vocational Education Reform coincides with a delicate situation in the country's economy and the promises made by the Ministry approximately two years ago are losing credibility. Instead, there is evidence of a significant reduction in the expenditure of each vocational training school, lack of attention by the Administration to vocational teachers, and an inadequate and inappropriate training programme for them.

I do not wish to be pessimistic in conclusion, but the panorama, at the present time, is quite discouraging. The general feeling among teachers who fatalistically await the Ministry of Education's implementation of the transformations so necessary in a totally exhausted system, responds to a very common experience in our country where we are waiting for something to change so that everything remains the same.

REFERENCE

Sanchez Fierro, J. (1994) La formación continua, asignatura pendiente, *Comunidad Escolar*, 24 January.

20 University reform

Oliver Boyd-Barrett

In the ten-year period following the election of the PSOE to government in 1982, the number of university students doubled from 669,848 to 1,295,585. Fifty-three per cent of students in 1993–4 study social science and law; 21 per cent, engineering and technology; 10 per cent, humanities; 7.5 per cent, experimental science; 8 per cent, health sciences. Short-course registrations constituted 32.5 per cent of the total. Three out of every 100 inhabitants in Spain study at university, and the number is growing at the rate of 8 per cent a year. Largest universities were the distance-teaching university (UNED) (100,000) and the largest Madrid university, Complutense (126,149). Of the other universities, twenty-three had registrations ranging between 15,000 and 40,000; and sixteen had registrations of less than 15,000. Just over 51 per cent of all students were women (a much higher percentage than for lecturing staff) with a much stronger predominance of women in social sciences, law, the humanities and health. In addition to Spain's forty-one public universities (of which four began teaching in 1993), there were four Catholic and three other private universities – now permitted by (1991) legislation, on condition that any such private provision offers a minimum of eight degree titles, delivered by a teaching force of whom at least 50 per cent must have doctorates and 60 per cent must be full-time, and that the teacher–student ratio is no worse than 1:25. Two new private universities for Madrid were approved in 1993. Each autonomous community now has at least one state university, and Andalucia has a university for each of its eight provinces.

Considering Spanish education as a whole since the 1960s one can detect three major periods of transformation. The first was transformation of demand by the public for education services, with the growing enthusiasm for university education as the proper channel of social mobility. The second was a transformation of response while the public authorities tried desperately to reduce the gap between demand and available quantitative resources. The third and most recent is a qualitative transformation of content. This does not denote that resource issues no longer exist, or that all controversies surrounding the legal framework, the relationships between Central Government, autonomous communities and the institutions. have been resolved. But it does point to a new confidence, a sense that the challenge of mass education has been met and will continue to be met, despite all the associated problems, and that at last the attention of the educational administrators and politicians must settle on the central question and purpose of education: what shall be taught, why and how?

Up to 1970, the Spanish university system was possibly the most centralized and bureaucratized in Western Europe. The *Ley Moyano* of 1857 had consciously applied the centralized French pattern to Spain and this model remained more or less intact for over a hundred years, only to be strengthened in its intensity by the period of Franco's rule. Up to 1970, therefore, university education was a state monopoly, its curricula ordained by the Ministry, functioning primarily to channel the children of the élite into the élite professions. Research was not an important priority or activity in Spanish university life. Franco purged university ranks of those who were not or were thought not to be sympathetic to the new regime. Teachers had to be members of the national movement, the *Falange*, and to possess certificates of loyalty to the regime. Church influence was strong. All students were obliged to belong to the approved student union, and to study religious, political and physical education.

The 1969 *Libro Blanco* considered that university courses were not meeting the social needs of the day. Subject-teaching was traditional, excessively theoretical, over-dependent on textbooks and magisterial lectures, with no resources for newer educational media, and assessed by examinations which were little more than a test of memory. There was little teacher–student contact. Research was neglected. Too much power lay in the hands of the established, tenured professors, the *catedráticos*. The 1970 Act aimed to give universities a greater measure of autonomy, but prescribed in detail how universities were to be organized and how curricula were to be planned and taught. It sought to strengthen the department as the most important institutional locus for teaching and research, as a means of reducing the arbitrary and often reactionary power of the *catedráticos*, and with a view to providing a more realistic management framework than the unwieldy faculty. The planning of course decisions about the organization of teaching, timetables and resources were to become departmental responsibilities. The Act called for more collaboration between teachers, more staff–student contact, the organization of tutorial groups, and greater reliance on continuous assessment.

The period between 1970 and the Law of University Reform of 1983 witnessed further considerable growth in demand for university education and in resource supply, although supply failed to keep up with demand. Student enrolments which had stood at only 69,000 in 1957 doubled to 142,000 by 1966, doubled again to 355,000 in 1970, doubled yet again in the period to 1981 to reach 670,000, and then doubled one further time in the period to 1994.

Many provisions of the 1970 Act were not translated into practice.

Benito (1986) complained that despite the improvements in the numbers of universities and the opening up of many university colleges, these new institutions resembled the original universities in their structure and teaching. He noted that curricula continued to be organized in uniform cycles of three and five years. The diploma, introduced in 1970, had not really taken root beyond the field of primary teacher training. Villanueva (1983) declared that the university system had not evolved in the way required by society in response to scientific, technical and social demands, and bemoaned a 'serious deterioration in quality' due, above all, to the lack of specialized teachers. Curricula had remained static.

The 1970 law appeared to have been unsuccessful in implanting the departmental structure within university life, though it was more import-ant in some institutions than in others. Maravall (1984) even states that the departments had suffered a notable deterioration in the recent years prior to the 1983 law of reform. McKenna (1985) notes that the depart-ment, which had been first introduced in 1965, did not really 'gel', as chairs (the *catedráticos*) were simply relocated within departments. With-out more adequate resourcing the 1970 law in itself was unable to combat the consequences of overcrowding and its calls for more staff–student contact, tutorial grouping and continuous assessment were simply pious hopes. The measure of autonomy granted to universities amounted to little in curriculum terms. As McNair (1984) observed, the syllabus for each course was still prescribed by the Ministry. These were considered by an advisory committee of university heads – rectors – on whose advice the Minister would either reject them or issue a decree approving them. But approval was not readily given.

The socialist education minister primarily responsible for the LRU of 1983, José María Maravall, wrote that until recently:

> There had persisted the old traditional structure based on a limited number of courses of equal or almost equal duration, to which corres-ponded on a one-to-one basis a limited number of faculties, circling around professors rather than departments, with rigid curricula com-prising subjects to which teachers were attached sometimes in per-petuity, with a completely inadequate third (doctoral) cycle and more often than not suffering a total divorce between teaching and research.
>
> (Maravall, 1984, p. 113)

Maravall claims that his LRU, for the first time in Spanish history, recog-nises that science and culture require liberty and autonomy. The three basic principles of the Act are the concept of a public university, regu-lation of a system of separate competitive establishments and a more powerful departmental structure.

The LRU aims to give universities autonomy in statutory, academic, economic and personnel terms. The *claustro académico* (senate) has the power to elaborate or modify statutes, to elect the Rector and formulate the main teaching lines, subject to the budgetary approval of the *Consejo Social*, a mixed body of university and community representatives. Universities can award degrees for courses which they have designed but which are subject to general conditions established for all universities laid down by the national *Consejo de Universidades* (representing university rectors and community interests at national level), the autonomous communities and the State itself. They are also given the freedom to award their own non-degree certificates for specific courses. Autonomous communities can establish new universities, subject to Ministry guidelines and national plans for higher education.

Inevitably the institutional reality is more constraining than ministerial rhetoric would allow. The process of legislative passage in itself gave some clues as to the nature of its own contradictions. The law was 'elaborated' within only five months, although it is true that similar laws had been much debated but not implemented by the previous centre-right government. University rectors only received copies of the draft legislation two weeks in advance of parliamentary discussion. The story, possibly apocryphal, is told of the university rector who complained to a Ministry spokesman about the poor level of Ministry consultation with the universities, only to be told that the universities no more needed to be consulted than delinquents needed to be consulted over criminal justice legislation.

LRU essentially addresses the issue of the balance of power between the State, the autonomous communities, community interests and the institution, as well as the balance of power within the institution. Certainly within the institution very important changes have been made in the direction of greater democratization (with rectors, deans and departmental heads subject to election) and there are improved democratic links between institutions and the wider community through the *Consejos Sociales* and the *Consejo de Universidades*. These bodies will have an ever more significant role upon the completion in 1994–5 of the process of transfer of powers in the control of the universities from Central Government to individual autonomous communities. The autonomous communities have the power to approve the statutes of the universities, and have control of the purse-strings as 80 per cent of university finance derives from the State, but then in turn the autonomous communities must negotiate with the Central Government the overall annual transfer of money from the centre to each individual community. Through their power to set up new institutions the communities can also alter the competitive climate within which institutions operate. Academically, as McKenna points out, the institutions continue to operate within the existing system of national degrees and titles:

> Central government in consultation with the *Consejo de Universidades* decides which university degrees are to enjoy national status and deter-

mines their basic curricular configuration and requirements. Universities must register national degree curricula with the *Consejo*, but institutional diversification within general norms is encouraged.

(McKenna, 1985, p. 467)

Although the LRU represents the second legislative attempt at reform of the universities in thirteen years, there were many who still felt that real reform had yet to be achieved. Quoted in *El País* (26 January 1988), one professor, Urbano Espinosa, complains that 'LRU . . . has generated miserable cantonalization, intellectual provincialism, bureaucratization of conscience and general clientelization; it has slowed down the rhythm of work and the level of intellectual effort'. This critic was particularly incensed by LRU's substitution of (supposedly) open competition in preference to the previous system of national examinations as the means of staff selection, with a view to granting universities greater autonomy. Despite counter-measures intended to ensure that a majority of each five-person selection committee should be chosen on a lottery basis from universities other than the university making the appointment, the system had been open to widespread abuse as departments conspired with each other to fix it in favour of their preferred internal candidates.

The scale of abuse was greatly exacerbated by the inability of the Ministry to solve, to the universities' satisfaction, the problem of the huge growth in non-tenured staff over the 1970s (the 'PNNs'), a force which by the early 1980s had come to represent 60 per cent of the entire university teaching force. PNNs were finally phased out by 1988 with the possibility of re-entry to new staff categories. But domestic recognition of longstanding personal debts has helped corrupt what otherwise should have been an impartial system of selection. In reality there have been a number of scandalous appointments whereby established external experts have been turned away in favour of relative unknowns from within institutions. Between June 1991 and January 1992, 91 per cent of all appointments were filled internally (and in some instances the figure was 100 per cent). Comparative figures for 1986 and 1988 were 83 and 88 per cent, showing a serious worsening of the problem. In 40 per cent of cases there was only one candidate; in 70 per cent of cases fewer than four and in 30 per cent less than three. Proposals for modifying the composition of interview panels were approved early in 1994 by the Spanish cabinet (*consejo de ministros*) and will lead to legislation to clarify, update and amend the LRU, in the form of a *Ley de Actualización de la Ley de Reforma Universitaria*. Under the new law, selection committees would comprise five members of the relevant academic discipline, of whom one, the president, would be nominated by the university and the others would be chosen by lottery from among all universities.

The proposed new legislation also rationalizes staffing structure so that there will be a clear distinction between permanent staff of civil servant status, and contractual staff, and a third group of assistants and teaching assistants. Contractual staff can include emeritus professors, associate professors (who are not part of the university but outside experts who bring prestige to it temporarily, and who complement basic teaching), visiting professors and a category of teaching partner, recruited to help out full-time to meet specific needs for up to eight years. Permanent staff include university professor (*catedrático* or *titular*), university school professor (*catedrático* or *titular*), the teaching assistant (*profesor ayudante*), requiring a *licenciatura*, and, at the bottom of the hierarchy, the assistant (*ayudante*) regarded as a 'training' post while the holder works to complete a doctorate – this would constitute the first stage of a university career. Measures have been introduced for additional remuneration for professors who are deemed to show good research productivity, as evaluated by a special tribunal using criteria that pertain to quality, creativity, originality, contribution to knowledge and capacity to stimulate.

Voicing a different dissatisfaction with the original LRU, Juan Garcia Sentandreu (*Papers*, June 1985), a professor of the University of Valencia, complained that the university statutes 'subject all university work to the *cultura nacional del País Valenciano* without mentioning anything of Spain and thus detracting from the universal implications of the term "university" '. Thus he argued that the statutes, reflecting the transfer of power from central to regional government, further distance the university from real social needs. The vice-rector of the University Polytechnic of Valencia is reported as saying that 'one can't make a reform along Anglo-Saxon lines with a third world economy' (*Papers*, June 1985), expressing widespread scepticism about the Government's ability to provide adequate economic support for its reforms.

Joan Romero, Director-General of *Coordinacion y alta Inspección* of the Ministry, complains of 'antiquated curricula' (*Papers*, February 1986). The Secretary General of the *Consejo de Universidades*, talking to *Papers* in June 1987, illustrated his curriculum worries by reference to engineering degree titles which he claimed had not changed since the 1920s when telecommunications was added. Nor had the content itself changed as much as it should have done, often lacking relevance and social interest, with insufficient updating and inter-disciplinary orientation. He further complained of inflexibility, over-standardization and obsolete pedagogic criteria.

These sentiments find support also among students. A survey of university students in Valencia published by *Papers* in June 1986 outlined their complaints. Students were not happy with the system of teaching, said that academic fees were too high, and considered that universities had become degree-giving machines with little time for research. Many students felt that their expectations had not been met; they felt defrauded. Other problems include overcrowding, the impossibility of direct teacher–student relationships, the oppressive ambience of the university environment, lack of facilities, poor preparation of lectures, obsolete curricula and excessive stress on memorization. Many of these complaints resembled the criticisms of the 1969 *Libro Blanco* seventeen years previously. A contributor to *Comunidad Escolar* (Garcia de Leon, 1990) considered that university teachers are untrained and overworked, with too much dependence on research staff for teaching, and evaluation of teaching too dependent on unreliable administration of student questionnaires.

LRU mainly had to do with regulating the structure of university control. By 1987 the Government had begun to tackle the problems of curriculum reform. This in turn may have reflected a pessimism at central level about the likelihood that LRU would actually deliver quickly enough in terms of curriculum modernization. Alternatively, it may simply have reflected the surviving assumption that when it came to seemingly urgent issues the centre was still in firm command.

Reform of the *'planes de estudio'* involved the appointment (in 'secret', as the critics complained) by the *Consejo de Universidades* and in line with general Ministry directions of seventeen expert teams (almost one for each of the existing faculty divisions recognized by the Ministry) to modernize content and devise new degree titles. More precisely, the objectives, as stated by Maravall (CE, 23 September 1987), were to keep teaching up to date; adapt the curriculum to community standards, needs and demands, both of Spain and of Europe; to diversify the educational offering at this level, increase the number of degrees and widen others; and to respect the autonomy of universities. It was envisaged that by the end of the reform process the total number of recognized 'long-cycle' (4 to 5 years) degree categories in Spain would have risen from 65 to 150. In addition, many more shorter courses would have been generated. The first batch of proposals, fifty-five, were sent out in October 1987. Controversially, the universities were given four months to consider them and make their counter-proposals. Exasperated ministry officials were inclined to the view that if reform had been left to the universities nothing ever would have happened. By the spring of 1988 no counter-proposals had been received by the *Consejo*. Upon final confirmation of the reformed and new degree titles universities were to be given a period of three years in which to adjust their existing course structures. Between 1983 and 1993 over 500 plans of study had been standardized by the *Consejo*, out of a 1993 total of 1,400 degrees: 159 'long cycle' (*licenciaturas*), studied by 70 per cent of students, 322 'short cycle' (*diplomaturas*) and 21 post-graduate.

The urgency with which the Ministry proceeded in relation to university curricula reflected growing central government anxiety that the country should be ready for full membership of the European Community by 1992, by trying to ensure the preparation of a competitive, élite work force and the regulation of a university system roughly in line with the rest of Europe. In practice, the speed of reform and the quality of its implementation depend on the system's ability to confront grave resource deficiencies. These include lack of adequate administrative support (only 19,562 administrative staff as against 40,000 teachers and 900,000 students – i.e. 5 per cent) (see *Educación* section in *El País*, 22 March 1988). University libraries are under-equipped, with shortages of specialist staff, poor speed of service (with students often unable to browse through shelf stock but having to order *all* books they want, either to consult briefly or to study in depth, over the librarian's desk), and difficulties of classification and maintenance of archives. Many libraries are not centralized in one place: instead, each department may have its own library. This may make for convenience in some cases, but greatly adds to overhead costs, and reduces scope for inter-disciplinarity.

The problem of the PNNs, the legacy of non-tenured staff, had formally been solved by 1988, but the university system continued to be carried largely by under-qualified staff. Poor pay, meanwhile, encouraged many staff to 'moonlight', although at present the Ministry is anxious to rationalize this process by making firmer distinctions between part-time and full-time staff. Laboratory facilities are inadequately funded, with too few technical support staff. A considerable proportion of all research money continues to be channelled outside the university system to industry or to state-controlled research centres. Research money for universities is distributed via the *Comisión Interministerial de Ciencia y Tecnología* (CICYT) but there is strong feeling in the universities that they should be responsible for decisions to do with the analysis and appraisal of research proposals.

An OECD report commissioned by the Ministry to report on Spanish university education on the eve of its entry to the Common Market had positive things to say about improvements that had been introduced since 1970 (see CE, 9 December 1987). The report identified three challenges facing the universities arising from integration into the common market: the need to add a strong international dimension to curricula (up to this point in time rather provincial in scope); to adapt curricula more effectively to professional demands; and to reinforce scientific and technical research. The biggest problem affecting the universities was the seeming inability of the economy to assimilate graduates appropriately. Too few students (then only 20 per cent, but 40 per cent by 1994) were taking short (generally three-year) courses; too few (6.1 per cent) were registering with the technical universities and their number had actually been falling while the numbers going into law and letters were rising sharply – an absurdity, in the opinion of the report. It considered that students were unevenly distributed across the available universities, a factor that contributed to overcrowding in some (41.5 per cent of all students were concentrated into the campuses of Madrid and Barcelona). There were too many students in humanities and social sciences, not enough in basic sciences and technology. The report also considered that academic fees should be allowed to rise. This they have done, leading to substantial student unrest in the autumn of 1993, when the Government raised fees by an average of 12 per cent (when the rate of inflation was officially 4.5 per cent). It was argued in justification that in 1985 university fees had covered 21.5 per cent of university costs, but that this had fallen to 17.5 per cent by 1993. Expenses in the period 1985–93 had increased 418 per cent, direct grants to universities by 310 per cent, but fees only by 188 per cent (CE, 22 September 1993). Factors contributing to high costs were identified by the OECD as the official length of degrees (5–6 years for *licenciaturas*), made worse by a high rate of repeats (e.g. average length of time to complete in the University of Santiago de Compostela was eight years, with a 'success' rate of 45 per cent) and high drop-out rates (above all in the first year).

With 30 per cent of all 18 to 24-year-olds registered for university in 1986 (up from 20 per cent in 1975), Spain has achieved a high level of access to university study, higher than most other countries of the OECD block with the exceptions of the USA, Belgium and Holland, and on a par with France and Germany. Increases in fee levels have been perceived as a threat to this record. Another increasing threat has been the introduction of quotas on particularly well-subscribed courses. Nearly all faculties in Madrid and Barcelona now have such quotas, and 72 per cent of all Spanish university places on offer in 1994–5 were subject to such quotas.

The maintenance of university entrance examinations (for the university faculties, but not required for the university schools which offer only courses leading to *diplomaturas* – the main route for entry to primary teaching, which base entry upon successful passage through the *Bachillerato*) has been very unpopular among students, not only because they can and do restrict access (though most students, 85 per cent, who sit for them, pass; and of these between 76 and 86 per cent get places in accordance with their first or second options) but because of widespread concern that standards between the entrance examinations of different universities are too variable. Measures were approved in 1993 for a more just and rigorous selection process, one which would ensure that students have sufficient opportunity to demonstrate that they have acquired a minimum level of knowledge and ensure comparability between schools, both private and public. The mechanism for achieving this reform was to be through change to the composition and functioning of the tribunals which judge the results and apply the criteria, e.g. introducing exclusive dependence on subject specialists; ensuring that the same markers do not mark scripts from the same schools in successive years; and improved complaints procedures.

The urgent need for moderation of standards between universities is intensified by the gradual introduction during the 1990s of the '*distrito compartido*', a proportion (maximum of 10 per cent in 1994) of university places reserved for candidates proceeding from regions other than the university's own 'catchment'. University entrance examinations in Cataluña have been standardized since 1991 through a body created by the *Consejo Interuniversitaria de Cataluña*, a consultative organ of the Department of Education of the Administration.

REFERENCES

Benito, A. E (1986) Multi-Campus Universities in Spain, *West European Education*, vol. 18, part 1, pp. 79–86.

Garcia de Leon, M. (1990) Tribune Libre, *Comunidad Escolar*, 1 May.

McKenna, J. (1985) University Reform in Spain: New Structures for Autonomy and Accountability, *Comparative Education Review*, November, pp. 460–76.

McNair, J. (1984) *Education for a Changing Spain*. Manchester: Manchester University Press.

Maravall, J. M. (1984) *La Reforma de la Enseñanza*. Barcelona: Laia.

Villanueva, J. (1983) The Structure, Promotion and Appointment of Academic Staff in Spain, *European Journal of Education*, pp. 259–68.

Glossary

AGLI	Associación Gallega por la Libertad del Idioma
ANPE	Associación Nacional del Profesorado de EGB
BUP	Bachillerato Unificando y Polivolente
CA	Comunidades Autónomas
CAP	Certificado de Aptitud Pedagogica
CCEG	Confederación de Centros de Educación y Gestión
CCOO	Comisiones Obreras
CE	*Comunidad Escolar*
	Consejo Escolar
CECE	Confederación Española de Centros de Enseñanza
CEP	Centros de Profesores
CERI	Centre for Educational Research and Innovation
CGEC	Consejo General de la Enseñanza Católica
CIDE	Centro de Investigación, Documentación y Evaluación
COU	Curso de Orientación Universitaria
CPR	Centros de Profesores y Recursos
CSIF	Confederación Sindical Independiente de Funcionarios
DCB	Diseños Curriculares Bases
DES	Department of Education and Science
EDICE	Editorial Instituto de Ciencas de la Educación Salamanca
EGB	Educación General Básica
EI	Educación Infantil
EP	Educación Primaria
EPA	Educación de Las Personas Adultas
ESO	Educación Secundaria Obligatoria
ETP	Educación Técnico Profesional, Enseñanzas Técnico – Profesionales
FERE	Federación Española de Religiosos de la Enseñanza
FP	Formación Profesional
FPB	Formación Profesional Básica
FPE	Formación Profesional Especifica
GMS	Grant-maintained school
ICE	Institutos de Ciencias de la Educación
IEA	International Association for the Assessment of Educational Results
INCE	Instituto Nacional de Calidad y Evaluación
INEM	Instituto Nacional del Empleo
IU	Izquierda Unida
LEA	Local Education Authority
LGE	Ley General de Educación
LMS	Local Management of Schools

LODE	Ley Orgánica del Derecho a la Educación
LOECE	Ley Orgánica por la que se regula el Estatuto de Centros Escolares
LOGSE	Ley Orgánica de Ordenación General del Sistema Educativo
LRBAL	Ley Reguladora de Las Bases del Régimen Local
LRU	Ley de Reforma Universitaria
MEC	Ministerio de Educación y Ciencia
MRP	Movimientos de Renovación Pedagógica
MSC	Manpower Services Commission
NVQ	National Vocational Qualifications
OECD	Organization for Economic Cooperation and Development
PP	Partido Popular
PSOE	Partido Socialista de Obrero Español
SCAA	School Curriculum and Assessment Authority
STE	Sindicato de Trabajadores de Enseñanza
TEED	Training Education and Enterprise Division (of the Department of Employment)
UGT	Union General de Trabajadores
UIMP	Universidad Internacional Menéndez Pelayo
UNED	Universidad Nacional de Educación a Distancia

Index